MAGNETIC CITY

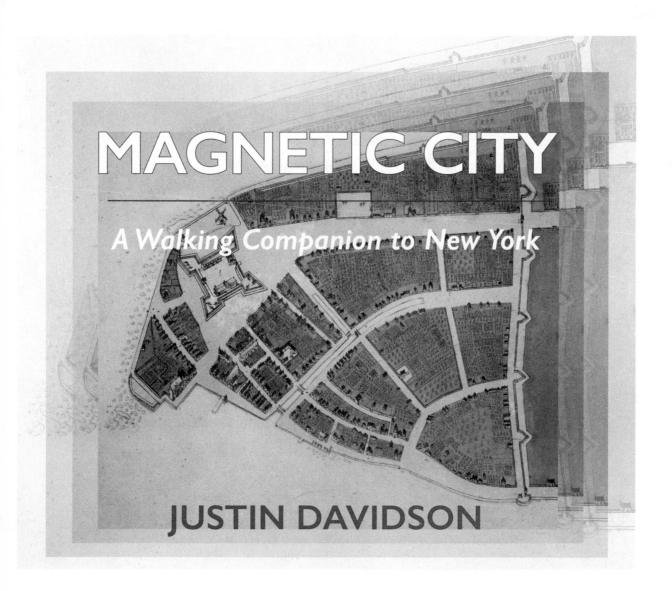

MAGNETIC CITY

A Walking Companion to New York

JUSTIN DAVIDSON

SPIEGEL & GRAU

NEW YORK

Published in the United States by Spiegel & Grau,
an imprint of Random House, a division of
Penguin Random House LLC, New York.

SPIEGEL & GRAU and Design is a registered trademark
of Penguin Random House LLC.

Portions of this work were originally published in *New York* magazine
and its associated websites, *Vulture* and *Daily Intelligencer*.
An earlier version of the Introduction was originally published
in *Jeff Chien-Hsing Liao: New York* (Aperture, 2014).
A short section of "Walk I: City of Money" was adapted
from an article originally published in *Newsday*.

LIBRARY OF CONGRESS CATALOGING-IN-PUBLICATION DATA
NAMES: Davidson, Justin.
TITLE: Magnetic city : a walking companion to New York / by Justin Davidson.
DESCRIPTION: New York : Spiegel & Grau, [2017] | "A Spiegel & Grau trade
paperback original"—Title page verso. | Includes index.
IDENTIFIERS: LCCN 2016041362 | ISBN 9780553394702 (paperback : acid-free
paper) | ISBN 9780553394719 (ebook).
SUBJECTS: LCSH: New York (N.Y.)—Description and travel. | Walking—New York
(State)—New York. | New York (N.Y.)—History. | Historic buildings—New
York (State)—New York. | Historic sites—New York (State)—New York.
Architecture—New York (State)—New York. | New York (N.Y.)—Buildings,
structures, etc. | BISAC: TRAVEL / Hikes & Walks. | ARCHITECTURE / Regional.
| HISTORY / United States / State & Local / Middle Atlantic (DC, DE, MD, NJ, NY, PA).
CLASSIFICATION: LCC F128.55 .D38 2017 | DDC 974.7—dc23 LC record available
at https://lccn.loc.gov/2016041362.

Printed in the United States of America on acid-free paper

randomhousebooks.com
spiegelandgrau.com

2 4 6 8 9 7 5 3 1

FIRST EDITION

To Ariella, my magnetic north,
and Milo, my city kid

*The soul of the city was always my subject, and it was a roiling soul,
twisting and turning over on itself, forming and re-forming,
gathering into itself and opening out again like blown cloud.*

—E. L. DOCTOROW, from *The Waterworks*

CONTENTS

INTRODUCTION

If you had fled New York when the World Trade Center site was still a pile of smoldering rubble and first returned when a new one was needling the sky, you would have found that the city had changed its skin. During the dozen years from 2002 until the end of 2013, when the people's plutocrat, Michael Bloomberg, was mayor, a metropolis famed for its lively grubbiness acquired a fresh glow. Graffiti migrated to other cities or was confined to designated zones like the 5Pointz development in Long Island City. Central Park's lawns were lacquered in pool-table green. The once-pervasive fug of cigarette smoke cleared, replaced by pollen clouds from hundreds of thousands of new trees. (Respiration remains a problem but only at certain times of year.) Every time an old stone building fell, its rusticated quoins, wrought-iron curlicues, and carved brownstone lintels were replaced by the uniform smoothness of glass. At dusk, mauve sunlight ricocheted off the Hudson River and inflamed all those mirrored façades. Suddenly, New York looked cleaner, lighter, and shinier: a city that could be made new again each morning with the stroke of a squeegee.

Some of that newness was deceptive. The shiny-skinned metropolis was draped over a century-old subway and a sclerotic circulation system of rusty water pipes and fragile gas mains. Periodically, a building crumbled or a rainstorm crippled the sewers, reminding all New Yorkers that they lived in a city of a certain age. But the seductive sheen had a substance to it, too, like the many coats of high-gloss paint that build up on a prewar kitchen's walls. Crime fell, crack crested, and the worst of the drug scourge migrated to previously wholesome places like Vermont. Overt racial conflict abated, and middle-class couples were emboldened to stay rather than make a run for the suburbs as soon as they bought their first bassinet.

New York reasserted itself as a magnetic city, drawing all kinds of people for all different reasons, from all over the world. The preposterously rich came shopping for ninetieth-floor estates that they left vacant virtually year-round. Their extravagant demands (combined with new technology, the scarcity of land, and the open-ended premium that developers could charge for views) inspired an architectural form that was new to New York: the anorexic-supermodel tower, hyper-tall and spectacularly skinny. The less pampered came, too. Indigent immigrants, freshly laureled college grads, nurses, retirees, writers, and middle-aged refugees from the ranch-house life—everyone needed a portion of that precious resource, square footage. The tide brought companies as well as individuals. The cream of Silicon Valley, like Google, Facebook, and Twitter, discovered their need for a Manhattan beachhead. Financial firms that had dispersed to New Jersey office parks found themselves slinking back into town. TV producers renewed their love of New York so passionately that they pressed Midtown into service as a fake Chicago for *The Good Wife* and made the Brooklyn neighborhood of Ditmas Park impersonate Iowa City—Iowa City!—in *Girls.* Then there were the tourists, millions upon millions of them, ambling too slowly and four abreast, infuriating the locals—but also buoying cultural institutions and broadcasting New York's status as a global object of desire. New Yorkers could count on being envied.

The gloss and the frenzy represented real change, much of it for the better, some of it disastrous, none of it forgone. Years after 9/11, New Yorkers continue to live with the event's afterimage engraved in our prefrontal cortex. But we have forgotten the ensuing gloom—the worries that nobody would ever again want to live or work in a skyscraper, that Manhattan was doomed as a financial capital, that those who could flee would, and that those who had already fled would never return. Despair and resilience are recurring motifs in the history of a city that has regularly been battered, doubted, cursed, and loathed, only to battle its way back to glamour. In 1835 a fire destroyed virtually the entire business district; within a few years, a stronger, less flammable city emerged. At the end of World War II, New York had the world's busiest port and most productive factories. Three decades later, shipping and manufacturing were both moribund, the municipal government could barely pay its bills, and the East Village teemed with punk rockers' nihilistic screams.

But another quarter century later, New Yorkers discovered that while they were hard at work again—now mostly in offices rather than on factory floors—they also inhabited a city optimized for leisure. A greenbelt of parks curled along once-begrimed docks, studded with sunbathers from May to September. Fun, it turned out, feels better when it takes place near water, and now the city's five hundred miles of shoreline were lined with places to drink, skateboard, play *pétanque,* watch outdoor movies, and learn aerial trapeze. Goofing off became serious business. The pastimes of the underpaid were wondrous to behold; production assistants and aspiring cartoonists, magazine interns and fashion apprentices: all had enough money coming from somewhere—their parents, presumably—to drive real estate markets and keep restaurants humming. Sometimes it was difficult to distinguish work from leisure. In the vast Brooklyn plants that had once churned out battleships and cardboard boxes, young men with extravagant facial hair now refined their hobbies—making chocolate, distilling moonshine, brewing flavored ales—into viable businesses. Brooklyn transformed from a blue-collar outer borough into the epicenter of the literary world and a global synonym for artfully disheveled cool.

This frantic pursuit of pleasantness dispossessed many and enraged more. Gentrification became a term of daily opprobrium, as the prosperous horned in on one neglected neighborhood after another. Gentrifiers grumbled when gentrification failed to stop with them. Longtime New Yorkers complained that their beloved city's history was being erased, its character homogenized, its sins diluted; even its accent was fading. Others groused that the forces of preservation had gone into overdrive and that the Landmarks Commission was frantically coloring in the map with ever-larger historic districts that were forever frozen in time—architecturally, at least. The commission stood accused of turning the city into a 1:1 scale model of its former self—not New York, but "New York."

What really got people to complain in chorus—and gave Bloomberg's successor, Bill de Blasio, his theme—was money: too much of it in some places, not enough in others. Ever since the days of the Dutch, money has been the source of the city's energy, the reason for its existence, and the engine of its growth. In the first decade of the twenty-first century, the geyser of capital got out of control. Manhattan's towers sprang ever higher, but all the frenzied construction couldn't bring real estate prices within reach of ordinary mortals. Working stiffs drifted to the outer boroughs or the inner 'burbs, while the homeless population topped sixty thousand, far more than would fit in Yankee Stadium.

The city's glory is its perpetual complexity and contradiction, which is why those who love it most do the most complaining. If you stay long enough, you get to grumble in one decade about junkies and criminals taking over the streets and, in the next, that they have fled, taking authenticity with them. The city's failures evolve but never vanish, and a sense of nostalgic pessimism dogs even periods of uplift. These oppositions can't be reconciled; they're part of the magnetism, the specialness that no preservation agency can safeguard and no epidemic of banks and drugstore chains can erase. The city is constantly being tugged between the forces of memory and amnesia. Every un-renovated tenement is an offense to someone's sense of progress, each new building a desecration of someone's childhood. We fret because the city is changing too quickly and also not nearly fast enough. But, outside occasional periods of disenchantment, one constant remains: New York is not quite ample enough for all the people who want to be here.

Each year, the population and the skyline reach new peaks, and so does the number of visitors. The new World Trade Center stands at the symbolically resonant height of 1,776 feet (including its spire), and the number of New Yorkers steams toward nine million. Cranes seem to be in constant use, executing their asynchronous, slow-motion rooftop dances. Asian cities boast taller towers and more manic demographic growth, but New York has left its crazed adolescent years behind. It now has the luxury of growing slowly into its extravagance. And as it does, this aging dowager of a megalopolis convinces the world that it is young again, and vibrant, a place of myth and magic and possibility.

MAGNETIC CITY

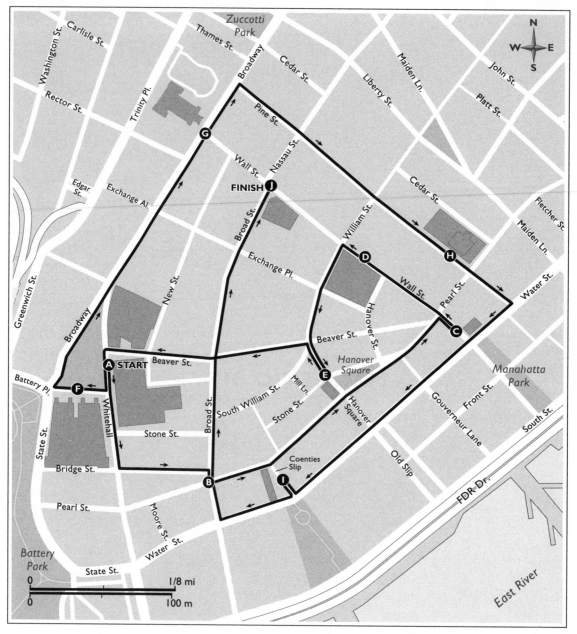

A Bowling Green

B Pearl St. and Broad St.

C 82 Wall St.

D 55 Wall St.

E India House, One Hanover Square

F Alexander Hamilton U.S. Custom House

G Broadway and Wall St.

H 70 Pine St.

I Coenties Slip

J 23 Wall St.

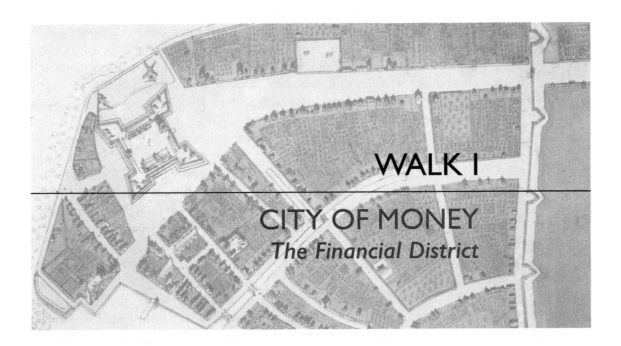

WALK I

CITY OF MONEY
The Financial District

From the earliest days of urban Manhattan, how much you made mattered more than who you were. The Dutch who arrived in the seventeenth century did not come to do God's work, or to glorify a king, or civilize natives, or escape persecution. They came because they spotted a good business opportunity. In his indispensable book about New Amsterdam, *The Island at the Center of the World*, Russell Shorto traces the tolerant, capitalistic character of modern New York all the way back to its roots as an outpost of the Dutch West India Company. This single-minded preoccupation with finance has its obscene side, a truth you can hardly miss on a quick walk around a city where some people spend more on cuff links in an afternoon than others earn in a decade. But it has also molded a city where fanaticism gets few footholds, where eccentricities and freedoms thrive. To walk around Manhattan is to stroll among piles of unimaginable wealth, transfigured into houses and towers and parks—a metropolis ample and weird enough to attract people who don't care about money at all.

Money is the juice that nourishes New York's growth. It flows through the world's ducts, converges on the Stock Exchange, and gushes through Midtown banks, where it's converted into Manhattan real estate, luxury goods, and tax revenue. Despite close competition from London and Tokyo, New York remains the world's financial capital, and the cataracts of cash that fall onto the concrete city splash about and irrigate our expensive amenities. The rich drive up prices and wield power in blinkered and capricious ways. But they also enjoy, and pay for, parks and concert halls and hospitals and universities. The sums that circulate through the municipal treasury—nearly $80 billion in 2016—mean that New York's affordable-housing program, its police department, schools, parks, public library systems, and network of bike paths are all far and away the largest in the country.

And so I come looking for New York's grasping but generous soul in the Financial District, where the city began, where the geological force of money has sculpted artificial canyons and laid down sedimentary deposits of architecture. This is where the trade in hemp and sugar and slaves eventually gave way to equities and bonds. It's where, when money fled in the 1970s, art crept in; where, when the money returned, it carried along a new tribe of downtown dwellers, who made room for play in a neighborhood built for work.

> Begin at **A**, Bowling Green.

I wander through the parklet called Bowling Green, the flat clearing where, tradition has it, Peter Minuit bought Manhattan from the Lenape inhabitants in 1626. Some cities trace their identities to an act of conquest (Mexico City), a royal charter (Versailles), the consolidation of political power (Beijing), the course of a river (Cairo), religious fervor (Boston), mythological lore (Rome), or the migrations of refugees (Tel Aviv). New York's founding document is a real estate deal. Each side traded away something of modest value: Minuit handed over a collection of hardware and other European goods. In return, the Lenape recognized the obvious fact that they were sharing an abundant wilderness with a handful of confused whites. From the moment of that transaction, this spot has always been about business. Here the Dutch West India Company built its defensible headquarters, really just a crumbling mound of packed dirt they called a fort. And here began the northbound Native American trail, which the Dutch adopted as their own main drag (Heere Straat, or "Gentlemen's Street") and the British later called Broadway.

> Walk two blocks south on Whitehall Street, turn left on Bridge Street and, after one block, right on Broad Street where it meets Pearl Street at **B**.

I thread my way to the unpromising corner of Pearl and Broad Streets. It's nothing much to look at now: a slightly claustrophobic intersection, presided over by Fraunces Tavern, the eighteenth-century hostelry built on a soggy "water lot." (It was already an ancient establishment in 1783, when George Washington went there to celebrate while the last British troops fled.) I can just barely make out Manhattan's original topography in the way the pavement slopes gently down toward Pearl Street and then flattens out where it hits what in the seventeenth century would have been shallows. Pearl Street was called Dock Street then, and it was both the edge of New Amsterdam and its center. This is where I find a wormhole to New York's remotest past.

Standing amid the high-rises, inhaling exhaust, I try to conjure up the mingled odors of brine, tobacco, and tar. I strain to understand how the colonists' urgent desire for financial success gave Manhattan its earliest form.

The grandest home in New Amsterdam: Peter Stuyvesant's house, called White Hall

Here, Peter Stuyvesant's two-story mansion sat beside serried shops, wooden homes, taverns, and warehouses. Ships were moored at the sole wooden dock that poked into the East River. Sailors unloaded their cargo, hauled it across the dirt road to the Dutch West India Company, and lifted it into the upper-level storeroom by a pulley fastened to the brick façade. Colonists from a country under perpetual threat of drowning knew to keep their valuables raised.

Dutch New Amsterdam was hardly more than a rustic hamlet, but already neighborhood dynamics were visibly at play. The Castello Plan, a 1660 map that details the location and function of every one of the 370 buildings, makes it clear that a stretch of waterfront nearest the pier functioned as the epicenter of urban activity. Governors, slaves, and smugglers landed on this hectic stretch of riverbank. A doctor, Hans Kierstede, lived at one end of a row of warehouses; on the other, the hatter Samuel Edsall kept his shop next

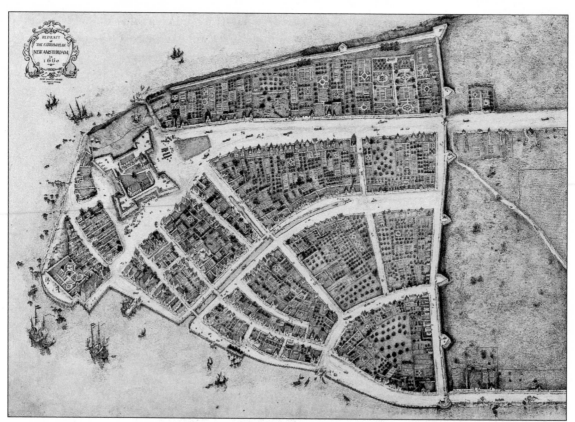

New Amsterdam in 1660, shown in the Castello Plan, redrafted in 1916 by John Wolcott Adams and Isaac Newton Phelps Stokes

to Nicholas Jansen's bakery. Asser Levy, apparently Manhattan's first Jewish resident, operated a slaughterhouse at the end of Wall Street. (The record is silent on whether his butchering operation was kosher.) But the main attraction sat on the corner with the Heere Gracht canal: Hans Dreper's tavern.

Even this tiny nub of the future megalopolis had suburbs. On the map, the gabled houses thin out to the north and west, facing roads but backing onto gardens, yards, and fields. Governor Stuyvesant commuted two miles on horseback every day from his exurban estate in Greenwyck (later anglicized to Greenwich Village). By the time the British took over in 1664, the city had already developed some of the maladies that still pit neighbors against one another: slums, ethnic conflict, and NIMBYism. Poor Dutch holdovers from the old regime clustered along Broad Street's side alleys, and in an early imposition of zoning, authorities insisted that cobblers take their foul-smelling tanning pits and get out of downtown.

Ah, the reek of early New York. You could construct a whole alternate history of the city through pollution and garbage. Both have always been plentiful, as always when you cram large numbers of people together. Today, we tend to think of trash as an expensive excretion, shipping it far away and paying other states to take it. In the past, though, New York treated garbage as a resource and managed to squeeze out of it the most valued yield of all: land. That's the reason Pearl Street sits two blocks back from the water now. Soon after England took over, the city began colonizing the damp ground between high and low tides and inaugurated the local tradition of the public–private partnership by turning over this newly created property to owners who promised to improve it with wharves, streets, and a seawall. That didn't always happen. Often the owners just built their houses and ignored the rest.

As the island became more urbanized, it produced immense quantities of rubble and refuse. In 1811, the Commissioners' Plan decreed that Manhattan would grow along a rectilinear grid, so hills were leveled and cliffs blasted away to make the terrain conform to the map, creating tons of debris. As the population grew, the tonnage of trash exploded: Between 1856 and 1860, its volume increased 700 percent. Huge loads of ash, offal, manure, dead horses, and household garbage were carted to the water's edge and loaded onto floating "dumping boards" and into the shallows and slips, where they gradually alchemized into real estate. The slow process haloed the city in stink, but in the long run it proved to be the most profitable form of recycling.

Big public works have helped the island expand: Every bucketful of dirt and stones scooped out to make the subway tunnels needed somewhere to go, and usually it wound up at the water's edge. It's been rare, in recent decades, for a virgin neighborhood to surge from the muddy flats, but in the late 1960s the western edge of the Financial District did: Battery Park City was mapped out on Hudson River landfill to provide rental housing for workers in the future World Trade Center and the Financial District. Today, the Twin Towers are gone and many of Wall Street's old office buildings have metamorphosed into condos, but Battery Park City has passed through its frontier stage and its antiseptic phase, evolving into a vibrant waterfront district, one of the only residential areas in New York that hug the river quite so close.

For most of the city's history, the river was where the money—and therefore the action—was. In 1979, Madonna arrived in New York and told a cabbie to take her "to the middle of everything." He dropped her at Times Square. But if she had stepped off a vessel at Burling Slip in around 1800 and wanted the same thing, she would have been pointed toward Tontine Coffee House, at 82 Wall Street.

Built in 1793 by the city's first stockbrokers as a place for business, it also served as an inn, a dining room, and a market where dealers traded whatever was for sale: molasses, investments, political influence, news—and, we must not forget, slaves. That pestilential trade predated the building. From 1711 to 1762, the city ran a dockside slave market, collecting taxes on every sale of a

< Walk four blocks along Pearl Street, turn right on Wall Street, and go to No. 82, **C,** near the corner with Water Street.

The center of everything: Tontine Coffee House in 1797, on the left in a 1910 engraving

human being. The open-sided market hut was torn down, but by then the slave business had moved a few steps away. "The steps and balcony [of the Tontine] were crowded with people bidding, or listening to the several auctioneers," a visitor reported. "The slip and the corners of Wall and Pearl-streets, were jammed up with carts, drays, and wheelbarrows; horses and men were huddled promiscuously together, leaving little or no room for passengers to pass. . . . Every thing was in motion; all was life, bustle and activity."

Standing in front of the stodgy brick-and-stone office building where the coffeehouse used to be, I can almost experience the scene: the urgent, mysterious rituals of exchange, the sense that greed, ambition, and civic pride were all concentrated on the house's cramped porch. The frenzy accelerated after the 1825 opening of the Erie Canal, when New York Harbor became a vestibule for the American hinterland. Soon, tides of bankers, brokers, lawyers, bookkeepers, and politicians sloshed daily between the docks and the grand new marble Merchants' Exchange on Wall Street. The buildings are gone, but the money-fueled intensity remains.

One December night in 1835, a security guard smelled smoke. In one of the many jammed warehouses downtown, some scrap of wealth awaiting shipment caught fire—a bale of cotton, maybe, lit by a dropped cigar or a spilled oil lamp. In minutes, the frigid wind off the harbor tossed the flames from window to window and roof to roof. Firefighters flailed and pumps seized up; near the shore, the East River was frozen solid. Crowds frantically hauled valuables to the Old Dutch Church, a solid brick building. It was said that a couple of hours later, when the fire swept into the nave, feeding on pews and salvaged ledgers, someone rushed to the doomed organ loft and played Mozart's *Requiem* as the flames rose. More likely, hot air rushed through the pipes, producing eerie unmanned blasts. When the fire finally burned itself out on the second day, Lower Manhattan was a charred hellscape. The Merchants' Exchange and the Tontine Coffee House were gone. Dozens of ships, cut loose so the flames wouldn't leap aboard, drifted offshore like so many Flying Dutchmen.

Lower Manhattan has been shaped by crisis and rebirth: the Depression, the fiscal crisis of 1975, the 9/11 attacks, the financial meltdown of 2008, Hurricane Sandy. Each time, the city has retooled. And as we try to prepare for the next onslaught, it's worth recalling the devastations of the past and how resiliently New York reacted to them. In fact, the 1835 fire—like the Chicago fire and the 1906 San Francisco earthquake—jolted the city into foresight.

Two centuries after the city's founding, this was still a rough, hurried place slapped together out of salvaged timber and hand-molded brick. The generations who built New York had their eye not on posterity but on the immediate future, when loans came due and investments might pay off. After the fire, with most of the seventeenth- and eighteenth-century city wiped out, New York reseeded itself. Businessmen built a more lavish and durable set of storehouses, banks, and exchanges. They began to think in terms of permanence. Fire codes were rewritten. Water was piped in from upstate. Two days of total destruction were a blip when what mattered most was that the flow of goods, people, and credit remain unobstructed. Just three years after the fire, in 1838, the SS *Sirius* chugged into New York Harbor, eighteen days out from Ireland, winning a transatlantic race with the *Great Western,* which came from Bristol, England. The era of the steamship had begun, and the pace of commerce accelerated again. It's hard to look back on those years without admiring the creative energy of capitalism. Fires recurred, and destruction was a fact of life—but so was the craving for wealth that expressed itself in urban design.

No single building represents the tenacity, adaptability, and grandiosity of the post-fire spirit more than 55 Wall Street, built in 1842. With their exchange incinerated, the city's merchants needed a new place of business, and so they immediately commissioned the architect Isaiah Rogers to design a temple to trade. The four-story, full-block structure, fronted by a row of massive Ionic columns carved out of Quincy granite, has the look of timeless stability.

< Walk up Wall Street, away from the water, to **D**, No. 55.

For decades, the neoclassical style had been the standard for town halls, schools, and, of course, banks, reassuring the public that ancient aesthetic principles translated into equally conservative practices. A few older merchants may have remembered the rickety riverside enclosure where slaves, flour, and cornmeal were bought and sold; this new white monument to staid permanence drove home the point that trade had outgrown its grubby bazaar phase and begotten its own upstanding institutions. Merchants could no longer operate by dint of informal gatherings on a crowded porch or in a noisy tavern. They now had echoing hallways, high ceilings, massive columns, ornate cornices, and enormous quantities of granite. That's what real money looked like.

55 Wall Street, Merchants' Exchange, now Cipriani Wall Street

Of course, buildings are commodities, too: The exchange moved out in 1862, replaced for a while by the Customs Service, where Herman Melville toiled, dreaming of distant seas. At the end of the century, National City Bank took over and had McKim, Mead & White outfit it with a second colonnade and sumptuous interiors. Today, it's an event space—one of the few dining rooms in the city that can comfortably seat eight hundred; on gala nights, amplified speeches echo incomprehensibly around the ornate vaults.

> **Turn left on William Street, then walk three blocks to E, at One Hanover Square.**

It's in the nature of New York ambitions to be quickly surpassed. Grandiosity comes to seem timid, dignity turns shabby, and each generation's glories sooner or later need to be rescued from obsolescence. Take the sober coffee-colored Italianate mini-palazzo at One Hanover Square, designed by Richard Carman in 1854 to house the Hanover Bank.

To a European businessman who stepped off a steamship from France in

One Hanover Square,
Cotton Exchange
(today India House)

the 1850s, the bank must have looked like a sorry bit of pretense. In Paris, plain-vanilla neoclassicism was giving way to over-the-top excesses that would shortly produce the grand, hyper-ornate opera house, the Palais Garnier. Here in New York, one of the most august financial institutions in town was named for the British royal family. And yet that bank occupied a cramped building with windows jammed so tightly up against the corner that there was no room for proper quoins. Besides, it was faced not in marble but with ugly dark sandstone that started crumbling as soon as it was installed. New Yorkers called it brownstone and used it to clad thousands of row houses, because it was cheap and local and because a handy worker could almost carve it with a pocketknife. Edith Wharton described the city of her childhood in the 1860s as "this little low-studded rectangular New York, cursed with its universal chocolate-colored coating of the most hideous stone ever quarried." But though Wharton deplored it, demand eventually exhausted reserves of the most popular variety, Portland Brownstone. Today's homeowners in Brooklyn and on leafy Manhattan side streets have to restore their façades with a look-alike composite.

Hanover Bank quickly outgrew its headquarters, and in 1871 a group of New York businessmen bought it as the seat of the city's first Cotton Exchange. Before then, independent agents moved the product from field to market, and when the Civil War stopped up the flow, they began negotiating the sale of confiscated cotton before they actually got their hands on it. Some called those promised shipments "futures"; others called the practice of selling them a shell game. After the war, fifty prominent New Yorkers realized that if they formed a club and kept in touch with their counterparts in the English port city of Liverpool by cable, they could stop depending on shady Southern brokers. The modern commodities market was born. One Hanover Square has suffered many abuses and modifications, but it's been recently restored, and today it looks much the way it did 150 years ago, even if nothing around it does. The Cotton Exchange has moved away, and a different kind of cozy business club has taken its place: India House, an organization dedicated to the fine art of lunch.

> Walk back up William Street to Beaver Street, turn left, and go back to Bowling Green, where F, Alexander Hamilton U.S. Custom House, stands on the south side of the square.

If business was going to erect properly dignified quarters in which to accumulate capital, the government, too, was going to need a place to skim off its share. Until Congress instituted the income tax in 1913, the vast majority of the federal treasury's revenue came from import duties, and its most productive golden egg–laying goose was the port of New York. Accordingly, customs officials generally occupied the finest available building, starting with a neoclassical structure at Bowling Green, directly on top of the old fort. In 1907, after meandering around Lower Manhattan, the Customs Service circled back to Bowling Green and built itself a home of its own: the Custom House, designed by the celebrated Cass Gilbert. By then, New York thought of itself as a global power, and its institutional architecture reflected that attitude.

The Alexander Hamilton U.S. Custom House

Gilbert built the government a Beaux Arts temple to taxation. In America, commerce paid for art, and here art gave thanks. Daniel Chester French sculpted four continents striking various allegorical (and stereotypical) poses along the façade: A vigorous and windblown America looks as if she's about to spring to her sandaled feet, while a topless Africa slumbers. The rest of the building is encrusted with wreaths and reliefs, lending hectic grandeur to a public office building where employees labored over prosaic ledgers. The decorating didn't stop with Gilbert and French: In 1937 the painter Reginald Marsh adorned the rotunda with ebullient murals of New York Harbor teeming with vessels—this just a few years before war would choke off commercial shipping almost completely.

It may seem odd to get sentimental about a building designed for accountants, but I find the Custom House to be a moving example of the era's civic generosity. This was, after all, the people's spigot, whose flowing cash paid for a modernizing nation, and the architecture encouraged pride in collective prosperity. Today, we frown on public buildings that cost any more than they need to, since every dollar spent on luxe is, after all, a dollar denied to a social service. But the Custom House, like Grand Central Terminal, the New York Public Library, and the Metropolitan Museum of Art, was a flamboyantly egalitarian gesture. At a time when most New Yorkers lived in airless squalor, these were places where anyone, no matter how foreign or poor, could tread like an emperor in vast vaulted halls. What new structure these days offers such inclusive grandeur?

At around the same time that Gilbert was helping the government collect its due, he was also championing the ultimate in capitalist architecture: the skyscraper. In 1913, he completed the Woolworth Building, a dazzling white upsweep of a tower near City Hall, etched with Gothic tracery, studded with turrets, and topped with a copper crown. But already, years earlier, he had made it clear that reaching for the clouds was not primarily an exercise in artistic ambition or advanced engineering; it was a business venture. "The building is merely the machine that makes the land pay," he wrote in 1900. "The machine is none the less a useful one because it has a measure of beauty, and that architectural beauty, judged even from an economic standpoint, has an income-bearing value." Art, in Gilbert's view, existed to turn a profit. Maybe Gilbert was simply telling his patrons what they wanted to hear, but he was a consummate artist of commercial architecture, and his words jibed with the practical spirit of the times.

It was a spirit that horrified the writer Henry James. When I see the palisade of Lower Manhattan towers, I think of James looking at the same view more than a century ago. In 1904, he returned to America after spending twenty years in Europe, and he was shocked at the changes he saw. When he left, Trinity Church towered over the city the way One World Trade Center does today. When he came back and gazed on his hometown from the harbor, the church was barely visible, hemmed in by the first generation of skyscrapers, which he found unbearably crass. He abhorred the arrogance of wealth expressed in stone. In *The American Scene,* he fulminated against buildings we would barely consider tall but that he saw as omens of a baleful future. Skyscrapers, he thought, looked big but were as ephemeral as a paper fortune:

> Consecrated by no uses save the commercial at any cost, they are simply the most piercing notes in that concert of the expensively provisional into which your supreme sense of New York resolves itself. They never begin to speak to you, in the manner of the builded majesties of the world as we have heretofore known such—towers or temples or fortresses or palaces—with the authority of things of permanence or even of things of long duration. One story is good only till another is told, and sky-scrapers are the last word of economic ingenuity only till another word be written. This shall be possibly a word of still uglier meaning . . .

By contrast, he continued, "Beauty indeed was the aim of the creator of the spire of Trinity Church, so cruelly overtopped and so barely distinguishable . . . in its abject helpless humility . . ."

The Singer Building looming behind Trinity Church (1904–10)

James was eloquently, spectacularly wrong. More than a century later, that next word has been written and rewritten many times, and each time it is still the same neologism he hated: skyscraper. The waterways had made the land beside them so valuable that the only way forward was to build up. While James was off in Europe, the elevator had replaced the staircase. The buildings he objected to were the first architectural glories of the modern age, including the Park Row Building and the New York World Building (both on Park Row). The Singer Building at 149 Broadway hadn't yet topped out.

Had I been born into a different time, I might have shared James's curmudgeonliness. I might have looked up and seen those rearing towers as the product of real estate lunacy rather than infectious vigor. But from the steps of Gilbert's Custom House, the fruits of rapacious capitalism look

Standard Oil Building

pretty splendid now. On the west side of Broadway, at No. 25, is the 1921 Cunard Building, by Benjamin Wistar Morris and Carrère & Hastings. For most transatlantic passengers, this was where the experience began, and the Cunard Line's executives wanted it to be as glamorous as possible. The ticketing hall (now freshly restored and converted to a condominium lobby) was as ornate as a cathedral, its frescoed vaults warming the sunlight as they entertained the stiff-necked gawpers standing on line, dazzling them with representations of continents, winds, ships, and explorers. Across Broadway, at No. 26, is the almost contemporaneous Standard Oil Building, which Carrère & Hastings (again) designed for the Rockefeller family business. It's a white wedding cake of majesty, pivoting on its way up so that the nine-story base follows the meandering curve of Broadway and the tower aligns with the grid of streets.

This pair of white castles forms a colossal gateway, New York's equivalent to the columns guarding Piazza San Marco in Venice. As technology pushed bigger and bigger buildings farther and farther toward the clouds, architects had to adapt ancient forms to the outsize steel-backed skyscraper. Carrère &

Hastings stacked windows and multiplied arches, enlarged campaniles and layered cornices, all in an attempt to make a thoroughly new kind of structure look comfortably familiar. The Standard Oil Building is a Renaissance palazzo for a Medici-like family of magnates who operated on a new-world scale. The wonder of that scale took a long time to fade.

> Walk uptown on Broadway, past **G**, Henry James's beloved Trinity Church, turn right on Pine Street, and walk to **H**, 70 Pine Street, near the corner of Pearl Street.

In 1935, the photographer Berenice Abbott took a picture of the Fulton Street Dock that captures the gorgeous collision of New York as shipping town and financial capital. In the foreground, burly men in rubber boots push wooden hand trucks over the wet pier, oblivious to the gray Gothic castles rising into the mist-bright morning like opera sets. The skyscrapers belong to a different universe, and I can imagine the fishmongers glancing toward them every once in a while and clicking their tongues. They spent their own lives fixed on the horizon line; what would people want with those fairy-tale heights?

Berenice Abbott,
Fulton Street Dock,
1935

The tallest of the buildings that appear in Abbott's picture is 70 Pine Street, which opened in 1932 as the shock of the Depression was settling in. It's hard now to grasp the mixture of misery and dogged ebullience of those days, when a few towers raced glamorously toward the sky just as the U.S. economy was hitting rock bottom. In 1929, the Chrysler Building lunged past 40 Wall Street to become the tallest building in the world—until two years later, when the Empire State Building overtopped them both. Then the gas and electric company known as Cities Services built itself a contender at 70 Pine Street, designed by Clinton & Russell with Holton & George. The spire reached 952 feet, a respectable third to the Chrysler and Empire State.

In those breadline days, the building must have seemed obscene. Today, though, I stand across Pearl Street and gaze upward in admiration. The tower spears the fog, embodying the moody glitter of Gotham. At every level, something grabs the eye: the ornate metal doors, the limestone models of the skyscraper carved into the building's façade, the abstracted peaks stamped in metal above the lobby windows.

Hugh Ferriss, Imaginary Drawings, Philosophy, 1928

The tower's Art Deco energy emerged from the interaction of aesthetic fancy and legislation. In 1916, as new technologies threatened to turn Lower Manhattan into a dark forest of high-rises, the city began regulating the skyline. The law allowed greater height on wider streets and required buildings to recede as they rose, funneling sunlight to the sidewalk. Hugh Ferriss, the architect whose brooding renderings made him the Piranesi of New York, understood the romance embedded in the new zoning code. "Our future buildings, with their superimposed, receding stages, will produce as definite a sense of strength and unity as did the medieval cathedrals which, with their clerestories rising above their bases, were a similar example of setback construction," he wrote. Because new towers would rise above the four- and five-story undergrowth, "architects will design buildings, not façades. That is to say, architecture comes into her own."

Ferriss saw this development as a liberating force and a template for cities everywhere. "The most fascinating potentiality of the new laws may lie in their ability to finally bring forth the much-debated 'new style' in architecture. . . . We are not contemplating the new architecture of a city—we are contemplating the new architecture of a civilization." His rhetoric helped transform the zoning code into a spectacularly utopian tool. In 1929, he published his graphic manifesto, *The Metropolis of Tomorrow,* the book that shaped the dreams of architects, planners, comicbook illustrators, and Hollywood set designers. In a long essay with 108 drawings, he described a city of fantastical drama, in which pedestrians would move around by skyway and towers would have rooftop landing pads.

So when the first workers arrived at their offices a few years later, 70 Pine represented not just a challenge to economic catastrophe but also a statement of faith in the future of architecture downtown. As it turned out, that faith was misplaced. The Depression and World War II brought high-rise construction to a standstill. No new skyscrapers went up in the Financial District until the 1960s, and then they came in the form of straight-walled boxes. (Those towers, too, were born from the marriage of zoning and desire. In 1958, the completion of Mies van der Rohe's Seagram Building at 375 Park Avenue [between Fifty-second and Fifty-third Streets] made it clear that the old rules did not adequately account for new technology and a new aesthetic. Architects demanded the right to have their steel-and-glass shafts shoot straight up from the sidewalk instead of contorting themselves in tapering setbacks. In 1961, the city revised the zoning code, trading height for public plazas, like the one at the corner of Pine Street and William Street. This new arrangement created a lot of blocky slabs and dead streets.)

On September 11, 2001, 70 Pine Street became once again (but only for a while) the tallest building in Lower Manhattan. By then it was occupied by AIG, the mammoth insurance company that a few years later, during the financial crisis of 2008, nearly drove the world economy off a cliff. The financial-services industry stepped back from the abyss, but AIG moved out and went bouncing around the neighborhood. And so, like so many landmark office towers in the Financial District, 70 Pine was converted to condos.

The disaster of 2008 was not the first economic calamity to visit the area. Just as droughts and fires mold landscapes, so the *absence* of money has often shaped New York. It's an awesome thing to watch that vacuum sweep through areas of concentrated affluence, uprooting businesses, emptying storefronts, leaving streets depopulated and bleak. The Financial District is an especially sensitive ecosystem, a sort of wetlands of cash. When the money recedes, an invasive species creeps in, creatures who thrive on desolation and seek out the most uninhabitable spaces in every great, decaying city: artists.

> Continue down Pine Street to Water Street, turn right, and walk four blocks to 1, Coenties Slip.

The first wave settled at mid-century on Coenties Slip, a once-decrepit alleyway just off Pearl Street, squeezed between the receding fortunes of the shipping industry and the rising monoliths of finance. In the nineteenth century, Coenties Slip (like Peck Slip and Burling Slip a few blocks away) was an artificial inlet, a finger of water poking into the belly of Manhattan so that ships could be jammed in, unloaded, and readied to cross the world again. Preachers stood on the pier, or on the deck of a moored barge, and harangued sailors whose only address was a shipboard hammock. You couldn't ask for a more convenient church: Right after the sermon, the congregation made straight for the closest groggery, not twenty yards away. Eventually, land was even scarcer than ships' berths, and the slips were all filled in. In the 1950s, as the shipping industry started to collapse, Coenties Slip attracted a coterie of virtually indigent artists: Robert Indiana, Ellsworth Kelly, Agnes Martin, James Rosenquist, and Jack Youngerman all lived and worked here, making new art out of fragments and memories of a New York that was constantly slipping away. Indiana later became famous for the sleek steel LOVE sculptures that adorn corporate plazas all over the world, but early on he was working in a rougher mode, cobbling together sculptures out of planks, wagon wheels, and stencils.

"I didn't have money," he later recalled in an interview with *Index Magazine,* "so I would go out at night and pilfer this old wood from the demolition sites around Coenties"—beams from old buildings "which themselves had been built with wood salvaged from the masts of sailing ships. Lower Manhattan was almost destroyed by the fire of 1835, at the same time that sailing ships were becoming obsolete. The masts became columns on the ground floors of the warehouses." I find this cycle of continuity and destruction moving, the journey of a natural material from tree to ship, to building, to art.

Robert Indiana
in front of his
Coenties Slip studio

City dwellers dread urban decay; then, after it's come and gone, they treasure it in memory. People who lived in Lower Manhattan at mid-century recall a place that had lost its old purpose. The collapse of shipping was followed by the decline of manufacturing and then by a third punch to the city's fiscal health: The middle class fled to the suburbs, taking their taxes with them, and in 1975 the city flirted with bankruptcy. All of this was fine with artists, who treated the decrepitude as a playground. Holland Cotter, now the *Times*'s Pulitzer Prize–winning art critic but then a struggling freelancer, lived a few blocks from the World Trade Center in the 1970s, and he recalled the carnival atmosphere surrounding Red Grooms's and Mimi Gross's *Ruckus Manhattan,* installed in the lobby of an office building at 88 Pine Street:

> The enormous piece, every inch of it handmade, was in progress almost daily for seven months. Everyone downtown, from artists to office workers, followed its progress from the street, and lined up to have Mr. Grooms and Ms. Gross draw their portraits. The final product, with a crazily tilting 30-foot-high model of the Twin Towers

made from wood, paint and papier-mâché, was a big success. It was the right thing, at the right time, in the right place: a loving, leering walk-in cartoon of New York that let a bummed-out city feel good about itself.

Artists thrived in abandoned, incomplete, or undervalued spaces. Soil excavated from the World Trade Center's site was used as landfill for the future Battery Park City, and for a time those low, empty flats along the Hudson River proved an ideal canvas. Agnes Denes planted acres of wheat there, and her photographs of amber waves of grain at the foot of the colossal Twin Towers remain an enduring document of those strangely vibrant, improvised years. The enterprising organization Creative Time commandeered the resonant rotunda of the Custom House for new-music concerts. One of the early events was the world premiere of Alvin Lucier's *Music on a Long Thin Wire,* in which a steel thread stretched taut across the vast space was made to vibrate automatically by a pair of strategically positioned magnets. The result was a virtually endless, self-sustaining drone that could either heighten spiritual (and drug-induced) bliss or make impatient listeners want to scream. A neighborhood famous for its unabating frenzy had now discovered the joys of catatonia.

By the time terrorists tried to deal downtown a deathblow on September 11, 2001, the Financial District had already started transforming itself again. Banks were moving to Midtown, Battery Park City, Jersey City, and beyond, preferring the airier, brighter, more elaborately wired office space of new glass towers to the creaky behemoths of Wall Street. In their place, families started moving in, turning a daytime hive of worker bees into a round-the-clock residential district. Real estate brokers shortened the term Financial District into the more family-friendly FiDi. In 1970, only about seven hundred full-time residents rattled around the largely empty zone. By 2014, the population had climbed to forty-three thousand, and master bedrooms replaced corner offices. Those new arrivals brought new schools, playgrounds, restaurants, and fresh forms of luxury. Today, fantastically profitable tech companies lodge in former factories. The heirs to J. P. Morgan's white-shoe bankers are white-tube-sock investors who pore over their laptops at home, while the stolid workplaces of a century ago have become the palaces of self-indulgence.

> Continue along Water Street, turn right on Broad Street, and walk to J, at the corner of Wall Street.

There are few corners in New York City with a more sober history and a more fanciful present than the squat, forbidding little former bank at 23 Wall Street. Once, it was the epicenter of the financial world. In 2007, it became an icon of the designer life, the vestibule to a luxury residential building titled like an auteur's creation: "Downtown by Philippe Starck." With this

The center of
financial power:
J. P. Morgan & Co.,
a.k.a. "the Corner,"
at 23 Wall Street

project, Starck, the French designer famous for fusing baroque and modernist sensibilities into such objects as bulbous baby monitors, tooth-shaped stools, and wall-size rococo mirrors, intended to reinvent the Financial District. In place of marbled halls and hushed talk of investments, there were now gigantic gilt-framed mirrors and loud flaunting of wealth.

At the time that he was converting the bank and the office tower next door at 15 Broad Street to condominiums, Starck told me that he saw himself not as a designer but as the design guru for a new people: the "Smart Tribe," he called them, urban pioneers who would convert an area of stodgy office buildings into a new Bohemia. "My idea is to bring happiness, respect, vision, poetry, surrealism, magic—these are not values you find in Wall Street," he said. "Here is the center of the world, but it's also hell, so I want to create paradise. This is the Garden of Eden in downtown."

The building was erected at the behest of J. P. Morgan in 1913, and despite its staid stone exterior, it did represent extravagance of a sort. Having paid a fortune for the site, Morgan decided not to take the logical step of putting up a revenue-generating tower to house his bank. Instead, he built just the three floors he required to do business, tossing away a vast and valuable tract of vertical real estate.

These days, to approach "the Corner," as it is known, means braving a gauntlet of police officers in bulletproof vests, who guard the New York Stock Exchange. The juncture of Wall and Broad has been a terrorist target before. At noon on September 16, 1920, a bomb hidden in a horse-drawn cart exploded in front of the House of Morgan, killing dozens and maiming hundreds more. The bank's stonework still bears the scars from the blast. New York City wouldn't see such a gruesome attack again until another September day, eight decades later.

But walk through the austere portal and you enter a world of flamboyant frivolity. Starck restored Morgan's colossal Swarovski chandelier and reinstalled it in the adjoining 15 Broad Street, not as a lavish fixture far overhead but as a crystal cloud hovering inches from the floor. Central to the Starck philosophy is the idea of life as a form of theater and the designer as director. The former bank and office building combo made "a beautiful building in the center of an opera set," he said. "It's not architecture; it's a movie, it's opera, it's boiling life." The Financial District outside provides the urban décor, an exciting backdrop to luxurious domestic drama. Who wouldn't crave a principal role in this spectacle, populated by a crowd of extras costumed as policemen, tourists, brokers, journalists, and financial workers?

Life à la Starck consists of a series of camera-ready tableaux. In its new incarnation, the roof of Morgan's folly has become a poolside arbor in which to lounge with a cocktail and admire the muscular marble figures laboring in the pediment of the Stock Exchange across the street. The roof garden, Starck enthused, is "like an Italian villa on a lake. You're in the middle of a sculpture, in a garden in the middle of the world. It's an ecstasy trip."

The Castello Plan tells us that in New Amsterdam days a couple of simple houses stood on this corner, backing onto orchards and gardens and facing the Wall, the protective wooden fence that separated town from wilderness. And yet today, as I stand at this thronged intersection, where visitors from all over the world come looking for the brain stem of the world's multi-tentacled financial monster, I'm struck by how consistent the neighborhood's spirit has remained even as it has physically transformed beyond recognition. The global goods that flowed through the New Amsterdam waterfront; the raucous bustle of the Tontine Coffee House; the frenzied lading of steamships in the nineteenth century; the fortunes that, year in, year out, have rushed through these narrow alleys, enriching some and beggaring others—all that relentless pursuit of wealth has kept New York's oldest neighborhood perpetually young.

Interlude I
CITY OF STREETS

I don't need a groundhog to tell me when winter will ebb; I have the Hallelujah Man, a.k.a. the Glory Guy. When the days get longer and the ice starts to thaw, I can hear his chant float up to my apartment from the street. *Glo-ry. Glo-ry. Glo-ry. Jesus.* His seasonal return soothes me, and I look for him in the neighborhood. Wearing a dark suit and fedora and waving a hefty Bible, the Glory Guy patrols his twenty-block parish, delivering his telegraphic message of joy in a hoarse West Indian singsong. *God good. Hallelujah.* Occasionally he breaks into a gleeful shuffle. Street preaching is an ancient and worldwide calling, and yet to me this gentle man, who doesn't hector or cajole or ask for anything but just announces his delight, embodies some benevolent essence of New York. Tens of thousands of people live within earshot of his hollers or just catch a stray *glory!* as they walk past. Some react with indifference or irritation; others ignore him. Still others regard him with varying shades of gratitude. All of these reactions and interactions depend on a deceptively ordinary kit of urban parts: the sidewalk and the street. They form the Glory Guy's office and his church, the stage where we all perform for others the spectacle of our lives.

New York is in many ways an upstairs city, where life is lived in offices and second-floor dance studios, on roofs and fire escapes. But especially in summer, when staying indoors becomes a choice between rattling air condition-

Men laying brick to pave West Twenty-eighth Street, 1930

ers and asphyxiating heat, domestic life colonizes the street. Brownstone dwellers sit on stoops, tenement residents unfold picnic chairs on the sidewalk, office workers escape their cubicles to line up for food trucks, homeless people build encampments in church doors, and chess players settle in at park tables. New Yorkers of every hue and class have a stake in the streets and don't hesitate to claim it.

The great urbanist Jane Jacobs saw a graceful order in the apparently random interplay of lives and routines on the street. In the fifties and sixties, she lived in the West Village, which is now a neighborhood preserved in the aspic of a historic district, where the wealthy rub shoulders with the wealthier, but which was then a scrappy place of immigrants and artists, old and young. Jacobs studied the area's mechanics from her narrow townhouse on Hudson Street and concluded that an old low-rise neighborhood like hers maintained a benign equilibrium around the clock. Her famous phrase "eyes on the street" described an informal mutual-surveillance program that maintained security without intending to. The elderly kept an eye on kids playing on the sidewalks, shopkeepers knew their customers, and teenagers loitered in plain sight. "Under the seeming disorder of the old city," Jacobs wrote in *The Death and Life of Great American Cities,*

> wherever the old city is working successfully, is a marvelous order for maintaining the safety of the streets and the freedom of the city. It is

a complex order. Its essence is intricacy of sidewalk use, bringing with it a constant succession of eyes. This order is all composed of movement and change, and although it is life, not art, we may fancifully call it the art form of the city and liken it to the dance—not to a simpleminded precision dance with everyone kicking up at the same time, twirling in unison and bowing off en masse, but to an intricate ballet in which the individual dancers and ensembles all have distinctive parts which miraculously reinforce each other and compose an orderly whole. The ballet of the good city sidewalk never repeats itself from place to place, and in any one place is always replete with new improvisations.

New York's connective fiber of streets is special—in that they are pretty much the same. Most cities have one or two main pedestrian channels, a web of local byways, and various traffic arteries, which can be safely navigated only inside a two-ton case on wheels. New York, on the other hand, has a warp of avenues and a woof of streets, a tight mesh stretched over most of its surface. That arrangement frustrates drivers, but it rewards obsessional strolling. You could walk the entire length of Manhattan, from Spuyten Duyvil to South Ferry, without having to duck beneath an overpass or navigate a lightless moat of traffic. You could do it again . . . and again, each time choosing a different and equally pleasurable itinerary. You don't even need distance to get variety. Years ago, when I walked my son to preschool, four blocks away, I had my choice of half a dozen different routes and many minor detours. What makes the experience of walking in New York so distinctive is a mixture of mechanical regularity and human idiosyncrasy: the grid and the Glory Guy.

What the savanna is to the lion, the city is to the *flâneur:* a vast and complex habitat. In the 1860s, Charles Baudelaire ambled purposefully through Paris, an itinerant audience member for the urban phantasmagoria all around. He observed the trauma of modernization, as Baron Haussmann ripped out alleyways and replaced them with boulevards. Around the same time, Charles Dickens crisscrossed London, savoring the shocking stench of its slums, and Walt Whitman strode through New York, cataloging the ways that the city kept remaking itself:

> *Give me faces and streets! give me these phantoms incessant and endless along the trottoirs!*
> *Give me interminable eyes! give me women! give me comrades and lovers by the thousand!*
> *Let me see new ones every day! let me hold new ones by the hand every day!*
> *Give me such shows! give me the streets of Manhattan!*

The streets that Whitman demanded were still largely untamed—crowded, chaotic alleys and thoroughfares, patchily paved with cobbles, wood blocks, or gravel or simply covered in dirt. He would wade joyously into foaming currents of traffic, jumping aboard a horse-drawn omnibus and staying on until the final stop, treating his post as a seat in the theater of urban life. "How many hours, forenoons and afternoons," he wrote,

> —how many exhilarating night-times I have had—perhaps June or July, in cooler air—riding the whole length of Broadway, listening to some yarn, (and the most vivid yarns ever spun, and the rarest mimicry)—or perhaps I declaiming some stormy passage from Julius Cæsar or Richard, (you could roar as loudly as you chose in that heavy, dense, uninterrupted street-bass.)

When Whitman was rhapsodizing about the crowds and urban cacophony of the streets, New York and Brooklyn—different cities then, joined only by a ferry—had a combined population of just over a million. Today, nearly 8.6 million are crammed into five boroughs, but the *flâneur*'s fundamental experience remains the same. Protagonists of New York novels, movies, and TV shows are constantly wandering for hours. In Teju Cole's 2011 novel *Open City*, a Nigerian immigrant named Julius meanders with Whit-

Muddy street, Fifth Avenue at Thirty-fourth Street, 1901

manesque determination, trying to make sense of all the hugeness and variety by organizing his experiences and, essentially, geotagging his memories.

Walking through busy parts of town meant I laid eyes on more people, hundreds more, thousands even, than I was accustomed to seeing in the course of a day, but the impress of these countless faces did nothing to assuage my feelings of isolation; if anything it intensified them. . . . One night, I simply went on and on, walking all the way down to Houston Street, a distance of some seven miles, and found myself in a state of disorienting fatigue, laboring to remain on my feet. That night I took the subway home, and instead of falling asleep immediately, I lay in bed, too tired to release myself from wakefulness, and I rehearsed in the dark the numerous incidents and sights I had encountered while roaming, sorting each encounter like a child playing with wooden blocks, trying to figure out which belonged where, which responded to which. Each neighborhood of the city appeared to be made of a different substance, each seemed to have a different air pressure, a different psychic weight: the bright lights and shuttered shops, the housing projects and luxury hotels, the fire escapes and city parks.

New Yorkers walk and walk, cataloging the people whose paths we cross, noting architectural flourishes, eavesdropping on the accidental poetry stuttered into mobile phones:

Yeah, I know . . .

So he was, like, all . . .

Oh, didn't I tell you? She's totally . . .

I mean, IsaidIsaidsoIgo: Yo . . .

The sound of footsteps is the constant rhythm of New York's history. Omnibuses, streetcars, subways, taxis, Citi Bikes, jet packs—none of them ever could or will dislodge walking as the essential way of getting around. (And by walking I mean slow-speed rolling, too: Those who rely on wheelchairs, strollers, and electric scooters also have the pedestrian experience, since its essence lies in its pace.) That makes New York virtually unique in America, although the benefits of a walkable city are becoming obvious, and even cities engineered for cars are gradually retooling. Walking is woven into the city's DNA, partly—and paradoxically—because traffic often makes driving impractical. As New Yorkers heading crosstown like to quip: *Shall we walk or do we have time to take a cab?* One minute on foot will carry you the length of a standard north-south block—thirty seconds if you have long legs and are late for a meeting—and in that time you may have passed three hundred homes. All New Yorkers know that twenty blocks make a mile.

It's odd, if you think about it, that this city should be so conducive to aimlessness, given its Cartesian regularity. New York is a planned place, and planners design streets to be purposeful. As Google Maps points out every time we consult it, cities are full of starting points and destinations, linked by more or less efficient routes. But New York's street grid is also a well-oiled machine for generating randomness.

In the early years of the nineteenth century, when the city was growing breathlessly, officials believed that they could control its future by marking off the map with a ruler. New York then was tiny, by twenty-first-century standards. Today Houston Street defines the edge of Lower Manhattan; then it was called North Street and separated the city below from farmland above. But everyone saw that New York would keep swelling, though how fast or how far was a question for oracles and bookies. To help keep the process as orderly as possible, a committee of dignitaries decreed that it should one day roll northward along eleven parallel avenues, crossed by 155 streets.

The Commissioners' Plan of 1811 was far from the first urban grid: Ancient Romans, Spanish colonists, and the London architect Christopher Wren all saw the checkerboard as the ideal city form. But the New York plan was so comprehensive, so farseeing and influential, that it became a document of visionary rationality. It included no broad squares, no network of grand boulevards converging on monuments or seats of power. It paid no heed to Manhattan's uneven topography or existing property lines. Rather than allowing the wealthy to monopolize the highlands with huge estates while the poor huddled below, it forced future mansions and tenements into similar rows. The result was a masterpiece of straight lines, right angles, and numbered streets that set the adolescent city on a course of democratic uniformity.

This was in many ways an insanely geometric exercise. If the plan's exacting surveyor John Randel could stroll up Fifth Avenue today, he would nod with astonished satisfaction at how precisely perpendicular each intersection turned out, even where streets climb slopes or slice across long-vanished streams. The process wasn't gentle. In order to stick to those straight lines, workers blasted away importunate hills, filled in streams, sliced through farms, and moved entire houses—sometimes without disturbing the families or furniture inside. Of course, there was money in all this disruption. Property owners howled, until they discovered that opening a new street did wonders for the value of their land. Bureaucrats discovered a fabulous gusher of graft.

Edgar Allan Poe railed at the implacable advance of the urban grid on irregular nature. "These magnificent places are *doomed*," he complained. "The spirit of Improvement has withered them with its acrid breath." The regularizing of streets could be traumatic. It swept away virtually every trace of pre-nineteenth-century New York above Fourteenth Street. Pig farms, mills, breweries, groves, cow paths, steepled churches, and village squares were all obliterated. In their place, the commissioners crosshatched the island with rectangular blocks that they expected would soon be jammed with cheap and more or less uniform houses. They left no room for parks—only a military parade ground and an open market—partly because land was already too pricey to be left undeveloped and partly because the "large arms of the sea which embrace Manhattan Island render its situation, in regard to health and pleasure as well as to the convenience of commerce, peculiarly felicitous." Who needs a park when you have the East River? (Fortunately, a later generation of capitalist city fathers felt differently and took 778 acres off the voracious market to create Central Park.)

The plan envisioned an orderly New York but not a mind-numbingly repetitive one. The distance between the avenues varied so much that a simple crosstown walk could be disorienting. (*I've been walking for five minutes and I still haven't gotten to Sixth!*) And then there was the one diagonal disruptor, the road that didn't get the memo to snap into shape but instead kept snaking and dodging its way from one tip of the island to the other and beyond: the one that eventually became Broadway.

Mapping out Manhattan was not the same as making it real. It took decades to flesh out and fill in, and modernity did not follow a steady north-

Second Avenue at East Forty-second Street, 1861

Jacob Riis, Manhattan shantytown, 1896

ward march, as the commissioners had perhaps anticipated it would. In 1867, more than fifty years after the commissioners issued their plan, George Templeton Strong walked the freshly opened Madison Avenue in the Forties and found it "a rough and ragged track . . . rich in mudholes, goats, pigs, geese, stramonium. Here and there Irish shanties 'come out' (like smallpox pustules), each composed of a dozen rotten boards and a piece of stove-pipe for a chimney." The grid didn't get rid of poor neighborhoods, of course, and rustic settlements endured for nearly a century. A Jacob Riis photograph of a Manhattan shantytown in 1896 shows a board-and-nail village perched on an escarpment so steep that residents have connected the levels with ladders, as in a Hopi settlement in New Mexico.

Meanwhile, the meandering country thoroughfare called Bloomingdale Road was straightened into the diagonal slice of Broadway and evolved into a wide tree-lined boulevard. Ample medians attracted Sunday strollers, while paved roadways satisfied cyclists and kept the road clean, gracious, and quiet. In retrospect, it was the kind of ideal shared street that urban planners are trying to achieve today.

All through the nineteenth century, the city was part prosperous industrial metropolis, part impoverished village. Paved thoroughfares coexisted with squelching pathways. In the years before the Civil War, these two worlds— those of the burgeoning bourgeoisie and a discontented underclass—were hinged together at Astor Place. The writer Nigel Cliff describes the two vastly different worlds on either side of the austere, opaque Astor Opera House, built in 1847 to look as if it had been there forever. It's one of the ironies of New York history that a building that tried so hard to appear timeless and aloof wound up triggering a spasm of class warfare:

> With its serried columns, lofty pediments, and bluff stone walls, the theatre sat like a stern patriarch at the junction of the most showily wealthy and the most fiercely working-class districts of the city. On one side was Broadway and the mansion where John Jacob Astor had lived out his last years. . . . On the other side was the Bowery. As broad as Broadway but zipped in tow by the iron tracks and horse-drawn carriages of the Harlem Rail Road, it was lined for a mile with fruit stalls and roast-chestnut stands, tables of tinny cutlery and faded millinery, and rows of Cheap John shops where smooth salesmen hustled bulk goods from raised platforms to jostling crowds. . . . Flames smelling of turpentine illuminated glass signs advertising cockpits, rat-baiting arenas, boxing rings, dime museums, bowling alleys, and gambling dens, together with scores of taverns and beer gardens, some of which served firewater through a rubber tube straight from the barrel at three cents a gulp.

The Boulevard (later Broadway) near West Sixtieth Street, 1898

On May 10, 1849, a riot broke out in Astor Place, with twenty thousand brawlers driven bonkers by the English actor William Macready's interpretation of *Macbeth*. Rioters didn't just take to the streets; they actually *took* the streets, tearing up cobblestones and hurling them at police. And while Macready was declaiming about all our yesterdays lighting fools the way to dusty death, real people were being killed outside: twenty or thirty of them, depending on who was doing the counting. It was an episode of appalling hysteria but also a cathartic expression of popular unrest in which tragedy spread from the stage to the streets. In his book *The Shakespeare Riots,* Cliff details the flammable social mixture that exploded that night, disguised as violent theater criticism. Macready was English, and his rival, Edwin Forrest, who was playing *Macbeth* a few blocks away, was American; that ridiculous difference ignited poor, heavily Irish crowds against the city's Anglophile aristocrats. Despite the genuine horror, it's hard at this distance not to feel a certain wistfulness for a time when theater mattered that much, when the iron filings of New York's class resentments flew to the magnet of Shakespeare.

In a claustrophobic city, a large square where thousands raged and dozens died tends to acquire the status of holy ground. Tahrir Square, Tiananmen Square, Place de la Bastille—these open areas hum with political resonance years after the bloodshed, and history keeps adding fresh meanings. But New York's geography is always in flux, and Astor Place soon lost its symbolic charge. The riots took place at the juncture of the old haphazard tangle of alleys and the orderly new grid, on property that the commissioners had left blank in order not to irk the real estate powerhouse John Jacob Astor. The spot was a weak point on the map. Afterward, the city's political topography shifted, opening up an even greater chasm in New York's class structure. The cultural elite drifted away from the Astor Opera House, with its promiscuous intermingling of burlesque and classics, and toward the more elegant Academy of Music, a few blocks north at Union Square. As highbrow entertainment moved uptown, so did the center of public gathering, thanks also to Frederick Law Olmsted and Calvert Vaux's redesign of Union Square in 1872. Today, Astor Place is a clotted corporate zone, overshadowed by a glossy black prism of an office tower and populated with NYU students and the tech world's post-collegiate minions. It's hard to imagine a placid demonstration, let alone a mass mêlée, taking place there.

The Astor Place Riot was the rare episode of unrest closely tied to a specific location. New York has no central square, no obvious place of assembly, so the streets have served as a movable platform. Lacking a natural home, protests and celebrations often migrate, and each political moment defines its own geography. The first Labor Day parade, in 1882, began with speeches in Union Square. Starting with the 1886 dedication of the Statue of Liberty, ticker-tape parades proceeded up Lower Broadway. Eighty years later, Vietnam protests took place on the Columbia campus, in Washington Square, in Central Park, and at the United Nations. In 2011, the Occupy Wall Street movement took over a privately owned public space that most New Yorkers had never heard of: Zuccotti Park, which was named for a city planning commissioner and operated by a real estate developer. Three years later, after a grand jury declined to indict the police officer who placed an unarmed Staten Island man named Eric Garner in a lethal chokehold, a march against police brutality started at Washington Square, branched out over the Brooklyn Bridge and crosstown to the West Side Highway, and fragmented into various local protests. In a way, this lack of a focal piazza reflects some essential New York values: the healthy churn of newcomers and the natural flow of ethnic groups, which keep shifting the city's various centers; the urban dweller's refusal to be corralled or homogenized. From the imperial fora of ancient Rome to the boulevards of Haussmann's Paris, to Buenos Aires's Plaza de Mayo, authoritarian regimes have always found big, ceremonial spaces both dangerous (because they concentrate so many people in one place) and ideally suited to surveillance and propaganda (for the same reason). New York's decentralized mesh gives it a more flexible geography of dissent.

Everyone owns the streets; nobody can control them all. This means that free speech flows where it pleases. During the Republican National Convention in 2004, the NYPD corralled protestors into oxymoronic "free-speech zones," outrageously implying that the rest of the city was subject to censorship. It's not. New Yorkers loudly exercise their First Amendment rights on virtually every block, on issues that range from the soul's salvation to the suffering of the New York Mets. This can get tiresome. Activists of all stripes stake out busy blocks and waylay passersby. I've been accosted while carrying grocery bags or walking the dog and asked if I have a minute for gay rights, for justice and democracy, to save the children, to save the planet, to stop an assortment of wars, or to help out a high school basketball team. At first, just trudging on with a shake of the head feels churlish. I mean, if a quick street-corner chat could lead to a better world, who's too busy for that? Then the pleas start to feel intrusive. *The whales are going to have to wait until I get this milk into the refrigerator, and anyway I don't actually like your candidate.* But that daily confrontation, however annoying, is part of what makes a vibrant street.

Walking in New York means having no idea who will cross your path, what they believe, or how they will behave. Strolling is a succession of chance meetings, the vast majority of them superficial, some fortuitous. At times, a dense neighborhood can feel like a village, where you bump into friends or revive dormant acquaintances. At other times it means confronting a vast and entrenched homeless population. New Yorkers take this haphazardness for granted, but many Americans duck from house to car to office to mall without ever having an unplanned encounter. Other than vast steppes of roadway and parking lots, the American megalopolis provides little in the way of open-air commons. Under the Constitution, hectoring, preaching, and persuading in public are not only tolerated but virtually sacred activities.

And yet in a country where so few citizens walk, that freedom is purely theoretical—or, rather, it has moved online, where ideologues chatter past one another and nobody listens. On the street, you can shut your ears, avert your eyes, square your shoulders, and refuse to break your stride, but it's still almost impossible to armor yourself against interaction. You simply cannot speak only to people who share your background and your ideas.

A sidewalk where a lot of people stream past one another, some clamoring for attention, others trying to withhold it, represents the physical embodiment of free speech. That can make it a frightening place. Public space is a splendid tool to express the people's will, but it amplifies toxic ideas just as effectively as fine ones. Control of the streets is a form of power, but urban conflict is not always, or even mostly, a fight between the tyrannical and the oppressed. Just as often it pits one activist group against another, each trying to remake the city according to its own desires. One citizen's helpful hand-painted crosswalk is another's vandalism; one person's benevolent bike lane is another's encroachment. A flash mob of food trucks can be a delight or a plague, depending on your taste for soup dumplings or exhaust. Squares and city streets are agnostic—equally well suited to repression and peaceful encampments, ginned-up rallies and outpourings of popular outrage.

A city street is a place of encounter, freedom, and unpredictability, which also makes it a place of menace. Crime constitutes one perennial danger, though the falling rate of mugging, murder, rape, and assault has made a nighttime walk less perilous than it used to be. The long-burning conflict between vehicular and foot traffic has taken its toll, too.

In the earliest film of the city, from 1896, you can see pedestrians moving at a familiar brisk clip, stepping off the curb mid-block and darting between horse-drawn omnibuses. A few years later, wealthy early adopters tooled around the city in locally made automobiles like Ardsleys, Brewsters, and Simplexes, forcing walkers to scatter. On September 13, 1899, Henry H. Bliss stepped off a streetcar on Central Park West at West Seventy-fourth Street, where a taxicab mowed him down, granting him the melancholy distinction of becoming the first pedestrian in the United States to be killed by an automobile. (A historic marker commemorates the event.) Since then, speeding vehicles have crushed thousands upon thousands of people. More about that scourge later.

Despite that murderous legacy, driving has a rich tradition in New York. The first and fanciest automobiles were manufactured here and raced at the Sheepshead Bay Speedway. A century ago, auto showrooms on Broadway and Park Avenue rivaled couturiers for chic, and Studebakers were built in Times Square. In the thirties, Robert Moses laced the city with scenic highways.

Frank Lloyd Wright intended the corkscrew ramp of his 1959 Guggenheim Museum to evoke the romance of a parking garage.

William Phelps Eno, the patrician scion of a real estate family, liked cars and speed, both of which irked the police. Eno developed the country's first traffic code in 1903, when a relatively small number of vehicles were already creating worrisome amounts of chaos. He advocated traffic circles as a way of allowing cars to whip around corners and through intersections without having to stop. Police departments, on the other hand, "betrayed a common-sense conviction that speed was part of the problem, not part of the answer," as the engineering historian Peter D. Norton put it in his book *Fighting Traffic: The Dawn of the Motor Age in the American City.* Cops liked congestion because it slowed everybody down. Eno's way eventually won out, and it kept winning for the rest of the twentieth century. As more and more automobiles poured out of factories, they transformed the streets, prying turf from foot traffic and reorganizing the fabric of the city. The fact that cars could zoom meant that they did, and new rules codified drivers' desire to hurtle along at ten times the pace of a brisk walker. The authorities saw it as their job to keep traffic flowing. Engineers designed roads that encouraged vehicles to go fast; then they measured cars' actual speeds and determined limits accordingly. On a given stretch of road, if 85 percent of cars tended to travel at 40 miles per hour or less, that became the allowable maximum.

In New York, as in cities all over the world, moving cars along became an overweening goal. In the first decades of the twentieth century, Park Avenue was not the multilane speedway we see today, with north- and southbound traffic separated by a skinny, flowered median; rather, it was a landscaped pedestrian esplanade flanked by a narrow roadway and a wide sidewalk on each side. Then, in the late 1920s, officials decided that cars needed more space. They whittled down sidewalks and multiplied travel lanes. Much later, they coordinated traffic lights to ensure that traffic could glide along avenues unimpeded. But, of course, every attempt to untangle congestion simply created more of it. All through the 1960s, as the city and state built more bridges, roads, and wider streets, while simultaneously cutting funding for public transit, more people chose to drive, resulting in ever more monstrous traffic jams.

Nobody likes traffic—not drivers who have to sit in it, not pedestrians who have to brave it, not neighbors who have to breathe its noxious fumes. And yet it's become such an integral part of the New York experience that at those rare times when the streets empty out—Christmas morning, Super Bowl Sunday, during a snowstorm—the stillness feels creepy, even vaguely apocalyptic. Conjuring a New York without the counterpoint of moaning sirens, snorting truck brakes, irritable honks, and occasional percussive crashes is as difficult as imagining how dark the city was before electric lights.

To the composer John Cage, who lived at the corner of Sixth Avenue and Eighteenth Street from 1979 until his death in 1992, traffic noise was no nuisance but an invigorating symphony that permeated his imagination:

> I wouldn't dream of getting double glass, because I love all the sounds. The traffic never stops, night and day. Every now and then a horn, siren, screeching brakes—extremely interesting and always unpredictable. At first I thought I couldn't sleep through it. Then I found a way of transposing the sounds into images so that they entered into my dreams without waking me up. . . . Now I don't need a piano. I have Sixth Avenue, the sounds.

This may sound perverse or even sarcastic to visitors from quieter places, who freeze in shock at the decibel level in Midtown. But to Cage, the magic of traffic noise was that it was both constant and haphazard, rather like his music.

Stop what you're doing for a moment and listen: What you're hearing is Cage's world. The aleatoric buzz of a street corner, the din of TVs from various apartments mingling on a fire escape—Cage claimed it all. He explored the wondrous border zone between the intentional and the accidental, deploying electronic beeps, mathematical rhythms, scratched recordings, nature's moans, banged-on pots. He scored several works for ensembles of randomly tuned radios, guaranteeing music that sounds predictably unpredictable. And, of course, he famously recruited silence, or its approximate facsimile, in *4'33"*, though what really interested him was not the absence of sound but the hum revealed when we're forced to pay attention.

To a composer so attuned to finding beauty in apparent chaos, the city supplied an endless source of material—and not just because of its soundtrack. He liked the way millions of egos and trillions of individual decisions overlapped and intertwined in infinitely mysterious ways. "If you go down the street in the city you can see that people are moving about with intention, but you don't know what those intentions are," he said. "Many, many things happen which can be viewed in purposeless ways."

In a sense, Cage was the musical equivalent of the street photographers who roamed New York, cameras at the ready, to investigate that mysterious swarm. The photographer Andreas Feininger's *Noon Rush Hour on Fifth Avenue,* from 1949, practically illustrates Cage's remark about unknown intentions.

Looking at that impressively populated Midtown scene, you can almost hear the chorus of engines, the shrill cries and shouted chatter, the whole

Andreas Feininger,
Noon Rush Hour on
Fifth Avenue, *1949*

cacophonous soundtrack of thousands of people, each with a task to perform. There are two versions of the picture, taken seven minutes apart. (A lamppost-mounted clock on the corner of Forty-fifth Street acts as a time stamp.) At first it appears as if both photos show the same stream of people in suits and hats, squinting in the summer sun. Actually, in the interval, the lights have changed, the east-west traffic has disappeared, and the cast of characters has turned over completely. Examine the photo closely, and the undifferentiated mass of humanity resolves into thousands of unique personalities, each harboring different worries, aspirations, and perversions. At

12:28, a man in a white shirt, light jacket, and bow tie, with a pipe clenched between his teeth, has just crossed the street and marches steadfastly uptown. The half dozen people just behind him all pause on the curb and glance right, at westbound traffic, waiting for the moment to surge into the wake of a passing car. When I study the next version, taken at 12:35, I scan the faces for a smile and find none; it's serious business making time for an errand or a meal in the scant lunch hour, when just moving around is so slow. Everyone seems rapt and alone yet armored against the world. The women wear gloves and pearls; most men wear hats and ties. There are no slobs on Fifth Avenue at lunchtime.

Every minute of the day, the city lays down a contrapuntal weave of slams and low hums that changes over time. If you positioned a microphone at any street corner and left it there indefinitely, you would wind up with a minimalist opera decades long, about the gradual transformation of the city. Bells become horns, brakes screech to a different tone, and lowriders throbbing to salsa give way to SUVs shaking with hip-hop. Sidewalks that were once strafed by high-volume insults shouted from curb to curb now acquire a random chorus of one-sided conversations as people on cellphones march by. With a little practice, you could learn to date a moment in street life from the quality of its noise.

Noise always has something to say about New York. When my wife is on the phone with her mother, who is ten blocks away, she can hear an ambulance siren pan from the handset to the window, making the city feel like one giant noisy village. When my parents call from their home in Europe, the din acts as a vivid evocation of the place where they both grew up. In the TV show *Mad Men,* traffic noises function as a marker of class, getting louder on the dilapidated Upper West Side and fading to nothing in classier precincts. On a Saturday afternoon at the Red Hook Ball Fields in Brooklyn, where immigrants from Mexico, El Salvador, and a dozen other countries deploy soccer teams and food trucks, the music from assorted radios clashes with the Mister Softee ditty. That beautiful tumult speaks of children reared in overlapping cultures.

You might think that the appreciation of cacophony, mess, and crowds is a peculiarity of the artist—that, given the choice, most people would opt for a clean, orderly street with more trees on it than people. But you'd be wrong. The urban sociologist William H. Whyte did much of his fieldwork on a particularly noisome stretch of Lexington Avenue. Here's how he described the blocks between Fifty-seventh and Sixty-first Streets in the 1980s: "The sidewalks are narrow and crowded; their pavements are cracked, full of holes and subway gratings; they are obstructed by a host of badly designed light standards, parking signs, mailboxes, trash containers . . ." and so on, a litany of urban annoyances, food smells, noises, and ugly signs. "Why do people persist in using this street?" he asked, in mock exasperation. The answer, gleaned from hours of unglamorous observation, was that people (city people, anyway) are drawn to mess. "On Lexington Avenue the side of the street with the most obstructions and slowest going is the side that attracts the most people." Whyte, Jane Jacobs, Cage, and Feininger shared with large numbers of urban dwellers a love of randomness, noise, and interference. New Yorkers feel at home in the controlled chaos. We sense that we are part of it and enjoy the jangle and jostle that we pretend to hate.

Whyte earned fame, and a lot of money, in 1956, with his elegantly brutal takedown of corporate conformity, *The Organization Man*. It was only later that he applied his observational skills to the street, where he found that people follow patterns as predictable as those of ants. Whyte—whom his many acolytes still call "Holly," though he died in 1999—dispatched researchers, set up cameras, and took up positions himself to record the ways in which city dwellers used their habitat. Mid-century planning savants declared that architecture could transform lives by, say, dislodging the poor from their slums and filing them away in housing projects. Whyte believed they had it backward: Behavior should shape design, but you had to know how it worked first. He and his team staked out corporate plazas, squares, sidewalks, playgrounds, and a run-down block of Harlem to document how people used them. With wry humor, he watched New Yorkers being New Yorkers and found logic in their seemingly random habits. "It is surprising how many well-dressed people can be seen rummaging through trash containers, and not surreptitiously, either," he noted.

In 1961, the Planning Commission allowed developers to stack a few extra floors atop new office towers in exchange for providing public space out front. Most of those privately owned public spaces, or POPS, remained dismal and empty, and the commission wanted to know why. Whyte trained his cameras on the Seagram Building's plaza, one of the few genuinely popular POPS, and discovered that the act of congregating followed distinctive natural laws. "A busy place, for some reason, seems to be the most congenial kind of place if you want to be alone. . . . the number-one activity is people looking at other people." He found that lovers chose conspicuous spots in which to display their privacy. Men in suits held impromptu business meetings on street corners. People did not step aside to talk but rather placed themselves like boulders in a rushing stream, directly in the flow of foot traffic— "a friendly kind of congestion," he called it.

Whyte studied the way people sat, too, and came up with stupefyingly specific recommendations for making plazas friendlier. Place benches in groups; stack ledges so people can lean back on them, and make them wide enough for two rows of derrieres; keep planters low enough for the rim to double as seating. He showed that some crowded places feel peaceful, that some elegant places feel desolate, and that lunchtime crowds will never pack a given spot beyond its comfort level. Among his most influential discoveries was that if you provide people with movable chairs, they will move them, even if only an inch or two—not necessarily to find more shade, or warmth, or to change their point of view, but simply to take temporary ownership of a public space. Every time I shift a metal chair in a public park, I imagine Holly Whyte smiling slightly and making another mark on his clipboard.

His people-centered philosophy of urbanism took hold slowly, and mostly at Bryant Park, which several of his followers, led by Dan Biederman, rescued from neglect in the early 1990s. Then, in 2007, a pair of powerful women in the Bloomberg administration, City Planning Commissioner Amanda Burden (a self-professed Holly-ite) and Transportation Commissioner Janette Sadik-Khan, traveled to Copenhagen. They rented bikes and pedaled around, hunting for ways to make an ever-more-crowded New York feel more like a pleasant Scandinavian town. They saw Danes lounging by the waterfront, nestling beneath blankets and heat lamps in outdoor cafés, cycling everywhere, and driving little. Burden and Sadik-Khan also huddled with planning guru Jan Gehl, a scholar/activist in the Whyte mold. Gehl had studied and shaped Copenhagen's two principal urban experiments: the gradual conversion of its central traffic artery, Strøget, into a pedestrian boulevard, and the fostering of an extensive bicycle culture. Burden came back bubbling with ideas about pop-up cafés and waterfront seating. Sadik-Khan found the tools to start a revolution.

Running the Department of Transportation has generally been an anonymous and glamour-free position, especially since in the arcane bureaucracy of New York "transportation" does not include most public transit. Traditionally, the most visible part of the DOT's brief has been repairing potholes. Sadik-Khan had something else in mind. She saw that her portfolio covered a vast network of public spaces, which could be retooled not just to satisfy drivers but to bring in a more varied constituency of pedestrians, cyclists, bus riders, children, and seniors—everyone, that is, who ever goes anywhere in New York: Holly Whyte's army.

Sadik-Khan, who moves and talks so fast she can bewilder opponents with her enthusiasm, started transforming her domain by planning a series of commando incursions. Like a crew of roadway elves, DOT teams arrived at night and painted asphalt in different colors, turning messy intersections into pedestrian plazas. They deployed a low-tech armory of heavy planters and metal chairs to secure sit-down havens in the middle of traffic. At Gansevoort Plaza, they arranged blocks of salvaged granite into funky seating, protected by a phalanx of spherical nippled bollards. Across town at Madison Square, another loiterer's haven sprouted at a hazardous intersection.

Behind such tinkering with blacktop and hardware lay an attempt to change the way people see and use their city. Lane by lane, curb cut by parking space, in steps so scattered and incremental that at the beginning they hardly got noticed, people on foot were wresting control of the asphalt from those behind the wheel. It worked. Even on a chilly winter day, you can now take a sandwich and a book and sit in a sunlit patch on Broadway between Times and Herald Squares that once belonged to cars. On one side of this oasis, cyclists speed down their own green lane. Vans and trucks park on the other side of the planters, barricading the plaza from moving cars. Having lunch in the middle of Broadway can be disconcerting, but it sends a signal of pedestrian pride.

Sadik-Khan has been called a "guerrilla bureaucrat," and her experiments did have a revolutionary cast. On Saturday mornings in August, vehicles started to vanish from various streets. First, in local actions taken under the city's approving eye, parts of Montague Street in Brooklyn Heights and Bedford Avenue in Williamsburg became temporarily pedestrian. Then a seven-mile stretch of Manhattan, from the Brooklyn Bridge up Lafayette Street and Park Avenue to Seventy-second Street, was transformed into a motor-free *allée*. Children played in the street, a brass ensemble oompah-pahed, adults huffed along on their kids' scooters, and Pomeranians promenaded down the center lane. If you walk around the historic center of Rome, you come across eighteenth-century marble plaques that begin BY ORDER OF THE PRESIDENT OF THE STREETS. I always thought that was a marvelously grand and archaic title, especially since the edict that follows it is usually NO DUMPING GARBAGE. Later it occurred to me that the title applied perfectly to Janette Sadik-Khan. For six transformative years, she was New York's President of the Streets.

A street is a changeable thing. A trafficked avenue gets its sidewalk shaved to make room for more cars. A truck delivery route in SoHo becomes lined with boutiques. A dozen small businesses crammed into a single block on the Upper West Side vanish when a row of short, homely buildings is cleared and replaced by the usual bank-and-drugstore combo in the base of a high-rise monolith. In Queens, plastic awnings get stripped from doorways, an unmistakable sign of gentrification. The street is where we look for signs of a city's health and symptoms of urban disease. A permanent pothole, a darkened streetlight, a yawning garage entrance, a sidewalk that's too narrow or too wide, a vacant storefront, another with its windows blocked by posters or piled merchandise, trash bags frozen into ice-encrusted mounds—any of these smudges of blight can make the heart sink and nudge pedestrians into choosing a different route.

Sadik-Khan (and her successor in the De Blasio administration, Polly Trottenberg) treated the street the way a yogi treats the body: holistically, with respect for its delicate intricacies. Beneath the surface flow the essential elements of modern life: water, sewage, power, the Internet, television, telephone lines, and public transit. Bikes, trucks, taxis, and cars jostle on the roadbed. Sidewalks are for shuffling along, running late to a meeting, wheel-

A man and his dog take advantage of a CityBench.

ing hand trucks, passing out flyers, window-shopping, panhandling, jogging, waiting for a bus, standing on a corner to finish an argument, and sitting at dinner. For the first time, the city tried to account for this dizzying array of activities and speeds. Wider sidewalks kept foot traffic from spilling into the road; sidewalk cafés provided new audiences for the theater of the streets. Bumpy surfaces at curb cuts helped guide the visually impaired. These were not elitist prettifications aimed at reminding European tourists of their ancient town centers; they were tools for making the public realm more public.

The pedestrian revolution has not forgotten those who sometimes would rather stop walking for a while. "A dimension that is truly important is the human backside. It is a dimension many architects ignore," Whyte once observed. Planners and designers of urban space have often stinted on seating, leaving the rest of us to colonize ledges or to lean against planters. Around 2010, though, officials began to recognize the needs of the temporarily sedentary. New York has quietly become an excellent city for sitting.

A partial catalog of places that have been added to park one's behind in public includes the red glass stoop above the TKTS booth in Times Square, the stacked slabs of granite at Gansevoort Plaza, and the gray and red stone blocks lining the approach to the subway station at West Ninety-sixth Street and Broadway. The East River Esplanade offers low stone walls, waterside steps, pairs of wooden-slat chairs angled so as to encourage conversation, and barstools with views of the Brooklyn Bridge. Next to the pinwheel-shaped pavilion at Peter Minuit Plaza are seductively snaking "zipper benches," designed by the firm WXY. Rogers Marvel Architects fitted out subway grates along Hillside Avenue in Queens with undulating structures that divert storm water and invite lounging. The City Council adopted new rules for privately owned public stretches on the waterfront, which now include plenty of shaded benches and clusters of "social seating." Lincoln Center sprinkled part of its campus with movable chairs and lined it with high-back benches. The High Line has comfortable bleachers and wooden lounge chairs mounted on railway tracks.

The city also rolled out a program of sidewalk seating by request. For a while, New Yorkers could go to the DOT website and suggest a location for a sleek, sculptural CityBench designed by Ignacio Ciocchini (who is also responsible for the garbage cans and shop kiosks at Bryant Park). Each bench comes with three side-by-side berths made from a sheet of perforated steel, folded into a back and a seat, and demarcated by a low armrest to discourage sleeping. The benches look tough, cool, and modern, but the effect of installing a thousand of them on sidewalks in all five boroughs was to make the city a more relaxed, inviting place.

New York's more social streets have received a high-tech upgrade, too: Digital billboards pump out ads, and there's a cone of free high-speed Wi-Fi. When those kiosks started popping up in the spring of 2016, I located one on the corner of Eighth Avenue and Fifty-eighth Street, where I found a man who was jabbing the touch screen and enjoying himself immensely. "This is the best thing that ever happened in New York," said the man, who identified himself as Michael from Connecticut. "This is my plaything, man. It's the ultimate in free-ness!" Michael, who had few teeth but seemingly plenty of time, said he had been using the new kiosk pretty much constantly since it was installed the week before. He gave me a quick tour: free calling to any number in the country, a large 911 emergency button, two USB charging ports, an audio jack for headphones, and unlimited Internet access on the embedded tablet. "You like Steely Dan?" he asked, and in seconds we were dancing to a YouTube video of "Do It Again." Michael asked me for a dollar for soup, which I gave him; the Internet may be free now, but lunch isn't.

New Yorkers would prefer the rest of the world to think that we move at a constant lope, defying cars in intersections and pushing past slow-moving tourists. The truth is, some of us are also old or infirm or have only just learned to walk. Sitting is a social act, which makes seating a crucial element of a vibrant metropolis. That sort of inclusive thinking affects the minutiae of public design. Making public spaces safe, civilized, and navigable is a deeply democratic issue. If you think that the new street designs are just about giving spandex-encased bikers a high-speed lane of their own or providing tourists with café tables, then try shepherding a gaggle of preschoolers across a complicated intersection or pushing a walker across Broadway. You'll be grateful for every arcane bit of traffic engineering.

The recent alterations have had a measurable effect. Mayor Bill de Blasio signed on to Vision Zero, a Scandinavian-style program to bring down traffic accidents, and now your chances of getting mowed down by a heavy vehicle while crossing the street are probably lower than they have been since the first horseless carriages began put-putting down Fifth Avenue. Once-terrifying journeys have become more tranquil, not just in Manhattan's glittering zip codes but in every borough. Being a *flâneur* in New York remains as intellectually invigorating as ever; it's just no longer an extreme sport.

The project of reforming New York's streets is nowhere near complete. Riders, drivers, and pedestrians still act as if they belong to different tribes rather than people who switch modes. The city remains full of Rizzos banging on the hoods of aggressive taxis, indignantly yelling, *"I'm walkin' heah!"* Fury forms an elemental part of the New York street, a more timeless ingredient than cobblestones or asphalt. Everything else is negotiable.

WALK II

LIQUID CITY
The Seaport, Governors Island, and the Brooklyn Waterfront

On a mild spring afternoon, I'm lazing on an open-air deck chair on Pier 15, beneath the glass cliffs of Lower Manhattan. The view is an urban pastoral, a perfect panorama of post-industrial leisure, full of light and spray and color. Taxi-yellow ferries ply the glittering waves, the Brooklyn Bridge's cables segment the sky, and, a few hundred feet toward the island's tip, on the East River Esplanade, teenagers sit on granite bleachers, letting the water splash over their feet. Across the river, seminude sunbathers lie scattered on the grassy banks of Brooklyn Bridge Park. Yet I detect another image ghosted over this one: a black-and-white shoreline bristling with piers and tugs, and oil-slicked wharves teeming with dockhands.

When I walk around New York, past and future mingle with the present city. Tenuous grand plans laid out in shiny computer renderings merge in my mind with jumpy footage of people who died generations ago, men in dusty suits and soft caps, women encumbered by long skirts—silent throngs whose vitality still clings to the places where they spent their days.

The waterfront I never knew was a frightening, chaotic, and thrilling strip that smelled of coffee, coal smoke, spices, and horse dung. Whitman-like, I fantasize that's me in one of those ancient photos, an unrecognizable figure in the crowd, turned toward a river so congested with vessels that I could practically hop from deck to deck, clear across to Red Hook in Brooklyn:

< Begin at **A,** the upper level of Pier 15, East River Esplanade between Fletcher Street and John Street.

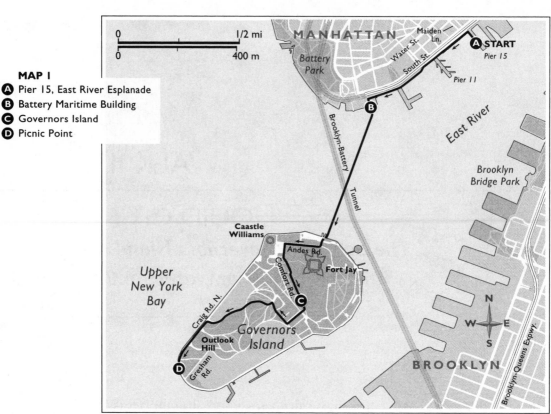

MAP 1

- **Ⓐ** Pier 15, East River Esplanade
- **Ⓑ** Battery Maritime Building
- **Ⓒ** Governors Island
- **Ⓓ** Picnic Point

MANHATTAN

Maiden Ln.

Ⓐ START
Pier 15

Battery Park

Water St.

South St.

Pier 11

Ⓑ

Brooklyn-Battery Tunnel

East River

Brooklyn Bridge Park

Caastle Williams

Andes Rd.

Fort Jay

Comfort Rd.

Ⓒ

Upper New York Bay

Craig Rd. N.

Governors Island

Outlook Hill

Ⓓ

Gresham Rd.

BROOKLYN

Brooklyn Queens Expwy.

N W E S

0 — 1/2 mi
0 — 400 m

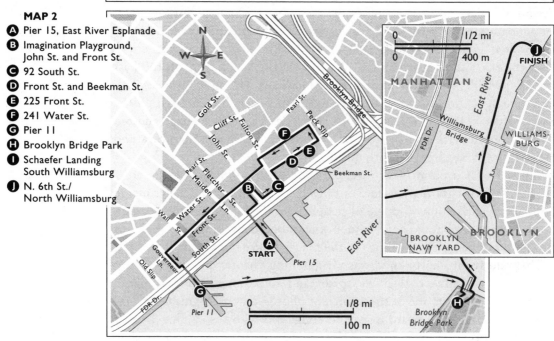

MAP 2

- **Ⓐ** Pier 15, East River Esplanade
- **Ⓑ** Imagination Playground, John St. and Front St.
- **Ⓒ** 92 South St.
- **Ⓓ** Front St. and Beekman St.
- **Ⓔ** 225 Front St.
- **Ⓕ** 241 Water St.
- **Ⓖ** Pier 11
- **Ⓗ** Brooklyn Bridge Park
- **Ⓘ** Schaefer Landing South Williamsburg
- **Ⓙ** N. 6th St./ North Williamsburg

N W E S

Brooklyn Bridge

Gold St.

Cliff St.

Fulton St.

Pearl St.

Peck Slip

John St.

Ⓕ

Ⓔ

Ⓓ

Beekman St.

Pearl St.

Fletcher St.

Maiden Ln.

Ⓑ

Ⓒ

Wall St.

Water St.

Front St.

South St.

Ⓐ START

Pier 15

Gouverneur Ln.

Old Slip

FDR Dr.

Ⓖ

Pier 11

East River

Brooklyn Bridge Park

Ⓗ

0 — 1/8 mi
0 — 100 m

Ⓙ FINISH

MANHATTAN

East River

Williamsburg Bridge

WILLIAMS-BURG

FDR Dr.

Ⓘ

BROOKLYN

BROOKLYN NAVY YARD

0 — 1/2 mi
0 — 400 m

Logs that have been herded down the coast from Maine are being driven toward the Steinway piano factory in Astoria; floating grain elevators bob back and forth from dock to train depot. Carts line up on the quays, waiting for their freight. Hour after hour, longshoremen keep heaving three-hundred-pound sacks, hoping not to be crushed beneath tumbling loads of cargo. This overpowering torrent of . . . *stuff* . . . rushes into nearby warehouses, which hold the world's abundance in immense dank chambers. "Cross the threshold and climb the stairways from one low-roofed loft to another, and you wander among foreign fields and breathe the airs of every zone," wrote a reporter from *Harper's Weekly* in 1877.

Pier 15,
SHoP Architects

Banana docks, 1905

Here are tier upon tier of hogsheads of sugar, perspiring molasses with the memory of the Cuban sun, and other hogsheads of old rum from Jamaica, beneath which the ground is greedily drinking precious oozings. Rows of dusty white barrels of China clay stand alongside rows of barrels of plumbago from Ceylon, whose black dust makes the floor all about as slippery as glass. Quadrangular piles of hides from Calcutta, the Cape of Good Hope and Buenos Ayres; redoubts of square gunny-covered boxes of lac gums from India, and kauri gum from Auckland; huge heaps of "allspice" pepper from Jamaica, and fiery bird-pepper and cloves grown in Zanzibar, in which the heat of those torrid latitudes seems concentrated . . .

The catalog goes on, enumerating imports that time has made mysterious. All that hoisting, hauling, stacking, carting, packing—the whole sweat-

Stevedores unloading a ship, 1877

lubricated machinery of consumption—makes today's waterfront seem sedate by comparison.

For a long time, I was barely aware that New York is a maritime city. In the early nineties, I lived in a landlocked part of Queens. I crossed the East River by bike daily, but I saw it mostly as a twinkling grid through the steel-grate roadway of the Queensboro Bridge. On some mornings, a damp, fishy breeze sneaked through our neighborhood, bringing a whiff of the Keys or the spray from a distant Atlantic storm. Despite these reminders, the presence of water in the city struck me as an archaeological relic. I knew that a canal still lurked beneath Canal Street and that pleasure boaters sailed in Pelham Bay. On weekends I might make an excursion to Coney Island, where the dilapidated amusement park and windy boulevards fronted an empty beach. For the most part, what I saw of the riverfront were stretches of stained concrete and sad sheds behind a chain-link fence.

But just look at it now. New York is a liquid city—a stunningly obvious fact that for decades was almost forgotten. It's as if someone glanced at a map twenty years ago and suddenly noticed its big blue center, ringed by a piecrust of boroughs. For a while, city officials took to calling the water New York's "sixth borough," and if it were actually granted that status, it would be the largest of them all—more than a quarter of the city's surface area. One reason the land here is so densely packed is that it's an archipelago, webbed by rivers, estuaries, inlets, bays, and channels. More than five hundred miles of coast meander through the metropolis, a shoreline more extensive and more varied than those of Seattle, Chicago, Portland, and San Francisco combined. It's not all piers and bulkheads, either. New York's shoreline has miles of beach, wetlands, gritty industrial stretches, and a lengthening necklace of waterfront greenery.

That realization has transformed the city, and there's no better vantage point from which to observe those changes than the second story of the double-decker Pier 15. The pier *is* one of those changes, a recent addition to the waterfront's infrastructure of pleasure, by SHoP Architects and Ken Smith Landscape Design. The upper slab rests on a pair of glass pavilions and is carpeted with a patch of aerial lawn. Ramps and stairs give it the feeling of a hilly landscape, and its highest point nearly lifts you into the rigging of the tall ship *Wavertree* moored alongside. In fair weather, especially on a weekend afternoon, the pier resembles a cruise ship's deck; stevedores have been replaced by sunbathers, and lunch-pail gruel by organic panini. But the jetty reaches the apex of its glamour at twilight, when a reddish glow emerges from the slats in the second story's undulating underside. This is relatively low-cost but high-level public architecture, a beautiful object and a viewing platform for the urban spectacular.

My eyes sweep around the panorama, starting at the footings of the Brooklyn Bridge and moving right. The Brooklyn-Queens Expressway clings to the cliffs below Brooklyn Heights like an electric wire stapled to a baseboard. Farther south are the cranes and gantries of Red Hook, where Arthur Miller set his 1955 play *A View from the Bridge*. Alfieri—the character through whom the story is told—sketches in the stevedore's habitat, with its envious view of Lower Manhattan: "This is the slum that faces the bay on the seaward side of Brooklyn Bridge," he says. "This is the gullet of New York swallowing the tonnage of the world." Alfieri would be confused by today's Red Hook, where the outward look of industrial decay mingles with post-slum pleasures. He could shop at the Fairway supermarket, which occupies a gorgeously restored Civil War-era warehouse; have lunch on the roof of Brooklyn Crab, which feels like a Hamptons outpost with panoramic views of the harbor; and furnish his house from Ikea. If he was feeling flush, he could stroll down to the cruise-ship terminal and board a vessel the size of a neighborhood, bound for the Caribbean.

From my vantage point on Pier 15, if I keep turning my head to the right,

I see the low distant rise of Governors Island, where the first Dutch settlers tried to make a go of their American adventure, before pulling up stakes and moving to the tip of Manhattan.

> Now you have two choices: Map 1: Walk south along the East River Esplanade to B, the Battery Maritime Building, and take the ferry to C, Governors Island; or stay at Pier 15, continue reading about Governors Island here but save a visit for another day, then continue on to Map 2.

The ferry to Governors Island leaves from the Battery Maritime Building, a lonely symphony in cast iron, steel, and Guastavino tiles, from 1909. The terminal recalls the days—which may be slowly coming back—when ferries constituted a crucial part of the city's transit system and deserved some decorative dignity. At the other end of the eight-minute ride, Governors Island is a maritime park unlike any other in the city, crouched low to the water yet close to the open sky.

On any given Sunday in summer, the island has the feel of an urban day camp—seasonal, boisterous, and irresistibly ramshackle. Thousands stream off the ferries from Manhattan and Brooklyn and fan out through the ex-military ghost town. Some grab a bike and circumambulate the island. Others picnic, watch glassblowing demonstrations, climb on sculptures, stand on line for jerk chicken, stretch out on hammocks, play miniature golf, explore the old fort of Castle Williams, and gaze at the disorienting marvel of the harbor views.

Governors Island has finally rejoined the city that was born there. The first Dutch arrivals camped on the wooded isle they called Noten Eylandt (Nut Island), and one form or another of the military monopolized it for the next four hundred years. When the Coast Guard finally moved out in 1996, leaving a collection of gracious nineteenth-century brick structures, some slablike barracks from the 1950s, and an abandoned Burger King, New Yorkers inherited 172 acres they barely knew existed and had no idea what to do with. In the ensuing years, a growing stream of visitors came to love the island's gracious but pleasantly derelict air, reminiscent of a spa resort past its prime or a boomtown once the silver dried up.

After a decade as a blank slate on which futurists and fantasists projected oversize desires—a replica of the Globe Theatre! A SpongeBob SquarePants hotel! A gondola to Manhattan! An offshore campus for New York University! Another Trumpville!—the backhoes finally got down to business, shoring up seawalls, running pipes and cable, re-roofing historic buildings, and, most dramatically, shaping a new landscape. The Dutch firm West 8 spent years observing the summertime crowds and their habits of leisure. Then the architects plowed that knowledge into an ambitious and spectacular but also freewheeling and improvisational landscape design.

Leslie Koch, the former president of the Trust for Governors Island, was canny enough to realize that one thing her little kingdom didn't need was an oppressively chic garden with look-but-don't-touch plantings. Instead, she demanded space designed for the way people actually behave rather than the way architects think they ought to. Circling the island with bicycles and cameras, she and her staff watched large families arrange picnic tables end to end, then spin apart and sort themselves by age. Young children piled into hammocks, commandeering them as group swings. Older kids biked freely on the carless paths or flipped Frisbees across the parade ground. Adults grouped deck chairs for conversation or else napped on lawns unsullied by dogs (which are banned from the island).

These observations shaped dozens of design decisions. Governors Island is now dotted with tables and recliners solid enough to withstand the crowds and the scouring, sea-salted air but light enough to be dragged around. The spot with the best full-frontal view of the Statue of Liberty became Picnic Point. An experiment in which a few movable hammocks were

The Hills, Governors Island, with Rachel Whiteread's concrete Cabin and Lower Manhattan beyond

sprinkled around an open area evolved into Hammock Grove, which looks like a cross between an orchard and a shipboard-berth deck. Most architects think visually. Good architects tend to all the senses. West 8 calculated the curvature of pathways and the height of signs to keep bikers moving but not too fast. Benches were given the butt test. Even the decision to create gathering spots for food trucks and stands, rather than build a permanent (and, perhaps, permanently mediocre) cafeteria, was ultimately a sensual choice. West 8's grandest stroke is the Hills, a range of artificial mounds on the island's southwestern corner. On one, a velvety expanse of grass invites children and boisterous adults to roll down it; another sends human missiles shooting down snaking slides. The tallest climbs seventy feet to a practically alpine lookout over the harbor, the Statue of Liberty, and the tip of Manhattan.

I'm back (or still) at Pier 15, the East River at my shoulders now, facing the FDR Drive. For decades, that highway severed the city from the East River so effectively that workers in the Financial District rarely considered bringing their sandwiches to the river at lunchtime—if they even realized that it was just a block or two away. But civilized urban living is like moss: It grows in the unlikeliest cracks. Parking and fences have been cleared away, and the space beneath the overpass has been given over to a bike lane. My gaze hits the great wall of the Financial District. It all seems so immense and perma-

<
Continue on to Map 2, starting, once again, at A, Pier 15.

nent, and at the same time so fragile. That's what I find so bracing about this spot where currents and currency flow together: The biography of the waterfront is a story of damage and resilience.

Think, for instance, about October 29, 2012, when a freakishly powerful hurricane named Sandy muscled its way into New York Harbor, pushing a fourteen-foot surge that swamped streets, flooded tunnels, tore up beach houses, drowned the unlucky, and left millions in the dark. For a while afterward, it appeared as though a demoralized city would turn inland again. Sandy was a meteorological fluke, but it was also read as a sign of the ferocity that climate change might bring. Suddenly, living close to the water seemed like an act of naïve defiance. The moral lesson of the storm seemed clear. We had disrespected the sea—built too close, too low, too blithely—and been punished for it. All those glittering apartment towers with their whitecap-flecked views were a mistake of the market. When the first waves hit, New Yorkers instantly understood the topography they had previously ignored, and any neighborhood with the word "Heights" in its name (Crown, Prospect, Washington) now had a comforting ring. The storm made it obvious why people had avoided soggy landfill, at least until low-lying factory areas like Tribeca were magically made luxurious.

But New York is too intertwined with its waterways to choose retreat. The Metropolitan Transit Authority, which had just spent half a billion dollars refurbishing the South Street subway station, got ready to do it again. It took a while, but eventually businesses started to reopen, residents returned, and stalled construction projects got moving. The Red Hook Fairway shut down, threw out its entire spoiled inventory, and restored its warehouse one more time. Sandy made it clear that the city resembles the shipwrecked boy in *Life of Pi,* sharing a lifeboat with a Bengal tiger. Like the beast, the water is beautiful, alluring, and vicious. We can't get away from it, we can't confine it, and we can't beat it back. The only option is a cautious love.

> Walk beneath the FDR Drive, cross South Street, turn right, and go one block to John Street, stopping in front of **B,** Imagination Playground. It occurs to me as I duck beneath the FDR Drive that two recent innovations—the dog run and the playground—especially would stun the dockworker or fishmonger of a century ago. Back then, few respectable citizens spent their nights by the seaport if they had a choice. Later, the Financial District pushed up close to the water's edge, and the great hive of money bees emptied out every weekday evening and repopulated in the morning. Then the banks, too, scattered, leaving an encampment of great stone skyscrapers too old-fashioned for the sleekest corporations to reuse. I find it hard to imagine making a life in one of those converted office buildings, pushing a stroller past the Stock Exchange, or doing my grocery shopping in the slot canyons between rearing towers. But tens of thousands of people do, largely for the harbor views. There are unmistakable signs of residential life:

A few blocks downtown, local dogs explore an elaborately landscaped park created just for them. And at the foot of John Street is Imagination Playground—not the standard assembly of colored steel gear but an environment conceived by the glitzmeister David Rockwell. Here on Burling Slip, a plaza once lined with shipbuilders' workshops, blacksmiths, and rope makers, kids can now assemble blue foam forms into multi-storied castles. Rockwell, who also designed sets for the Academy Awards and an assortment of amped-up Las Vegas dining environments, has created for children the sort of high-octane, full-immersion theatrical experience that he has regularly produced for adults. In a way, his playground continues the local tradition of refining raw materials into the stuff of culture. In the past, ships brought in sugar, cotton, and whale blubber; New Yorkers turned them into candy, gowns, and *Moby-Dick*. Now Manhattan itself has become a cultural product, a showcase of good living.

The corner of South and Fulton Streets is one of the most evocative corners in New York, even if its tangy, clattering romance has faded to a soft melancholy. The Fulton Fish Market kept the cobblestones slick and the traffic lively for 183 years, until 2005, when it moved to shinier—and less mobbed-up—quarters in the Bronx. The smells lingered for a while, but they've finally dissipated. Tourists pass through for an hour or two, breathing in the brine of nostalgia. I console myself with the thought that the seaport's heyday was always a lifetime or two ago; its fish was fresh, but the market glowed with gilded memories and was shadowed by gloom. Even in 1952, the

< Walk back to South Street, turn left, and go one block to **C**, No. 92.

Sloppy Louie's

New Yorker writer Joseph Mitchell described it as if he were writing its eulogy. "The smoky riverbank dawn, the racket the fishmongers make, the seaweedy smell, and the sight of this plentifulness always give me a feeling of well-being, and sometimes they elate me," he wrote in his *New Yorker* essay "Up in the Old Hotel." Mornings, Mitchell would feed his bliss at Sloppy Louie's, the greasy spoon at 92 South Street that remained much the same until it closed in 1998, with the old green cursive sign hand-lettered on the window.

Later in that essay, Mitchell ventures into the abandoned floors above the coffee shop, which had once been the Fulton Ferry Hotel. Until the opening of the Brooklyn Bridge in 1883 made the Brooklyn ferry obsolete, this was a crucial institution. Sailors, whores, fishermen, traveling salesmen bound for Long Island, carousing Brooklynites who missed the last boat home—all needed to stay overnight, within earshot of the gulls and creaking ropes. But by Mitchell's day the hotel was a mysterious relic, preserved by total neglect and in a state of almost sacramental decay. "Between the boarded-up windows, against the front wall, stood a marble-top table," he wrote. "On it were three seltzer bottles with corroded spouts, a tin water cooler painted to resemble brown marble, a cracked glass bell of the kind used to cover clocks and stuffed birds, and four sugar bowls whose metal flap lids had been eaten away from their hinges by rust. On the floor, beside the table, were an umbrella stand, two brass spittoons, and a wire basket filled to the brim with whiskey bottles of the flask type." Some years ago, when I retraced Mitchell's steps, some of the bric-a-brac was gone and the dust had grown even thicker, but little else had changed. Not many Manhattan interiors remain picturesquely vacant for quite so long.

> Walk up Fulton Street, away from the river. Turn right on Front Street and go one block to **D**, the corner of Beekman Street.

These streets have a movie-set quality, especially after Sandy flooded the area so badly that it turned into a ghost town for nearly a year. That period felt like a pause in a protracted siege on history. For years, white-collar palaces of concrete, steel, and glass have kept encircling the nineteenth-century workingman's zone. Now a wave of new development is closing in, and fresh prosperity is inching down from the upland zones. You can see it coming by looking up Beekman Street to the wavy high-gloss skyscraper rising a few blocks north: 8 Spruce Street, an apartment building designed by Frank Gehry.

With its crinkled-steel drapery that catches the sun and casts plunging shadows, Gehry's tower is an architectural diva. Beneath that extravagant costume is an unremarkable body: a T-plan apartment building standing on a brick box pedestal and turning a flattened profile toward the north and west. Gehry had planned a tall, twisting corkscrew tower, but that would have cost too much—especially once the economy dipped and the developers opted to erect a rental building instead of selling off condos. And so, he tucked quirky bay windows into the billows of that opulent metallic gown, which could practically have emerged from the Metropolitan Opera costume shop. It's a princess's robe, tailored to awe this straight-edged town.

The past's worn fabric can survive these glittering attacks only by adapting. On Historic Front Street, the artfully preserved block between Beekman Street and Peck Slip, the architects Cook + Fox spiffed up two-hundred-year-old brick buildings that weren't built to last, bound them with connective tissue, and repurposed them to house families instead of liquor and salted cod. Handle this kind of clever deception well and you have a city of layers instead of erasures, a place of complex textures and creative frictions, where the old and new don't just sit awkwardly side by side. Instead, they

< Continue on Front Street to E, No. 225.

Frank Gehry's 8 Spruce Street

mingle and converse, discussing the protracted, fervent relationship between New York and its waters. That passion has cycled through periods of manic energy, violence, abandonment, and elated rediscovery. On a plaque above 225 Front Street is a passage from the first pages of *Moby-Dick,* which opens in Manhattan with an evocation of the magnetic power of the sea:

> Circumambulate the city of a dreamy Sabbath afternoon. Go from Corlears Hook to Coenties Slip, and from thence, by Whitehall, northward. What do you see?—Posted like silent sentinels all around the town, stand thousands upon thousands of mortal men fixed in ocean reveries. Some leaning against the spiles; some seated upon the pier-heads; some looking over the bulwarks of ships from China. . . . They must get just as nigh the water as they possibly can without falling in.

Melville was born a short stroll away (at 6 Pearl Street, next to Battery Park), and writing those words in 1851, when the Front Street buildings were still young, he captured the ancient romance of the wharves. From the seventeenth century to the mid-twentieth, whenever it seemed that the bond between the port and the city had reached its greatest intensity, it intensified a little more. Fire, violence, economic depression, accidents, and planning blunders couldn't damage that relationship for long.

THE NEW YORK AND PORT

Shapeup at Pier 92, 1948

Moby-Dick isn't a treatise on the whaling industry, and Melville wasn't just talking about longshoremen; he was describing a primeval yearning for the open ocean. For the most part we city dwellers have domesticated those urges, channeling them into fishing piers, bike paths, and kayak launches. Even so, the force of that attraction has been powerful enough to turn a city inside out, so that every day New Yorkers gravitate toward the water with a little bit more bounce. I have mixed feelings about turning rough docklands into a zone of bourgeois pleasure, but there's no returning to the distant past of vendors shucking harbor oysters for a workman's snack.

> Continue down Front Street to Peck Slip, turn left, then left again on Water Street, and walk halfway down the block to F, No. 241.

The longshoremen who decamped in the 1960s assumed, correctly, that they were abandoning the waterfront to a future of ugliness and rot. But if they returned now, they would find themselves utterly disoriented: salt-crusted piers and gritty wharves have acquired a shocking wholesomeness. One oddly G-rated presence is 241 Water Street, which looks as though a white-paneled tugboat with a stubby smokestack has popped out of a cartoon and landed on top of a four-story brick warehouse. It was built in 1991 as a last-ditch headquarters of the Seamen's Church Institute, a pastoral and educational organization that was founded in 1834 to care for the spiritual needs of sailors. The seamen have moved on, taking their sins and their institute with them. Now the whimsical building (designed by the firm then called Polshek Partnership and now rechristened Ennead) looks as though it were designed for exacting children—indeed, its current occupant is the chicest of private elementary schools, the Blue School.

At the water end of Wall Street, Pier 11 serves the Brooklyn ferries, which Whitman sang and are now gradually returning, like a species crawling back from extinction. Travel by water proved its worth on September 11, 2001, when boats of all kinds helped evacuate the stranded, and again in the aftermath, when the PATH train connecting Lower Manhattan to New Jersey was knocked out of service for a while. Now new waves of high-rise development along the Queens and Brooklyn waterfront are reviving the river commute.

The first stop on the East River Ferry is Brooklyn Bridge Park, which even unfinished is already jammed with kids and adults enjoying themselves, shaping a generation's childhood memories. Though the young greenery still has a fragile, uncertain look, every basketball court is in use, every lawn dotted with people irradiating their bodies. This luxuriant chip of parkland at the edge of Brooklyn clearly draws visitors from well beyond its fringe of affluent streets. Not everyone is happy about that: The park's mostly white neighbors complain regularly about the noisy, mostly black teenagers who use the basketball courts; some have suggested replacing them with tennis courts. Still, peace mostly reigns. The borough's various ethnic and religious populations appear to have worked out a tacit time-share arrangement. On a midweek afternoon in summer, kids teem like minnows in the water park and avoid the scalding slides, while their minders (wearing chadors or sheitels, depending on the day and hour) huddle in the scarce shade. The sun-strafed picnic tables are full, the coastline hazed in the smoke from grilling meat.

All that indolence is hard-won. Two hundred years ago, when New York's grandees were planning exactly how the city should keep swallowing farmland and forest, they figured it would never need a park. The waterways that encircled Manhattan already met its needs for fresh air and open space, they thought, and so they gridded the map with streets, leaving only a couple of

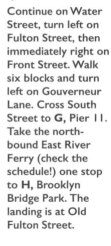
< Continue on Water Street, turn left on Fulton Street, then immediately right on Front Street. Walk six blocks and turn left on Gouverneur Lane. Cross South Street to **G**, Pier 11. Take the northbound East River Ferry (check the schedule!) one stop to **H**, Brooklyn Bridge Park. The landing is at Old Fulton Street.

Hoops with a view, Brooklyn Bridge Park

muddy parade grounds and potter's fields. The mistake became too obvious to ignore when wealthy families demanded a carriage course at least as pleasant as London's. By the mid-nineteenth century, that competitiveness had given birth to Central Park, which holds one of the keys to the city's livability. I'm there virtually every day, walking my dog, picnicking on a bench, biking to a meeting, or tapping this paragraph into my phone.

Today, as urban land becomes ever more rare and precious, the value of outdoor refuges has risen, too. More than half the world's population lives in exploding megalopolises. Superstar cities like New York, London, Seoul, and Tokyo are growing, too. And every member of those burgeoning millions craves a bit of friendly turf. These gilded cities have entered a new idyll of urban parks, made possible by a legacy of ugliness. Every city has its polluted waterfronts, abandoned train tracks, decommissioned military installations, or redundant highways—a whole smorgasbord of wastelands to be revived into verdant zones of leisure. Greenery has sprung up in areas that once lay dank and useless behind chain-link fences.

The grand old parks of Europe, like the Bois de Boulogne in Paris, the Tiergarten in Berlin, and the Villa Doria Pamphili in Rome, began as hunting grounds and suburban estates. The urban parks that came later are often smaller and tamer, planted on strips of salvaged land. Their charm lies in the inventiveness of the rescue rather than in their expanse. Each summer, Paris turns a segment of its riverside traffic artery into a string of temporary beaches called Paris Plages. Recently, it made the experiment permanent on the Left Bank: Now Parisians can stroll down former on-ramps to the Promenade des Berges de Seine, where gardens float on moored barges, children hold birthday parties in public tepees, and adults can retreat to sanctuaries installed in steel shipping containers.

At Brooklyn Bridge Park, the process of converting eighty-five acres of flat and filthy coastline into verdant hills and floating greenswards has been combative and long, and it's not over yet. The landscape architect Michael Van Valkenburgh remade an abandoned stretch of pitted concrete and crumbling bulkheads into a busy little Eden. Meandering walkways lead past hidden gardens and lurking sculptures. Six specialized piers jut out from a narrow ribbon of green, covering a range of habitats from cultivated meadow to tiny beach and soccer field. Still, the compromises show. The looping paths are short; the noise-blocking mound that screens off the BQE had to be scooted toward the water. Worst of all, the park shares the shore with several big, clunky buildings that will justify their existence by funding the park's upkeep for decades. Some neighbors condemn what they see as the unholy marriage of real estate interests and the public realm. And yet every patch of parkland is a small victory for the public's pleasure, a piece of earth left gloriously inefficient and perpetually unprofitable. Its only purposes are leisure and beauty, freely dispensed. Could there be a better antidote to the relentless pursuit of money, a purer assertion of democratic ideals, than a fabulously valuable square foot of soil given over to growing grass?

What is urban nature for? The answer to this question has both philosophical and economic implications, as Frederick Law Olmsted understood a century and a half ago. Living in cities, he said, can produce such vague but disabling forms of malaise as "'vital exhaustion,' 'nervous irritation' and 'constitutional depression' . . . excessive materialism, [leading] to loss of faith and lowness of spirit, by which life is made, to some, questionably worth the living." Cultivated landscape could alleviate these suicidal miseries: Trees saved lives. Today, we ask urban parks to do far more than just make us happy and healthy. They fight climate change, scrub toxins from the air, mitigate summer heat, absorb floodwaters, transform garbage dumps into nature preserves, promote democracy, welcome birds, and generate revenue to pay for their own maintenance. Parks are hardworking places.

The denser the city, the more open space it needs. New York has a lot of it—29,000 acres, or 14 percent of the city's land—but in many of its 1,700 parks, hope does battle with neglect. Shabby and unsafe parks undo Olmsted's virtues: They increase anxiety and infect neighborhoods with the spirit of abandonment and the potential for danger.

Living with this legacy of parks is a bit like inheriting a drafty castle: very nice, but who's going to pay for the upkeep? Michael Bloomberg's answer was that deluxe enclaves like Brooklyn Bridge Park could pay for themselves by partnering with developers and courting philanthropy. Less glamorous parks would have to rely on the city's dwindling largesse. Maintenance can't be outsourced, and its costs can't be traded for naming rights, but it is crucial, nevertheless. Healthy trees last for decades, well-planned green space almost never gets reabsorbed into the weave of streets, and investments in parks pay off over generations.

As I continue upriver, the ferry skirts the Brooklyn Navy Yard, an immense former shipbuilding facility that in recent years has been rescued from industrial ruin by a new wave of boutique manufacture. Exploring these three hundred acres is an exhilarating and slightly mournful experience. Decay coexists with vigor. Out beyond a battered pier, the Williamsburg Bridge executes its grand *jeté* across the East River. In an immense pre–Civil War dry dock, granite-walled and roomy enough for the Chrysler Building to lie down on its side, an oil barge is getting a fresh coat of red paint, while a giant tanker waits outside the imperial-scale gates for its turn to be spruced up.

After Secretary of Defense Robert McNamara shuttered the Brooklyn Navy Yard in 1964 (along with the Brooklyn Army Terminal, Fort Jay on

< For the end of this tour, you again have two choices: (1) Visit the Brooklyn Navy Yard, which is a little tricky to arrange. The entrance is on Flushing Avenue, an unlovely half-hour walk from Brooklyn Bridge Park, or half that from the next ferry stop, I, Schaefer Landing/ South Williamsburg. The only way to visit is by taking a scheduled tour organized by the yard's visitor center, called BLDG 92. (2) Return to the East River Ferry landing on Old Fulton Street, and take the northbound ferry two stops to J, the North Sixth Street/North Williamsburg landing, reading about the Brooklyn Navy Yard while on board.

Governors Island, and scores of other military facilities), it entered decades of ruinous neglect. The result is a scarred and fragile loveliness. I have wandered among the vacant, off-limits relics, feeling as though I had snuck into a haunted estate or the set of a post-apocalyptic movie. Weather and vegetation reclaimed the doomed houses along Admiral's Row (most of them eventually demolished to make way for a Wegmans supermarket). The 1838 hilltop hospital stands quiet and strong, faced in Tuckahoe Marble, the local stone that gives so many of New York's public buildings their pale, antique grandeur. The exquisitely detailed Surgeon's House, with its mansard roof and finely carved moldings, sits graciously reverting to a state of nature. It's fitting that a film-production company has designs on the whole creepy campus, not as a set but as a spiffed-up studio.

But the true beauty of this historic industrial park is that it's still an industrial park. The paradox of preservation is that often, the more you safeguard a building's appearance, the more its character changes beyond recognition. This is especially true of machine-age behemoths or buildings designed for a precise technological moment. We recycle silos as apartment buildings, turn power plants into parks, and install museums in empty factories. We protect the body and rebuild the soul.

At the Brooklyn Navy Yard, though, industrial spaces are being rejuvenated so that people can do what they have always done there: make things. All over, disused husks are being restored or rebuilt. Workers have punched hundreds of windows into the great concrete hulk of Building 77 and are converting its factory floor to a food hall. Products made in Brooklyn adorn homes, protect soldiers, illuminate streets, and sweeten coffee. Pee into a vial at the doctor's office and your urine may get sent here for testing. Spend a weekend morning at MoMA, meet friends for brunch, take a nap on your custom couch, turn on the air conditioner, order a gift online, wrap up the evening with *Saturday Night Live,* and it's possible that every luxurious and leisurely minute of that day will involve a company located at the Brooklyn Navy Yard. I once stood near the rafters of the Capsys Corporation's hangar and watched workers weld together the frame of a house, then shunt it to another station, where the concrete floor was poured. Other crews filled in walls, hung cabinets, and painted, until someone's future home slid along a set of tracks, ready to be lifted onto a truck for the trip to East New York. In June 2016, in a different vast hall, Hillary Clinton celebrated the moment when she became the Democratic Party's nominee for president.

During World War II, seventy thousand people came to work here every day, grinding out warships and materiel. A photograph in the yard's archives shows a platoon of grinning young Riveter Rosies marching through gates while their new male co-workers gawk. Today, the vibe is cleaner, greener,

Women join the shipbuilding force at the Brooklyn Navy Yard during World War II.

and more muted. Employees lock their bikes to stands designed and manufactured by one tenant, Ferra Designs, and find their way after dark thanks to solar-and-wind-powered streetlights designed on-site by Duggal Energy Solutions. Building 92, the brick-and-cast-iron Marine Commandant's House, has been expanded to contain a sleek multimedia exhibit about the yard. The military–industrial complex endures in the vestigial form of Crye Precision, a boutique purveyor of high-tech body armor for elite forces. Crye's vests are hand-sewn—originally by a few dozen skilled Chinese tailors who commuted from Sunset Park, a labor force that a century ago would have both lived and worked in a crammed Lower East Side tenement. As Crye has grown, it's taken over an immense former machine shop, one of several multimillion-dollar renovations that are stimulating the campus's rebirth.

The most visible changes to the waterfront have been the glittery stretches devoted to exercise and languor. But the city has been shoring up the working waterfront, too, convinced that even a post-industrial megalopolis can still nurture shipping, manufacturing, and other olden trades. The Brooklyn Army Terminal and Industry City in Sunset Park are being slowly resuscitated, too.

We know vanished civilizations by the biggest, brawniest, and most durable buildings they leave behind: Roman stadiums, Egyptian temples, medieval cathedrals, Renaissance châteaux. The last two hundred years have bequeathed to us an ungainly legacy of industry, and what we make of that inheritance helps define who we are. At the peak of the machine age, factories were emblems of human might, and artists like Charles Sheeler hymned their majesty and ruthless purpose in his paintings and photographs. Later, the decline of manufacturing in the West gave us a new Gothic landscape, and we have come to savor the poetics of abandonment: silent smokestacks, vaulted basilicas with missing windows, massive brick fortresses, concrete silos, weed-mossed trolley tracks, great steel trusses furred with rust.

> If you've saved the Brooklyn Navy Yard for another day, continue north on the ferry and get off at J, North Sixth Street/North Williamsburg.

After chugging beneath the Williamsburg Bridge, the ferry passes the old Domino Sugar factory, which has been brooding bittersweetly over the East River ever since it shipped out its last sack in 2004. For four hundred years, sugar fueled the process that made New York America's mercantile center: move raw stuff in, work on it, then ship it back out. In 1730, Nicholas Bayard opened North America's first sugar refinery on Liberty Street in Manhattan, which was a momentous event, and not just because it introduced the first generation of New York children to the joys of commercial candy. Ships carrying raw sugar from the Caribbean also brought other loads that scented the docklands' air: cocoa, molasses, limes, ginger, and tobacco. Sugar and shipping produced enormous wealth and plenty of waterfront places to spend it; watchmakers, booksellers, haberdashers, tailors, and other expensive ateliers hugged the docks.

The original Domino Sugar opened in 1856, and by 1870 it was meeting more than half of the nation's sugar needs. The factory burned in 1882, was rebuilt, and continued to refine sugar until 2004. The central brick building, the smokestacks, and the DOMINO SUGAR sign have been preserved by order of the Landmarks Preservation Commission; the rest of the decaying plant is being replaced by a complex of tech-friendly offices, skinny towers, affordable housing, a public waterfront, and streets lined with small, non-chain stores. But in the summer of 2014, before demolition began, the sculptor Kara Walker briefly took over one of the empty warehouses.

Kara Walker's
A Subtlety

In that cavernous space, where waves of granulated sugar once rose so deep and dense that for years nobody ever saw the concrete floor, Walker attached the head of a black house slave to the body of a giant sphinx, all of it made out of polystyrene coated with refined white sugar. The smell of burned caramel still lingered in the air from the old days, and the walls remained coated with a sticky residue, so it looked as though the structure were simply dissolving.

The title was a lyric artwork in itself:

A Subtlety
or the Marvelous Sugar Baby

an Homage to the unpaid and overworked Artisans who have refined
our Sweet tastes from the cane fields to the Kitchens of the New World
on the Occasion of the demolition of the Domino Sugar Refining Plant

Walker's work transformed the industrial structure into a para-religious one. When I visited the exhibition, I entered the dim basilica at one end and sensed the sculpture's presence in the distance before I quite got the measure of its size. I filed down the nave to the bay where she crouched, three stories tall, bathed in the pallor that flowed from a skylight above her kerchief-crowned head. There was only one way to exit: past her mountainous, proffered behind.

Morbid, grotesque, and weirdly adorable, *A Subtlety* invoked the mythic maternal nursemaid who catered to a white family's every caprice, while her bared breasts, cocked buttocks, and swollen vulva suggested that she had other duties, as well. Walker's sphinx was all about nurturing and sex, loyalty and ruthless trade. Walker re-created one of the great marble colossi of the ancient world, transforming it into a statuesque black woman who was whiter than white.

Before reaching the oversize figure, I passed a small army of life-size molasses boys balancing baskets filled with amber shards of crystallized sugar. Walker enlarged them from made-in-China tchotchkes discovered on Amazon. With their round limbs and big soft eyes, they were cute, in a Koonsian sort of way, producing Walker's desired effect of "giddy discomfort." They were slowly melting in the heat, their dark bodies oozing onto the floor.

We keep hearing these days about the poisonous effects of sugar on our brains and waistlines. Walker delved deeper into the historical ravages: the Southern field hands who grew and cut the cane, then hauled it to ships sailing north; the Northern workers in the refineries who purified the product until it was white enough to reimport for use on plantation tables. Today, refined sugar has gone from being the gentry's expensive consumer good to the scourge of poor communities, where obesity and diabetes have reached epidemic proportions. The residents of the future Domino towers will probably patronize the kind of pricey organic-food stores that dispense sugar in its rougher, more putatively authentic forms. They will look out of their floor-to-ceiling windows over a waterfront that is being remade in their image, cleansed of the toxins and sweat and violence with which New York was built.

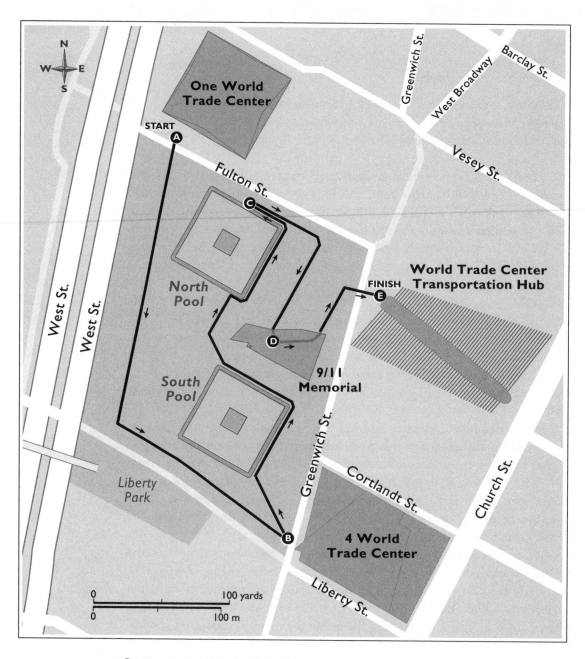

ⓐ One World Trade Center

ⓑ 4 World Trade Center

ⓒ 9/11 Memorial North Pool

ⓓ 9/11 Memorial Museum

ⓔ World Trade Center Transportation Hub

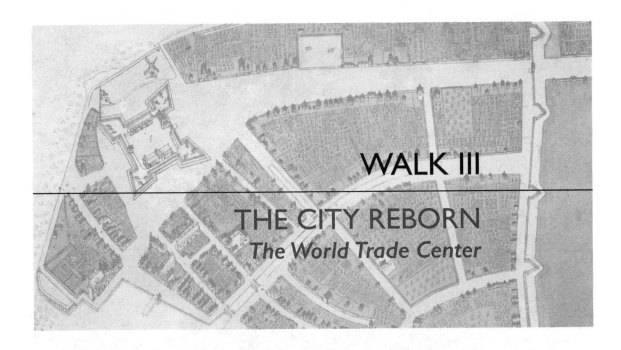

WALK III

THE CITY REBORN
The World Trade Center

On a frigid morning in 2012, I donned a plastic hard hat, pulled a fluorescent-yellow vest over my parka, and was admitted to the vast, swarming pit of the World Trade Center site. A crane swooped down to pluck a steel beam from a flatbed truck and reel it into the air, where it dangled like a plastic prize in an arcade game. All around, workers in color-coded vests and hard hats clambered over various quadrants of the site. In one vast hollow, steam shovels spooned away soil. In another, a naked steel cage was rising above a pick-up-sticks pile of conduits, subway tubes, train tracks, truck ramps, and interlaced foundations.

< Begin near the corner of Fulton Street and West Street, on the south side of One World Trade Center, **A.**

I stepped into a hoist clamped to the side of Tower One. It was a worrisomely low-tech method of transportation—no more, really, than a steel-mesh box lined with plywood and warmed by an electric blower. A dozen bulky men packed in around me, their voices booming and torsos thickened by layered sweatshirts, flannel, and fleece. The operator clanked the gate shut and we lurched upward. I got out on the ninetieth floor, then still a raw concrete slab topped by a thatch of bare columns and rebar. Someone had torn a hole in the netting that wrapped the exposed floor, framing the vista. Down below, the city seemed to be floating away, barely tethered, hardly real.

At the center of the structure, two cranes raced each other to the sky. A battalion of lathers, ironworkers, and welders lit the scene with blowtorch

9/11 Memorial Museum pavilion, with the transit hub and plaza reflected in the façade

sparks. One man gripped a thick iron rod that another banged with a sledge-hammer. It looked like a scene from some medieval illustration of labor—"The Blacksmythe's Forge." For no discernible reason, one of the workers lifted a cry of "whoo-whoo." Another answered him from across the slab, and soon dozens of men were hollering, filling the air a quarter of a mile above Manhattan with a primal group yodel. Then it died out, whipping away on the cold wind. When it was time to go, an older worker whose hard hat was entirely covered by a patchwork of American flag and 9/11 memorial stickers picked up a length of rebar that was lying on the floor and slammed it noisily against the hoist's metal frame to summon the operator. "Yo, Vince," he bellowed down into the void. "We got tourists." He let the iron bar bounce on the freezing concrete and marched back off to work.

As I thawed out on the way down, I felt that I had witnessed an unfathomably complex feat of craftsmanship, carried out on a pharaonic scale. This sleek technological marvel, where hushed offices would one day be as carefully lit and temperature-controlled as cases in a museum, was being hammered together by hand, like a Gothic cathedral. I was also watching emotion harden into form. The man with the stickers on his helmet was just doing his job up there in the icy air, but he was also helping to bring order to chaos, a mission that, like many construction workers, he may well have begun in the toxic rubble of September 11, 2001.

Twin Towers

For years, I stayed away from reminders of 9/11 and the weeks that followed. The most exhaustively recorded cataclysm in history yielded fictionalized movies, documentaries, YouTube clips, eyewitness accounts, TV news reports, police-radio tapes, and endless documentation. I avoided it all. Instead, I remained focused on the drama of reconstruction, returning to the site over the years to observe swarms of welders cauterizing the urban wound. I watched as the messy tangle of history and ganglions of infrastructure were covered over by a great concrete quilt and thin sheets of glass. Today, the site's subterranean realm serves overlapping but incongruous functions, few of which are visible from the street. Trucks enter a buried ramp where security agents can scan them for explosives. Subway and commuter trains click through their concrete tubes. And in a crypt seventy feet below street level lie some unidentified human remains.

The World Trade Center was never just another construction project, though at times it behaved like one. Those who followed it grew accustomed to a steady drip of frustrations. The list of delays, petty grievances, bastardized designs, exploding budgets, and truncated ambitions is too lengthy and depressing to rehash. The result is, on the surface, at least, a geyser of unflappable corporate modernism, a monument to business as usual. Walking

The 1,776-foot One World Trade Center, with the crouching transit hub

through the vast campus now, you might be fooled into thinking of it as the acme of rational design. The symmetrical, supertall Tower One rocketing skyward; the artful arrangement of prisms that makes up its much smaller but still colossal neighbor, Tower Four; the memorial's rectilinear voids—the whole complex exudes geometric cool.

When those buildings first started to rear up, shining, from the mire, the surprise was how much optimism they broadcasted. A year after my winter visit, Tower One had evolved into an immense festive skeleton arrayed in multicolored lights, like some kind of mutant lawn ornament. On stormy days, the wind literally howled through the open floors, producing an unearthly shriek that could be heard for blocks. The building was still raw, hopeful, and wild. The World Trade Center isn't just an achievement of government-subsidized capitalism or sophisticated engineering; it's a collection of enshrined feelings. Fear and defiance gave us the bulked-up skyscraper whose height of 1,776 feet, back when it was called the Freedom Tower, was determined not by any market or structural considerations but by the master planner Daniel Libeskind's penchant for historical symbolism. Preserved grief produced the memorial. The white, winged Transportation Hub embodies the need for uplift that fifteen years ago even hardened pragmatists craved. The horrific pit has been filled in, built up, and dressed in a palette of steel and pewter and charcoal and slate, a whole range of blacks and grays accented by reflective surfaces. Healing, denial, and commemoration battled for primacy and reached an uneasy equilibrium.

Maybe the results were bound to disappoint. The architecture of this site had to perform so many contradictory tasks—notably, to honor trauma while allowing business to continue as if nothing had happened. A multibillion-dollar complex of skyscrapers can accomplish many things, but it's not very good at dealing with paradox. Despite its complexity, the new World Trade

Center has two distinct realms: above and below, work and remembrance. The first demands a purposeful amnesia, the second an unyielding commitment to the past. When the office towers are all built and filled and humming, the tens of thousands who swipe their ID cards in the turnstiles each day must persuade themselves to forget the mayhem and the enduring threat. You can't make money in a graveyard, or on a battlefield.

When I next visited Tower One, it was nearly ready for tenants. I made the ascent indoors this time, in one of the warp-speed elevators that beam workers up to their cubicles from the white portal of the lobby. Now, instead of wind-scoured slabs of concrete, I found office floors soaked in daylight. The curtain wall's thirteen-foot panes of glass made the interiors vertiginously airy and gave the exterior an almost liquid seamlessness, as if the façades were coated in shellac.

Today, those offices contain the hum of work getting done, deadlines being met, approval being sought. It is a hive of mundane anxieties, designed to minimize historic drama, to make everyone forget the circumstances of its birth and the threats it guards against. The almost $4 billion skyscraper, designed by Skidmore, Owings & Merrill (SOM), tries to balance brawn and poise. Like the original Twin Towers, the structure is a rectangular block, only here each corner has been shaved away so that the building tapers from square base to smaller square top, passing through a series of octagonal floors.

There's a lot of mild deceit embedded in this building. Employees of the publishing conglomerate Condé Nast, the tower's first marquee tenant, can approach along a newly extended Fulton Street and enter through a handsome sheet of glass, as if this were just any corporate building. But the lobby doesn't open directly onto the street; it takes cover behind a blast barrier and backs onto an elevator core built as solidly as the Hoover Dam, with ultradense concrete six feet thick. The designers have made an attempt to cloak all the armor, but the message is clear: No soft targets here; anyone with malicious intentions should just keep moving right along.

The tower is unpeopled at the bottom and the top. The base is a massive concrete bunker, impervious to all the threats that the police department could think of. SOM has tricked out the first twenty floors of the façade with the architectural equivalent of rhinestones: pairs of glass fins, cocked at different angles and illuminated from behind, so that the surface glitters twenty-four hours a day. Inside, the lobby has an inadvertently sepulchral air. A collection of gaudy paintings struggles to enliven the high white walls, illuminated niches, and pale angelic light wafting down from above, but the effect remains subtly morbid.

There's more razzle-dazzle up top. The building proper rises just to the height of the original World Trade Center (a mere 1,368 feet), but it's capped by a 408-foot spire, the principal purpose of which is to win the title of tallest building in the Western Hemisphere. (And it did, after a lively debate in height-certifying circles over whether the mast qualified as an architectural element or just a piece of broadcasting equipment stuck on top.) What a strange griffin of a building, with its bulked-up base, its lean glass torso, and its elaborate ceremonial headgear.

> Walk counterclockwise around the memorial plaza, past both the North and South Pools, and stop near the corner of Greenwich Street and Liberty Street, in front of 4 World Trade Center, B.

Nowhere is the tension between buoyant gleam and gnarled history starker than in 4 World Trade Center, the tower by Maki and Associates. It's the epitome of the office building as gadget. The out-of-the-box sheen, corners sharp enough to shave with, surfaces so smooth and pristine that a fingerprint reads like graffiti, lines you could sight a rifle by—every detail and finish is calculated to stimulate pride (if you belong there) or envy (if you don't). The elevator hall's marble isn't just white; it's frothy and unblemished, as if Maki had skimmed off the cream of the quarry and discarded everything else.

To what end, this fetishized perfection? Maybe it performs the same consoling magic on the site's violent history as do hospital corners and gleaming uniforms: It neutralizes gruesome memory, substituting violence with order. From the upper floors, you can press yourself against the glass and squint past your feet to the memorial below. At the end of the workday, you step across the granite-paved lobby, slip through the glass membrane, and emerge onto a block of Greenwich Street that the old World Trade Center had obliterated and that has now been restored. Cross that, and you come to the memorial plaza and the pair of dark-polished wells of melancholy.

> Walk over to the South Pool.

Soon after the Twin Towers fell, the young architect Michael Arad made a dreamy sketch of two square holes in the Hudson River, with water perpetually flowing in from all sides. That poetic image, haunting in its impossible simplicity, evolved into the entry that won the design competition for the 9/11 Memorial. Later, Arad's imaginary sculpture of water and air (transposed to the site of the original towers) materialized into a pair of chasms clad in granite the color of shadow and then lined with a film of falling water. Inside each box is a second void, its bottom always out of sight. Names, incised in bronze, scroll around the lip of that austere vastness. The two pools share the same mournful shade, form, and dimensions but bear different roll calls of the dead.

The memorial plaza isn't an especially solemn place, most of the time. Families come to pay their respects and, having done so, aren't quite sure how to sustain an attitude of sobriety. Office workers stroll by, hollering into mobile phones. Tourists pause on granite benches to plan their next stop. Teenagers take selfies with the names carved in bronze and the big shiny towers beyond. The atmosphere is a mixture of uneasy reverence and casual cheer.

That's all as it should be. The plaza, with its hard pavers and soft canopy of oaks, was always intended as a verdant buffer between the temple and the street. It's okay that the impeccably tailored corporate design should gloss over the past and hide the saga of destruction, dismantlement, and rebuilding. For years, it was a no-go zone, cordoned off and largely invisible. Visiting the memorial plaza—something New Yorkers hardly did—meant obtaining passes and standing on line for airport-style security. Now that the fences have come down, crowds are once again flowing freely.

This might have been a far richer, greener public space if it hadn't immediately been co-opted by symbolism. From the beginning, bringing this part of the city back to life meant consecrating a big chunk of it to death. The emotions that followed the attacks—apocalyptic foreboding, looming grief, panic, determination, and the obsessive fear that memories would fade along with the state of emergency—imprinted themselves on the city in an oversize, irreversible way. Future New Yorkers will not share my generation's feelings, but the pair of geometric fissures in the middle of dense downtown will keep admonishing them that they should. Already those who barely remember and those who hardly knew stare down into the infinity of one pool and hear the exhortation "Never Forget." Then they walk over to the other and receive the message a second time.

The design's basic, ineluctable elements were already laid down well before Arad sent in his drawing. In January 2002, Monica Iken, a victim's wife, asked at a public meeting: "How are we going to honor those like my husband who died? How can we build on top of their souls that are crying?" That demanding expression of grief became an explicit political agenda a few months later, when then-governor George Pataki echoed Iken's demand that the lots where the Twin Towers had stood be dedicated to commemoration. The buildings' footprints, 212 feet on every side, "will always be a permanent and lasting memorial to those we lost," he promised, declaring them "hallowed ground."

By the second anniversary of the attacks, as the memorial-competition jury was sifting through thousands of proposals, the president of the Lower Manhattan Development Corporation, Kevin Rampe, made the exclusion even more specific and categorical: The footprints of the two vanished towers, he declared, would remain free of commercial structures "from bedrock to infinity." A few people wondered whether it was wise to plan a memorial while the pain was still fresh, before trauma had hardened into history, but it was already too late for equivocations. A succession of vows had already defined the memorial's shape, size, and location, plus its overriding aesthetic of emptiness. (The openings are in fact slightly smaller than the Twin Towers' footprints, but a tree was placed on the plaza directly above the stump of

<
Walk to the North Pool, C.

each supporting column, reproducing the original perimeter in symmetrical greenery.)

The site's master planner, Daniel Libeskind, initially conceived of the memorial as an eight-acre park dropped seventy feet below street level. (He later pulled it up to less than half that depth.) Arad wisely feared that such a plan would produce a grim pit in the middle of a space-starved neighborhood. What he wanted instead was a grand piazza at sidewalk level, where the city's life could churn around separate zones of mournful pensiveness. Those he envisioned as a pair of sunken cloisters, reached by ramp from the plaza, and a gallery running around the perimeter of each square, curtained by falling water. I can imagine that walking through such a space might have had a mellow beauty: shadowy towers and mottled light visible through a liquid veil, and the city's clangor softened by the fountain's steady thrum. But the idea of bringing visitors into the depths and communing with the names below ground, so central to Arad's conception, was tossed out, on practical and financial grounds.

Arad's clarity of vision did not exempt his project from the thicket of bureaucracies, budgets, rules, security fears, agendas, and political interests that dogged virtually every step of the redevelopment. The history of squabbles over how to arrange the names of the dead, for example, is not an uplifting tale. Still, Arad claimed that this grinding process wound up enriching his design. It's true that the simple squares are vibrant with understated detail. The names are not just carved but cut right through a thick bronze plate, the letters made of space and light. Water flows through channels spaced an inch and a half apart, forming separate filaments that merge as they fall. The dark granite of the fountains sets off the pale-gray pavers on the plaza, which alternate in rough cobbles and smooth planks of the same stone. The trees are planted in irregular rows that look random at first and then suddenly snap into orderly *allées*.

The fountains have a separate pedigree. They evoke the work of the earth artist Michael Heizer, who, at around the time the original World Trade Center was going up, sliced a deep wound in a Nevada desert and called it *Double Negative*. But the closest precedent to the 9/11 memorial is Heizer's *North, East, South, West,* an ominous set of cubical and cylindrical steel voids sunk into the floor of the Hudson Valley museum Dia:Beacon. Arad has merged Heizer's rough morbidity with tailored elegance. His huge cubes of nothingness—Arad's own double negative—take their place among the pinstriped canyons of steel and glass. Mid-century modernist architects fetishized such orthogonal precision, and their spiritual heirs—the ones producing all those tight-cornered office towers—still rhapsodize about the elegance of a straight line and a flawless edge. Ultimately, Arad's memorial belongs in their company more than in Heizer's, because he subordinates heroics to fastidious detail. In the end, the memorial winds up looking like a massively enlarged version of an antiseptic corporate plaza.

Designing the memorial was the first act in the drama of commemoration, but it occupies only a part of the void left by the destruction of 9/11. Part two is the 9/11 Museum, an even grander, more ambitious epic of memory.

In late May 2002, the place they still called Ground Zero had become an immense and pristine hole. Truckload after surreal truckload of mangled steel and ash and gruesome finds had been carted away, leaving a flat expanse of concrete and rock. One final column from the Twin Towers remained standing, a thirty-six-foot totem of rusting steel emblazoned with cryptic notes, duct-taped snapshots, and a running tally of recovered bodies. But even with the cleanup declared done, workers kept raking the floor with ordinary garden tools, hunting for some infinitesimal shard of human bone. Today, the floor, the column, and one of those rakes are reunited in the mu-

< Walk to the 9/11 Memorial Museum Pavilion, **D,** between the two pools. I suggest reading about the museum before you enter, though: You won't want any distractions in there.

seum, a huge and spectacularly painful institution slipped below the memorial fountains.

I had an early preview of what a museum might be like a decade ago, when I visited Hangar 17 at JFK Airport. There, crushed emergency vehicles, twisted girders, sections of the antenna, half a dozen bikes still chained to a rack, and a lump of fused metal, concrete, paper, and glass were all laid out in an improvised architectural morgue. The last column lay on its side, housed in its own dehumidified area. I found the hangar tour draining but also strangely reassuring. If the authorities treated all this detritus with such rever-

The last column standing at Ground Zero

ence, maybe one day the public would, too. Years later, though, the prospect of revisiting that archive of mass murder relocated to its place of origin made me fibrillate with dread.

The museum is buried beneath the crime scene. I enter through the silvery pavilion designed by Snøhetta, which has the pale sheen and fractured lines of a glacier in mid-melt. Daniel Libeskind had once imagined that the entire sixteen acres would have that icy, falling-apart look; this is a fragmentary remnant of that vision. As visitors line up outside, they can peer through the glass wall to the only traces of the ruined behemoths that penetrate above ground: two of the linked tridents that formed the towers' Gothic arches. Weathered but unbent, they thrust vertically past their new home's weave of angled struts, mute reminders of the original buildings' enormity. They also stand as signposts to the Stygian galleries below.

As I enter, I wonder where the museum experience will fall on the spectrum from anodyne to earnest to brutal. Virtually every decision in this enterprise has been controversial: the underground location, the inscription from Virgil's *Aeneid* (NO DAY SHALL ERASE YOU FROM THE MEMORY OF TIME), the ticket price ($24), the gift-shop souvenirs, the placement of unidentified human remains in an inaccessible chamber just off the museum's main hall, the inclusion of terrorists' photographs, the short film about the rise of Al Qaeda, and so on. The more I think about the task of perpetuating the recollection of that day, the more doubts flock: How can a museum chronicle unsettled history or interpret an event we don't fully understand? How can an exhibit be meaningful to those who were showered in ash that day and also to children yet to be born?

I walk down the long staircase into the minimalist Hades designed by Davis Brody Bond. A murmuring choir of recorded reminiscences from all over the world reminds me that 9/11 was a global event. The dark floors and austere aura make me wistful for the light above, but the architects have taken care to lead visitors gently into the depths. Underground spaces can be disorienting, but this one comes into partial focus at the first overlook. Shock arrives in ripples of recognition. A ramp winds down toward the foundations, where the cut-off columns that held up the Twin Towers sit embedded in Manhattan schist. A pair of building-size boxes containing the memorial's waterfalls and coated with glistening aluminum foam hang in the immense cavern like geometric stalactites. I have arrived at bedrock level, the floor of the concrete bathtub, separated from the Hudson River by a seventy-foot-high section of "slurry wall" so brawny and raw that it feels like the remnant of an ancient Mayan temple. It's here that the collapsing skyscrapers came to rest.

The tale that this museum has to tell is partly about dimensions—the inconceivable scale of murder, the size of the weapons, the sheer bulk of the targets, the worldwide aftershocks. Doing it justice requires a lot of space. As I stare at thick girders bent by the force of a speeding plane, I try in vain to conjure up the extremes of violence that formed it. The last column is standing upright again, proud and solitary in the great hall just as it was in the open pit—only now a touch screen allows visitors to zoom in to the scrawls and taped mementos and to read a digital text label for each one. After all, a museum's job is not just to preserve but also to explain.

In 2006, Alice Greenwald, who had been a director at the Holocaust Museum in Washington, D.C., was appointed to run what was then an amorphous institution with a laundry list of topics and a backlog of acrimony but no overarching concept, no consensus, no design, and not much of a collection. So Greenwald launched a series of exploratory powwows. "We brought everybody into a room," she says, "family members, survivors, first responders, landmark preservationists, architects, museum people—and we started with a set of very large questions about what a museum should be." From those conversations, the team arrived at a few fundamentals: that immense spaces should contrast with intimate chambers, that visitors should be free to create their own itinerary and bypass whatever content they chose, and that tissue boxes would be strategically placed.

The result is a bifurcated museum, split between the square footprints of the original towers, its two parts tucked beneath the twin memorial pools. Where the South Tower stood is the memorial exhibition, an outer room papered with the photographs of the 2,977 people killed on September 11, plus the six who died in the World Trade Center bombing of 1993. Table-mounted touch screens bring up details of the victims' lives, which can be projected on the walls of a separate room, an inner sanctum where the lost are remembered one at a time. In an audio recording, the Cantor Fitzgerald employee John Katsimatides's sister Anthoula teases him posthumously about his John Travolta dance moves: "They used to call him Johnny Bodacious," she recalls.

Beneath the North Pool, stowed in a climate-controlled zone behind glass doors, the historical exhibit is a tour de force of devastating authenticity. Its core is a minute-by-minute timeline of the events as we all observed them, starting at 8:46 A.M., when the first plane hit. In the confined spaces of the exhibition, you confront the experience of a city blasted beyond recognition. Firefighters, their landmarks, equipment, and buddies all gone, mill helplessly around, then start to search through the great pile for tiny caves where someone might conceivably have survived. Almost subliminally, the design leads you from small spaces to large, toggling between intimacy and awe.

Chief curator Jan Ramirez assembled a collection of mundane objects and digital traces sanctified by circumstance. We see the wristwatch that Todd Beamer, a passenger on Flight 93, was wearing when he muttered, "Let's roll," into an open cellphone, then organized a doomed rebellion against the hijackers. (The plane crashed into a Pennsylvania field.) We hear Sean Rooney call his wife, Beverly Eckert, just after the first plane hit to reassure her that the problem was in the North Tower and that he was fine. (He died.) We read a letter from Kenneth Feinberg, special master of the Victim Compensation Fund, informing Steven Morello that his father's life was worth exactly $62,135.41. We imagine the sensation of strapping on the *Phantom of the Opera*–like burn mask that Harry Waizer, who'd worked for Cantor Fitzgerald and was badly disfigured by fire, wore sixteen hours a day for a year after the attacks. We stare at a sealed store window, where jeans and sweatshirts coated in toxic ash form a wrenching diorama. These artifacts, too, reflect the scale of September 11, which didn't just rip a hole in history but also stole into separate lives.

The task of weaving photos, audio, video, and radar into narrative fell to Thinc, the exhibition design firm headed by Tom Hennes, and Local Projects, a multimedia design company founded by Jake Barton. This was the aspect I worried about most—that glossy screens and hyperactive graphics would distract from the experience they were supposed to enhance, or else not work at all. That danger isn't past—it's crucial that the machines are maintained with fanatical perfection—but the use of interactive technology is tastefully restrained. There are films but no sonorous narration, no added sound effects—just, as they say, the facts. The graphic palette, like the architecture, is mostly black and white. Every one of the interactive displays must strike a balance between vividness and consoling distance, and when they don't get it right, they err on the side of aloofness. "We don't ever want to re-create that day," says Tom Hennes of Thinc. "It's not about screams and sirens. You're at the site, but you never lose sense of the fact that you're there today, not back then. The there and then of the day comes through testimony, not immersive experience, which would be sensationalizing and exploitative, and potentially traumatizing."

At times, the sensitivity becomes glaring. A wall label near the entrance to one alcove states the stunningly obvious: PLEASE BE ADVISED THAT THE PROGRAM CONTAINS DISTURBING CONTENT. That description gets ratcheted up to "very disturbing" in the corner reserved for the topic of those who, faced with the choice between burning and jumping, chose the open air. I couldn't face that section on my first visit, but on the second I steeled myself and went in, to find familiar horrors: no videos or identifiable faces, only stills of distant plunging specks.

The museum averts its gaze in more insidious ways, too. The story that opened on a bright Tuesday morning at the start of the school year kept growing more tendrils. During Alice Greenwald's first year on the job, construction began on One World Trade Center, Saddam Hussein was sentenced to death, the war in Afghanistan raged, and drone strikes became an almost daily routine. The meaning of 9/11 continues to change, which means that the museum must be simultaneously definitive and open-ended. "We're a museum that doesn't presume to wrap it up nice and neat," Greenwald says.

In fact, it presumes too little. The exhibits hint at the complexity of the aftermath without tackling the thorniest topics. There are glancing references to conspiracy theorists and tensions between security and civil liberties. A gimmicky digital synopsis projected on a wall keeps recomposing itself, creating a new sequence of headlines every few minutes, but it all goes by too quickly to digest. Clips from on-camera interviews with dignitaries are interspersed with comments that visitors can contribute in a recording booth. But we learn little or nothing about torture, or rendition, or Abu Ghraib, or Tora Bora, or drone raids on Pakistan, or the Bush administration's spurious linkage of 9/11 and Saddam Hussein to justify the war in Iraq. We are spared Rudy Giuliani's constant campaign invocations of his leadership in the wake of 9/11.

As I thread my way through the skein of memories and outrage, it occurs to me that mine is the reaction of someone who was in Manhattan on that day. I am discomfited and unhappy—and that is the museum's strength. It's a tonic for the jaded and an antidote to denial. To visit is to volunteer for certain but tolerable pain. I wonder, though, what impact the museum will make on my son, who spent that morning happily playing dress-up on his first day of preschool, or what it will mean to his grandchildren. Hennes has thought about that question, though he offers no pat answer. "People will enter this place with all different narratives. There isn't one story of 9/11. There are thousands. The museum has to be a place where those stories can be told, and where they can be made coherent." But history is not, or not only, a subjective affair, and the museum's lasting power lies in the unadorned presentation of evidence. In one alcove, recorded voices from inside the towers segue one into the other, while illuminated pinpoints on a simple diagram indicate the speaker's position. We hear Orio Palmer, a fire department battalion chief who has climbed to the seventy-eighth floor of the South Tower, shout breathlessly into the radio to report "numerous 10-45s Code Ones"— fire department lingo for the dead. The realization that he will be next comes in a burst of weird, appalling immediacy. We are witnessing the instant of doom from the comfortable distance of time, and it's still not easy to bear.

All this healing has come at immense cost: $3.8 billion for One World Trade Center; $700 million for the memorial and museum, with another $60 million a year in operating expenses; $4 billion for the world's most expensive subway station, known as the "Flying Bird" and the "Stegosaurus."

<
Cross Greenwich Street to the World Trade Center Transportation Hub, E, which sits between Dey Street and Fulton Street.

The acerbic *New York Post* critic Steve Cuozzo, who took a special loathing to the station's architect, Santiago Calatrava, dubbed his design the "Calatravasaurus." I visited that, too, while it was under construction, and it was like standing in the center of a ruined arena or prehistoric observatory. Immense pieces of molded steel sat on plinths, like the bones of some giant fossilized beast. Above, curving steel fingers reached toward each other. The space between them framed a worm's-eye view of the surrounding skyscrapers, which seemed to converge toward a point in the sky. Calatrava's aesthetic emerged from the ruins of the ancient world—all those bleached, perfectly proportioned skeletons gleaming in the sun. That kinship was most obvious at this stage, before the openings had been glassed in, the two sides of the roof met, and the whole structure acquired its final pristine gloss—before, in other words, the structure got un-ruined.

In early 2004, Calatrava stood beneath the palm trees of the World Financial Center's Winter Garden and drew a quick sketch of a child releasing a dove. That was the showman's prelude to unveiling his design for the World Trade Center Transportation Hub, a great white bird that charmed a roomful of skeptics. Finally, after all the earthbound squabbles and depressing compromises, here was an expression of upwelling joy. Calatrava had recently joined the rarefied ranks of celebrity architects. Then in his early fifties, he was still young in a profession with a notoriously lengthy dues-paying stage, but he had a clutch of flamboyantly energetic projects under his belt. His white-steel bridges flung themselves across rivers and ravines like ballerinas in mid-leap, a concert hall in the Canary Islands tossed back its sweeping coiffure, and his lakeside addition to the Milwaukee Art Museum evoked both ship and whale diving into the spume.

He promised a phantasmagoric piece of urban theater. Commuters would emerge from beneath the Hudson River into an architectural daydream. In Calatrava's design, sunlight filtered through layers of glass and burrowed down to the platforms below ground. A few steps up the escalator, and the city's towers appeared through a curving transparent shed. A public plaza wrapped itself around the station and beneath the building's soaring canopies, merging the lobby with the street. Here, at the edge of the memorial's sober acres, would be a place for crowds to mingle: a full block of exuberant urban chaos capped by a stunning, luminescent structure. The station he spoke of preened, arced, and spread its wings; the spiky extensions were designed to flap a little when the roof parted along its spine, opening the atrium to the sky.

It's difficult to remember at this remove how desperately those of us who watched Calatrava perform his magic trick with a Sharpie wanted him to uplift the process of reconstruction. We craved something better than a plain old New York–style real estate deal, and that's what he promised.

A lot has changed since then: Towers have risen, trauma has been enshrined, and the scar tissue between the site and the city has slowly begun to heal. And Calatrava is suddenly, stunningly out of fashion, amid reports of leaky roofs and wobbly bridges and budgets gone kablooey. He has turned from a humanist hero into the emperor of self-indulgence, pilloried for invoking facile metaphors from nature, for randomly defying convention, for pushing against the limits of buildability, for bequeathing intolerable maintenance burdens, for indulging in visual razzmatazz instead of just getting the job done, and, mostly, for erecting budget-guzzling luxuries. A man of grandiloquent visions and erudite charm, he managed to cajole unsuspecting bureaucrats on both sides of the Atlantic into buying more than they could pay for. He sometimes sacrificed practicality on the altar of amazement.

It didn't help that, after terrorist attacks on railway targets in London and Madrid, he had to thicken the hide on his glass cocoon. Along the way, the cost leaped from the huge to the inconceivable. The word "obscene" was tossed around. Those who applauded him in 2004 later came to feel a little foolish, as if Calatrava had performed a conjuring trick on them and picked their pockets at the same time. But he did neither. He had an idea, and everyone loved it. It still seems like a good idea, a boondoggle perhaps, and an overpriced architectural gadget, but still a thing of awe and wonder.

If those of us who felt the exhilaration of that day understood the financial implications better than the Port Authority had, would we have swallowed hard and rained brimstone down on the design? Maybe, but hardly anyone did. Like most critics, I waxed rapturous: Calatrava, I wrote, had conceived "an optimistic emblem of flight as an answer to airborne disaster." I still feel that way. It seems miraculous that Calatrava's daydream should now finally exist, altered yet recognizable. Its frame is a little less lithe, its skin a little less smooth, its concept more mature. What remains is an extravagantly idealistic creation unlike any in New York. It challenges the city's public architecture to rise above habitual cut corners and rectilinear repetition. The cost of beauty is often high.

The station disrupts the World Trade Center's relentlessly Cartesian arrangement. It roosts at the foot of towers, steel-veined wings almost brushing an adjacent façade. Sitting aslant the grid of streets, it pivots toward the morning sun. The Transportation Hub is a buried, tentacled affair, stretching toward both rivers and linking the PATH with eleven subway lines, but the part that pokes above ground is the Oculus, the building's great white eye. Observed from a high floor of a neighboring address, it seems to squint—especially when the retractable skylight blinks—and the wings metamorphose into lashes. Does any work of architecture in New York turn such an expressive face to the clouds?

Dancer in the Oculus

Calatrava originally designed the wings to dip, a ludicrously literal flourish that was wisely scrapped. What remains of that urge is the illusion of motion contained in every view. Outside, the eye is drawn up and out in a parabolic swoop. Along the exterior flank, the parallel columns appear to accelerate like bicycle spokes. In the PATH Hall that extends beneath the memorial plaza, steel lines flow horizontally, undulating across the ceiling to make an underground chamber feel like a dive beneath the waves.

The Oculus merges a flock of organic allusions, but its most astute homage to nature lies in the way it makes visible the forces of gravity and shear. Calatrava began with a basic engineering tool, the bending-moment diagram, which shows the stresses on a cantilevered beam. Those calculations gave him the shape of each rib: an enormous boomerang that he could balance on one tip with the other tilted toward the sky. He lined up all these freestanding sculptures and attached them at the elbows, creating a pair of immense arches along the spine. If the whole massive ensemble seems held together by nothing at all, it's because the Oculus is effectively a pair of separate clamshell-like structures, lightly joined at either end. You could knock one half down and the other would barely budge.

> Enter the Oculus at the west entrance, pause at the overlook, and take the escalators and stairs down to the white marble floor.

The large hall competes with Grand Central Terminal in its vaulted drama, but if you stand in the center and look up, the effect is more Pantheon-like: The eye finds a feather-shaped length of air instead of a central arch. The site's master planner, Daniel Libeskind, had imagined a "Wedge of Light," a frame for the rays that fall across the site at 10:28 A.M. every September 11—the moment when the second tower fell. Calatrava, honoring that idea, has the sun slice through the open skylight. And the rest of the year, when the vault isn't serving that particular Stonehengian function, it still allows a generous portion of sunshine to cascade down into the hall.

Cost is an objective fact; value isn't. Whether you consider this station splendid overkill, an ugly boondoggle, or a lasting work of genius depends on a host of intangibles. Granted, you can move one hundred thousand commuters in and out of New Jersey every day a good deal more modestly and cheaply. (Penn Station manages five or six times that number of passengers.) But the Hub serves an area that is both the oldest and the newest part of town and keeps changing in ways that planners have never been able to predict. There's a good chance that more commuters will arrive as new offices materialize, old ones become apartments, and the neighborhood acquires residents who will flow through the Oculus in search of dinner, a shirt, or a meeting spot. I doubt it will ever feel empty. In the end, we are left with a structure that must endure a century or more. Calatrava's skeletal dove joins the tiny circle of New York's great indoor public spaces, serving not just the city that built it but also the city it will help build.

*Lower Manhattan
seen from the
S.S. Coamo, 1941*

Interlude II
CITY OF TOWERS
The Skyline

In the summer of 2014, New Yorkers started to notice a new presence on the Midtown skyline: 432 Park Avenue, an unrelenting concrete grid of ten-by-ten-foot openings stacked like cubbyhole units. Unpromising buildings under construction were nothing new, but this one just kept getting taller and taller, adding a new floor every week. By fall, it spindled far above the tallest part of the city, dwarfing even its Fifty-seventh Street neighbor, One57. Only a few months earlier, that brand-new thousand-footer had seemed monstrously tall, but compared with 432 Park it shriveled into insignificance. Suddenly you could see the 1,400-foot rod of 432 Park from almost anywhere, dominating the city's silhouette as forcefully as a campanile looms over an Italian hill town.

A bell tower performs many tasks: It projects the spiritual and worldly power of the Church, calls the faithful to Mass, announces feasts, mourns deaths, keeps time, and acts as a unifying symbol of community. The Park Avenue apartment tower, on the other hand, represents only its investment value. It's hardly even a place to live, only an extremely expensive safe-deposit box where the global ultra-rich can quietly park their cash. The design, by Rafael Viñoly, looks like the product of rationalism gone insane, a linked chain of tic-tac-toe games reaching into the sky. Some architects love it for that reason. Making a large and complex structure look this simple is a stag-

432 Park Avenue redefines the Midtown skyline.

gering task. The result eventually placated me, too. I have grudgingly started to appreciate its rigor and lack of showiness and the fact that it's the rare new tower that isn't curtained in glass. As the building grew, it grew on me. Perhaps today's children will one day consider it a landmark, not to be tampered with. Every iteration of the New York skyline is an abomination to one generation and an inspiration to the next.

Not since the days of Art Deco has New York experienced a growth spurt like the one that's stretching it now. Burly office towers have begun to crowd Manhattan's once low and open West Side. The newest downtown skyscrapers push over the tops of slightly older skyscrapers. Thousand-footers may soon pop up in Brooklyn and Jersey City, New Jersey. In Midtown, Viñoly's colossus will soon get more company, too.

Why do these new buildings have to be so tall? For starters, because a sky-scraper is a money machine. It's what happens when a team of developers, cost analysts, insurers, engineers, architects, brokers, investors, and lenders makes a collective determination that physics and market forces, fused into one enormous hunk of a building, will probably yield a profit. But that's only part of the story. When buildings consist of nothing more than the output of bookkeepers' jottings, then every effort to maximize profits yields the same result: a maxed-out skyline of utter monotony.

Fortunately, in high-stakes construction, pragmatism has its limits. Profit-and-loss calculations can never quite account for a set of deeply irrational instincts, which is why some of New York's tallest towers soar well above the point of diminishing returns. The Rutgers economist Jason Barr has quantified the "status effect": how much higher some skyscrapers rise than the profit motive would justify. The Empire State Building, Barr estimates, is fifty-four stories taller than pure number-crunching suggests it should be. The race to erect the world's tallest skyscraper endowed the Chrysler Building with thirty-seven extra stories and its rival, 40 Wall Street, with twenty-nine. Barr doesn't follow his reasoning to the logical conclusion: If the single-minded pursuit of profit ruled alone, we would have a stumpier city.

Thank goodness, then, that greed is not the only source of the skyscraper's addictiveness; so is the primal urge to climb and stare at a more distant horizon. That drive intensifies at certain times, and those variations get mapped onto the skyline. After periods of stasis, the spiritual lust for height returns, producing an ever more spectacular urban silhouette, a dynamic work of collective genius. There's something sublimely crazy about this cycle. Builders keep building because they believe, sometimes foolishly, that even if a project makes no economic sense at the moment, it will pay off someday. To erect a tall building is to proclaim one's faith in the future, and the skyline embodies that confidence multiplied many times over. It's a seismograph of optimism.

The results are not always inspiring. All through the twentieth century, Manhattan grew by dint of ugly architecture, punctuated by the occasional marvel. Every celebrated skyscraper rose amid bundles of mid-rise mediocrity. Each masterpiece-producing boom also threw off acres of stupefying repetition. It's an old story. Once again, a new generation of towers is crowding out the sky and shadowing our open space. Their domineering mass can kill street life and choke off the smaller-scale city at their feet. They dump more hordes on crowded subway platforms. Today's juggernauts block our view of yesterday's juggernauts: We are losing sight of our icons.

Some of these are practical objections, some selfish. But if many New Yorkers see each new tall building as another oppressor, it may be that their reaction is partly visceral, an instinctive revulsion couched in complaints about traffic, construction noise, and neighborhood character. The writer W. G. Sebald attributed a deep-seated fear of enormousness to the title character of his 2001 novel *Austerlitz,* and described it as practically a law of nature:

> No one in his right mind could truthfully say that he liked a vast edifice. . . . At the most we gaze at it in wonder, a kind of wonder which in itself is a form of dawning horror, for somehow we know by instinct that outsize buildings cast the shadow of their own destruction before them, and are designed from the first with an eye to their later existence as ruins.

These days, you can see that bleak process play out again in Downtown Brooklyn, where canyons of cheap window walls and protuberant air conditioners rise along Flatbush Avenue. It's hard to fathom how sentient beings could have devoted so much time, money, and enthusiasm to producing such drear. Well, not that hard: Everyone follows the path of least resistance and then moves on to the next job. The result is an orgy of indifference. When a newcomer does sport a dash of design, it only accentuates the sadness. Consider Brooklyn's temporarily tallest building, 100 Willoughby Street, a.k.a. the all-rental AVA DoBro, which SLCE "designed" for AvalonBay. The architects couldn't do much about the monolithic mass, but they did speckle the façade in an assortment of blue panes, so that it looks as though the builders had raided an odd-lot store. (Blue-glass patchwork has become a mystifying mini-trend.)

And yet, once again, massed ghastliness could also give birth to a masterpiece: the future tallest tower in Brooklyn. The Williamsburgh Savings Bank held that title for eighty-five years, before being deposed by a series of unworthy successors. Happily, the next claimant, a thousand-foot tower at 9 DeKalb Avenue, designed by SHoP Architects, could be one of the most sensitively detailed and spectacularly expressive additions to the New York (not just Brooklyn) skyline since the Seagram Building. Most towers grab height; this one earns it.

Like most great urban architecture, the design emerges from a thicket of local constraints. The scarcity of lots, and the difficulty of assembling them, forced SHoP to squeeze its seventy-three-story spire on a triangle it shares with an unofficial landmark, Junior's Cheesecake, and the officially designated Dime Savings Bank. The bank, originally designed by Mowbray & Uffinger in 1906, expanded in 1932 into a geometric layer cake: a round cupola on a hexagonal base, enclosed by another hexagonal banking hall, inscribed in a triangular site. SHoP's designers extended the same grid onto the adjacent lot and massaged it into a composition of nested and overlapping hexagons. The faceted forms get smaller on their way to the top, like a bundle of pencils of varying lengths. From below, the arrangement of staggered setbacks and vertical piers evokes an abstracted sandstone butte, gorgeously scored by erosion.

Despite the Western allusion, this is unmistakably a New York building—or will be, if it gets built the way it was designed. Tubes of varied sizes and profiles run up the exterior like crazy organ pipes, growing thicker and darker as they shoot into the sky. The tower doesn't pretend to dematerialize in a cloud of light, mist, and glass, as so many clunky supertalls wish they could. Instead, virtually every vantage point reveals multiple façades, all of them textured and sinewed. An assortment of dramatic flourishes—the chiaroscuro of blackened metal and brazen glints, the Batman-ready ledges, the syncopated rhythms of windows, the spiky crown—add up to a new kind of Gotham Gothic.

These charms may not be enough to placate Brooklynites who fear that giants are trampling their borough. When 9 DeKalb Avenue opens, its thin-air penthouses will look out over a four-to-eight-story borough stretching from Newtown Creek to Coney Island. What is to prevent one super-scaled building from leading to the next, until they invade the leafy brownstone shires? Plenty, for now: zoning regulations, the distribution of subway lines, the existence of historic districts, and the power of money to fight money. These barriers can crumble, though, and so the best way to preserve low-rise Brooklyn is for Downtown to succeed by growing up rather than out. A great skyline remains concentrated and confined, its towers made meaningful by borders, its scale a contrast to be savored, not feared. Height is not in itself a problem. Managed well, it opens the way for a constantly growing but geographically confined metropolis to expand. New York reconstitutes itself all the time, nourished by a regular supply of invention, and the day we consider the skyline complete and untouchable is the day the city begins to die.

Taller buildings won't ruin New York, but too many terrible ones can. We need the exceptions, the Empire State and Chrysler Buildings, designs that captured the imagination before they could turn a profit. When you're putting up a multibillion-dollar tower that's a quarter mile high, it had damn well better be a work of art. That's a challenge: Overweening realities of technology, zoning, and real estate arithmetic don't leave much leeway for frills like beauty. The difficulty of making an elegant, symbolic presence out of an immense vertical structure has been vexing architects since the beginning of the skyscraper age.

"Problem," declared the great architect Louis Sullivan in 1896: "How shall we impart to this sterile pile, this crude, harsh, brutal agglomeration, this stark, staring exclamation of eternal strife, the graciousness of those higher forms of sensibility and culture that rest on the lower and fiercer passions?" Sullivan knew from experience that in large, expensive buildings, aesthetics struggle to assert themselves.

The earliest skyscraper designers groped toward a way to translate traditional opulence into a vertical style. They enlarged European precedents, piling up palazzos and cathedrals into layered buildings encrusted with giant cornices, columns, and pediments. Sullivan's generation divided the tower into three parts of varying symbolic significance: a column's base, shaft, and capital; a tree's roots, trunk, and branches; a drama's exposition, denouement, and conclusion. Sullivan saw the three parts as the natural, and therefore excellent, consequence of the job a building does: high-ceilinged shops on the bottom, in the middle a warren of offices repeating as many times as necessary, topped by a windowless attic housing mechanical systems. "Form ever follows function," he declared, a formulation slightly less terse and much less stylistically prescriptive than the modernist battle cry it engendered: *Form Follows Function!*

In recent years, that imperative has yielded two comically distinct types of glass super-skyscrapers: the fat office building, with a girth ample enough to accommodate a trading floor; and the skinny residential shaft, just thick enough for a full-floor duplex. Think of them as architecture's Laurel and Hardy.

Today's urban workplaces have little to do with the elongated masonry pyramids of the twenties or the spare blocks of the sixties. In the new business behemoths—the Bank of America Building at One Bryant Park, for instance—a few indentations or judicious asymmetries set off tautly seamless skins. Vertical folds in a curtain wall resemble slits in a satin gown worn by an elephant. These are not so much whims of style as they are forms shaped by technology and the demands of the most valued tenants. The corporate culture shaped by financial firms dictates the need for enormous, column-free floors and high ceilings. Large, populous floor plates mean more high-speed elevators, which get packed into a thicker concrete core. Glass walls keep the inner cubicles from feeling sepulchral. Office towers' most dramatic advances take place in their innards: You can practically date a skyscraper's vintage by the air quality in its offices, the speed of its elevators, and the softness of its lighting. These features also affect the building's mass. Contemporary air-conditioning ducts take up space between floors, meaning that eighty stories need a lot more height than they once did. Unsentimental efficiency is raising a crop of ungainly monoliths.

Sullivan assumed that only the office building warranted great height, but the most radically double-edged innovation of recent years is actually the ultra-tall *residential* tower. If you've ever gazed southward across Sheep Meadow in Central Park, you know that the plutocratization of the skyline has gotten under way. Along Fifty-seventh Street, lanky residential towers are lining up for Central Park views like an NBA team craning to peer at a new iPhone. From each $100 million penthouse, the park looks virtual and screen-like, a glossy rectangle of green, populated by tiny avatars. Between 432 Park Avenue (at Fifty-sixth street) and One57 (at the corner of Fifty-seventh Street and Seventh Avenue), the gracious old building that for ninety years was known as Steinway Hall, where Carnegie Hall performers came to choose their pianos, is getting a new identity and a new neighbor: 111 West Fifty-seventh Street. There's hope for that one: the old foyer and showroom will become the building's lobby, which SHoP has adorned with a bronzed feather of a tower, tricked out with glazed terra-cotta tiles. But the supremacy of 432 Park will last only until the completion of the Nordstrom Tower, near Broadway, a 1,550-foot scene-stealer by the supersizing virtuosos Adrian Smith and Gordon Gill. (They also designed the world's currently tallest tower, the Burj Khalifa in Dubai.) When it's done, the Nordstrom Tower will clear the top floor of One World Trade by a healthy margin.

I evaluate tall buildings not stylistically, or by how well they serve those who pay the bills, but by how sensitively they integrate the different spheres of interior, street, and skyline. A few residents occupy a tower that tens of thousands walk by every day and millions see from all around. Those separate scales impose different aesthetic demands, all equally important. It used to be a given that a great building met its private and public responsibilities with equal panache. But because today's economics permit a tiny number of largely absent people to have a disproportionate impact on the skyline, these buildings invert the rationale that propelled skyscraper construction for more than a century. Instead of packing the largest number of people onto the smallest patch of earth, they fill up the skyline with sparsely populated habitats for oligarchs who, if they live there at all, roam across their parquet tundra, hollering for their mates.

Yet it's not enough just to gape at these towers' bravado or grumble at the arrogance of the hyper-rich gobbling up the sky. Like it or not, the elongated condo is an ever-more-assertive category of New York architecture, and it, too, can function as a form of public art. The combination of slenderness and height means that skyscrapers can sprout from modest lots, minimizing their impact on the street and narrowing the shadows they cast. The fact that they contain the caviar of real estate means that they can afford the luxury of being good. Since we have to live with the follies of the outlandishly wealthy, we should at least insist that they pamper themselves in a way that also enriches the city.

New York's founding credo is that you get what you pay for, and what you pay for is yours. But in such a dense city, the rest of us also get what you pay for, and we help pay for what you get. A mere $90 million or so buys a nice duplex perch, but the people down below must bear the aesthetic cost—and in some cases the financial cost as well: One57 benefited from an outrageous $66 million tax abatement. In theory, developers pay for their portions of sky and light with architecture worth looking at. In practice, they judge design by their clients' taste for glitz—which explains One57's façade, done in fifty shades of azure by Christian de Portzamparc. It's a luxury object for people who see the city as their private snow globe.

Such buildings fail when they treat New York as an amenity for prospective buyers and the architecture as nothing more than a marketing tool. On the Fifty-seventh Street side, the building pours out of the sky in parallel ribbons that undulate as they fall, then go rippling out above the sidewalk in a wavy canopy. That's the conceit, anyway. But a building doesn't liquefy just because computer renderings promise that it will. In the physical world—the one where Hurricane Sandy crippled a crane that dangled perilously on the roof for months—One57 looks like a stolid arrangement of beveled blocks upholstered in silk and satin stripes. Up top, the rounded crown suggests a menacing helmet. It's as if Darth Vader had dressed up for a charity ball.

Today's priciest dwellings abound in light and sky, and little else. Through transparent casings, they offer the illusion of levitating just beneath (or sometimes in) the clouds, turning billionaires into creatures of the air. The layouts of these crystalline crows' nests afford nowhere to retreat from contact with the sky. They offer the fake thrill of exposure but no shelter from the glare. No wonder the owners don't spend much time there, when they have their choice of cozier homes. And yet builders of super-fancy apartments have nothing else to offer clients that would justify the expense. It's hard to imagine how high the ceilings would have to be, how glossy the kitchen, or how noiseless the air-conditioning to make an apartment here feel like a good deal. At these financial altitudes, the views are a hedge against the future. If you look out the window and feel like a full participant in city life, then you probably live low enough to have your sunlight blocked by the next round of construction. Billionaires want assurance that that isn't going to happen.

When I stared out the window of a still-unoccupied eighty-seventh-floor apartment in One57 (asking price $67 million), the city appeared vivid but unreal. My eye drifted to the vague horizon: the shadowy silhouette of the Poconos, the gantries in the Port of Elizabeth, the misty hills of Staten Island, and the low haze of Garden City and the Rockaways. The residents of billionaire aeries are happy to see those places from afar but have little interest in what goes on there. Meanwhile, their actual neighbors' lives play out at ant level. The hyper-wealthy pay immense premiums to live so high that they can hardly see anything at all.

Why, then, would anyone choose to live atop an observation platform where violent winds make opening a window unwise? For a taste of store-bought divinity. A view is power, a form of majestic surveillance—and you can enjoy it, too.

On the dark afternoon of December 20, 1932, the photographer Berenice Abbott took the elevator to one of the highest man-made points in the world in order to chronicle a completely new sight. The Empire State Building was just eighteen months old, and from the eighty-sixth floor Abbott beheld the city of towers from above. She left her shutter open for fifteen minutes dur-

ing that fleeting stretch between sunset and 5:00 P.M., when she knew that office workers would start to click off their lights. Her wait in the cold, windless air yielded the famous *Nightview*—the ultimate modern vision, blending stillness and movement, regimentation and sublimity. In the photo, hundreds of foreshortened towers shoot up toward the camera, each one a grid of luminous little squares, each square a person about to go home.

I thought of that picture when I stood on the hundredth-floor observation deck of One World Trade Center, where the Empire State Building looks at once immeasurably distant and close enough for me to reach out and snap off its spire. The view is practically astronautical. From here, the city below recedes into abstraction, a gridded 3-D map. The effect is not grandeur but its opposite: The inhabited world has been miniaturized for your viewing pleasure.

To look out over a great, complicated metropolis from this height is to try to give landscape a meaning, to press it into the service of an argument. On the evening after Hurricane Sandy hit, the photographer Iwan Baan went up in a helicopter and took a photo of a stunningly darkened Manhattan, with just one corner incongruously alight. It's a parable of resilience, the twenty-first-century answer to Abbott's celebration of modern existence. The bright city may have lost its gleam for a moment, but it will never flare out completely.

If exclusive towers like One57 sell the view as a unique possession, an observation deck rents it by the hour. Legends, a company that manages skyboxes and stadiums and now runs the World Trade Center deck, has turned it into a high-tech spectacular. Before you get a glimpse of an actual place, you follow a winding path through cheesy synthetic bedrock, complete with trickling water, then ride an elevator where a time-lapse panorama zips through four hundred years of New York history—wooden farmhouses giving way to brick, cast iron, terra-cotta, and glass. When you emerge on the hundredth floor, you watch a two-minute multi-screen montage of cabbies, crowds, and subways. Then the curtains lift and—*voilà*—behind all that razzle-dazzle, spread out before you in its weighty three-dimensionality is . . . well, on a foggy day, nothing much, actually. But if you have the good luck to visit on a soft, perfect afternoon when a light haze purples the Catskills and flatters the sharp contours of Midtown, then New York looks like a gorgeous stage set. All the theatricals serve to palliate the $34 admission and encourage people to feel they are doing something more exciting than just gazing out the window. They also help distract from the fact that this is what people saw through shattered windows on September 11, 2001, the scene that hundreds jumped into rather than face the flames.

Like a panning shot in a movie, such a godly view creates the illusion of omniscience. In *The Hunchback of Notre-Dame,* Victor Hugo brings the reader up to the cathedral's roof to summon a view of Paris in 1482: "The spectator who arrived, panting, at this pinnacle, saw a dazzling abundance of roofs, chimneys, streets, bridges, squares, and clock towers. Everything drew to the eye at once." Hugo leads the reader over a thirty-page excursion, landmark by landmark, neighborhood by neighborhood, building up a virtuosically detailed portrait of a city that is at once sweeping and minute. His description reads like the verbal version of a CGI-enhanced film scene, in which objects moving deep in the background maintain their HD clarity.

Real life presents a trade-off between distance and detail. You can spot an upper-story window a few blocks away and gauge its height and distance accurately. Pick a point on the horizon, though, and you have no way of knowing whether it's one, five, or twenty miles away. Your sense of depth disappears. There's nothing quite like comparing a cartographic city view with an actual map to make it clear that both of them lie a little. From where I watch, the Empire State Building stands hip-to-hip with 432 Park, though they are in fact more than twenty blocks apart. But the view also tells me what a map neglects to mention: that you could swing by zip line between the Woolworth Tower, near City Hall, and Frank Gehry's 8 Spruce Street without hitting anything; that the spaces between buildings are cushioned in foliage; that the natural beauty of New York's waterways endures.

The urge to see everything at once has often intruded into art. Sometime around 1600, El Greco followed a mule track into the hills around the Spanish city of Toledo, watching the way its buildings spilled down the ravines. No one perspective corresponded to his ideal of his adopted city, its ecstatic steepness and religious intensity. And so, for his famous *View of Toledo,* he whipped up a divine lightning storm, switched the location of the Alcázar and the cathedral to heighten the drama of the composition, and invented a compound across the river as a monastic retreat for the city's patron saint. The World Trade Center pursues a slightly different kind of viewpoint multiplication, using technology instead of fiction. Visitors can stand on a circular "window" in the floor and look past their feet to the traffic on West Street a thousand feet below—except that they're really standing on a solid concrete floor and what they're seeing is a live camera feed projected onto a screen. Another $15 will get you the use of an iPad mapped with forty landmarks: touch one, and the camera swoops low over the city, zooming in on, say, Zabar's or Yankee Stadium, with a ten-second description by the novelist Jay McInerney. Like Hugo and El Greco, Legends' view-management system rejiggers distance for the sake of drama and clarity.

The potion of technology, ambition, viewlust, and economics that brought us to this point keeps getting more and more potent. So the question presents itself: How high will it lift the skyline? By global standards, and by the standards of all that's possible, New York's hugest buildings aren't really that big. From the Empire State Building in 1931, at 1,250 feet tall, until Taipei 101 in 2004, the roof of the world rose just four hundred feet. Then, in 2010, it jumped another thousand feet, to the half-mile-high Burj Khalifa, a godlike spike in the desert. Its usurper is already under construction: The Kingdom Tower in Jeddah, Saudi Arabia, will hit the one-kilometer mark (or 3,280 feet) when it's completed, theoretically in 2018. The pace of supertall construction has accelerated recently, and if there is some theoretical or practical ceiling beyond which nobody will ever build, engineers haven't found it yet. "I don't see a limit other than people's chutzpah—arrogance, actually," says Ken Lewis, a principal at Skidmore, Owings & Merrill who managed the design of One World Trade. Arrogance is useful: A sizable segment of the architectural, engineering, and construction professions depend on it for inspiration and employment.

The mile-high skyscraper makes a little more sense to build than it did sixty years ago, when Frank Lloyd Wright imagined such a thing as a habitable sundial in the middle of Chicago called the Illinois. That idea couldn't be realized at the time, and it remains hypothetical. A mile-high skyscraper would still be financially ruinous, slow to construct, and inefficient to operate, but that doesn't mean it will never be built.

"Going big has been a trend ever since the pyramids. It has little to do with practicalities," says Jay Siegel, an executive and engineer with Allianz, the company that might one day insure this Hubris Tower. The technology of supertall buildings is a bit like genetic testing or nuclear energy: a volatile form of power. Technological capacities have outpaced our judgment. We know we can do it, but we don't know when *not* to do it. And so some preposterously wealthy mogul, most likely in South Asia or a Gulf emirate, will eventually move into a penthouse so far above the earth's crust that the air is thin, gales hammer at the glass, and the elevator ride to the top is inadvisable if you have a sinus infection. A mile's not science fiction. It's not even an outer limit.

From a mile up, the world looks the way it does from an airplane, at the point during takeoff and landing when you can pick out an individual car beetling along a highway. In the not-unimaginably-distant future, this will be the view from someone's breakfast nook. I asked William Baker, the SOM structure guru who figured out how to make the Burj Khalifa stand up, how he would respond if a developer with limitless resources came to him and said: "Okay, time to quit screwing around with ten stories here and a hundred feet there. Let's build the mile-high tower."

"Yup," he answered. "Okay." (Baker is originally from Missouri, and he is frugal with words.)

"How about a mile and a quarter?" I pressed.

"Yeah, we'd figure it out."

"And at what point do you stop being able to figure it out?"

"I'm not sure. A mile would be twice the Burj. For now, let's double what we have. Then we can figure out how to double it again."

It's easy to wave away architects' impractical fancies: Wright's mile-high Illinois, which in his drawings looks like the Burj Khalifa's grandfather; also X-Seed 4000, a two-and-a-half-mile-high takeoff of the Eiffel Tower, and TRY 2004, a vertical city in the shape of a pyramid, both of which were designed to rear above Tokyo. But there is something irresistible about that phlegmatic bravado, the Midwestern matter-of-factness with which an experienced structural engineer like Baker suggests a whole new era of loftiness. For Baker, the mega-tall tower is really a new species, not just an inflated version of the skyscrapers of yore. He cites the biologist D'Arcy Thompson, who, in his 1915 classic, *On Growth and Form,* described with mathematical elegance the relationships between shape and size in nature. Different orders of magnitude require different skeletal structures. You can't just inflate the Empire State Building and get its mile-high successor, any more than you can multiply a mouse to produce an elephant. Double the height and width of a blocky tower and you wind up with a dark-bellied leviathan, in which many occupants labor so far from windows that they might as well be stocking shelves in an Amazon warehouse. Instead, engineers have had to invent new structures, the kind that narrow from a sprawling mall below to a cozy penthouse palace.

That tapering comes at a cost. Each additional floor on top requires expensive extra concrete and steel down below, but it also gives back little. "When you look at the square footage gained by going up higher, at some point you could just build another building next door. There is a height where it no longer becomes economically feasible," says Siegel, the Allianz executive. For a century, the rise of skyscrapers was propelled by an inexorable formula: the higher the cost of land, the higher the number of stories needed to pay for it. At a certain point—where, exactly, is a moving target—this logic falls apart. Instead, another craving takes over: the need for immensity.

Building at high elevations may seem like a rational enterprise, but it's more like an extreme sport, filled with potential dangers. Piping junctions can snap, high-pressure hoses burst, cranes collapse, fires rage beyond reach. Wet concrete can start to harden on its way up to its destination. Even a minute shift in the earth below the foundations can knock a building askew.

In the first phase of skyscraper development, the greatest limiter of height was gravity. But as towers poked farther and farther into the sky, engineers had to deal with the more erratic forces of earthquakes and weather. A light breeze on the fourth floor can magnify into a gale on the 104th, and even infinitesimal vibrations can make people feel ill. Wind slams into a tower from one side, then splits into two arms. When the two streams whip around the building toward each other, they create vortices that spin off in a regular rhythm (a phenomenon called "vortex shedding"). Under the right conditions, the building will start snapping back and forth or humming like a guy wire, the vibrations increasing to intolerable levels. One common way to counteract that phenomenon is with a tuned mass damper, an immense ball suspended in the upper stories. A popular YouTube video shows how, during the massive Sichuan earthquake of 2008, an eight-hundred-ton ball of steel at the top of Taipei 101 swayed in its harness like an infant in a baby bouncer. When the top pitched left, the ball swung right, keeping the tower from moving much at all. (432 Park Avenue incorporates a similar system.)

Wind can also sculpt a high-tech tower the way it does a Bryce Canyon hoodoo. After placing a scale model in a sophisticated wind tunnel, architects try to disperse the onslaught by varying the obstacles at different heights, carving out channels right through the tower, adding fins, and softening curves. If supertall towers have gotten less symmetrical and more textured, that's not all for show: It's also a way of "confusing the wind," a poetic phrase for creating calculated chaos.

The multiplicity of forces waging war on high-altitude architecture means that supertall buildings are necessarily designed from the guts outward. For decades, the tallest buildings have been collections of separate structures, fused in ever-more-complex ways. Chicago's Willis (née Sears) Tower consists of nine square tubes bundled together like fasces. More recent colossi make use of the core-and-outrigger system, in which an immense steel truss links a powerful concrete trunk to thick columns at the edges. For the Burj Khalifa, Baker worked with the ex-SOM architect Adrian Smith (one of the designers of the Nordstrom Tower) to develop a buttressed core, in which three companion buildings, each with its own corridor, share a central spine, rather like three lanky drunks leaning on a lamppost. A mile-high skyscraper would most likely be a cheerleading squad of three or four towers standing hip to hip, with a companion on their shoulders. Which system gets used for which tower depends not just on its height but on how much land is available at the base, how close the nearest seismic fault line is, and the proportion of spaces for work and play.

Persuading a megastructure to remain vertical is only step one; the next job is getting thousands—even tens of thousands—of people in and out of it every day without each of them having to budget elevator time. Traditional steel cables are strong but so thick and heavy that a coil longer than about 1,500 feet becomes unmanageable. That simple physical fact dictates that to get up to, say, the 120th floor requires switching elevators—which means designing a sky lobby, fattening the core with additional shafts, and increasing the length of time it takes to get in and out of the building. Or that used to be true. A few years ago, the Finnish elevator company Kone inaugurated a lightweight carbon-fiber cable called UltraRope, which, at least in theory, could double the length of a single elevator ride to a full kilometer. If it lives up to its billing, that could make high-rises thinner, lighter, and far more energy-efficient—so that if you lived in a penthouse two miles high, you'd have to change elevators only twice. At this point, the limiting factor is not the technology of vertical transportation but the human body. A fast elevator can glide smoothly and silently into the skies, but if you're riding it with a head cold, it will be murder on the sinuses. Nothing a Finnish engineer can do about that, except possibly pressurize the cab, though for now that remains a futuristic form of comfort.

Seen from New York, the notion of a mile-high tower can seem like a distant, screwball real estate venture, like an indoor ski slope in the desert or a fake Manhattan in China. "If we can build plenty of fifty- and sixty-story buildings, do we need any 120-story buildings?" asks the architect Jamie von Klemperer, who has an interest in the answer, since his firm, Kohn Pedersen Fox, is designing the sixty-five-story, 1,500-foot One Vanderbilt, going up next to Grand Central Terminal.

But just because there are no current plans to push a building's height from profitable to narcissistic doesn't mean it won't happen. Manhattan is where global egos—and foreign money—come to roost, and there's no telling what monuments they will choose to erect. Even a single Manhattan block could accommodate a 2,500-foot tower. A super-block (like, say, where the much-loathed Madison Square Garden now sits) could support something much bigger than that.

Even if the next generation of super-skyscrapers is built in other parts of the planet, it will still affect New York just by virtue of its existence. The world's tallest towers are outliers by definition, but extreme height has a normalizing effect on slightly less extreme height. A few thousand-foot towers have already made their eight-hundred-foot sidekicks commonplace. Two or three contestants for the mile-high mark will sow an underbrush of half-milers. New York may never again boast the world's highest anything, but the mere existence of thin-air buildings halfway around the world will surely pull the local skyline upward, too.

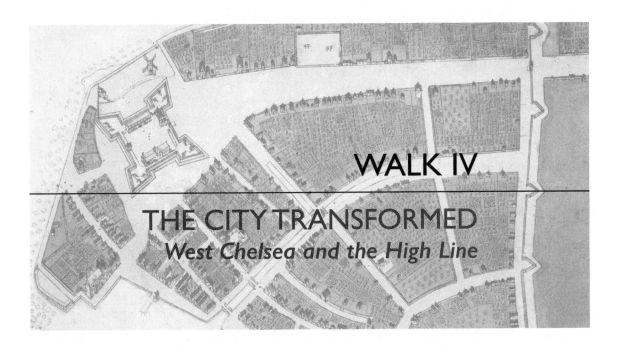

WALK IV

THE CITY TRANSFORMED
West Chelsea and the High Line

Dawn comes late to the West Side of Manhattan. The first sun skims the skyline, sneaks past the shadows of the Midtown towers, and reaches out into the Hudson, before doubling back toward the piers. One morning in the early 1970s, just as daylight was starting to smudge the night's sharp outlines, a small boy climbed into his grandfather's meat truck parked beside the Gansevoort Destructor Plant, a comic-book name for a garbage incinerator. There, at the western end of Gansevoort Street, beneath the elevated highway, the city petered out in parking lots, crumbling piers, and the oily river. The old man had finished the same routine he had been conducting for decades so that the city's butcher stores and steak houses could start the day well stocked.

Warehouse workers had hosed down the streets, washing away the animal blood and the rich odor of offal, and giving the cobblestones a film-noir gleam. From time to time, an elevated freight train shuddered overhead, whining to a halt at the Gansevoort Street Terminal. At that moment, the boy saw a man emerge from a door. He wasn't a butcher: Instead of a blood-stained apron, he was wearing shiny black leather. One detail stuck in the boy's mind for decades: the glint of morning light on the man's diamond earring, a grace note of glamour at the end of a night's labor. It would be years before the boy grasped the double meaning in the area's name, the Meat

<
Begin at the southern end of the High Line: Take the staircase or elevator at Gansevoort Street and walk one block north to **A**, Little West Twelfth Street.

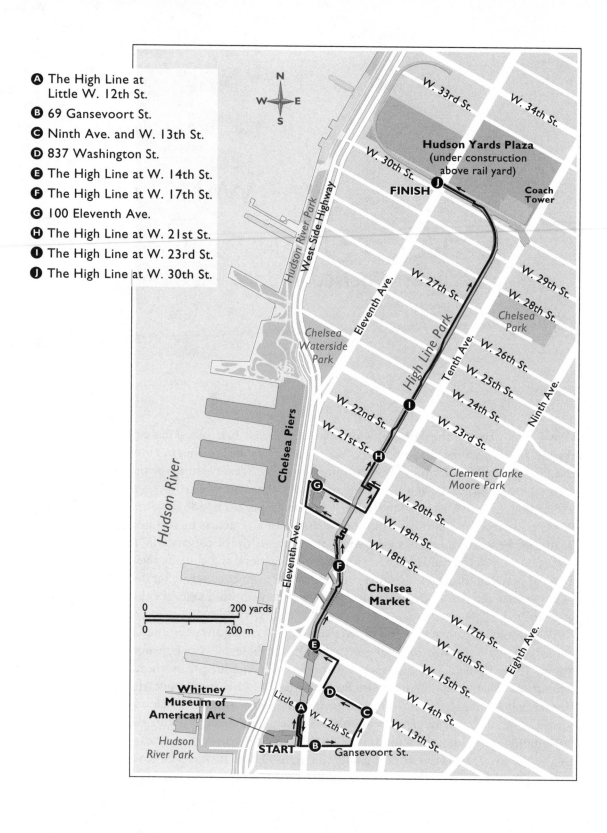

A The High Line at
  Little W. 12th St.
B 69 Gansevoort St.
C Ninth Ave. and W. 13th St.
D 837 Washington St.
E The High Line at W. 14th St.
F The High Line at W. 17th St.
G 100 Eleventh Ave.
H The High Line at W. 21st St.
I The High Line at W. 23rd St.
J The High Line at W. 30th St.

Market, or understood that some men were drawn to the nocturnal traffic in live, rather than dead, flesh.

Forty years later, that boy, Eric Latzky, now a successful arts publicist, is standing on the High Line, looking down on the last remaining building full of wholesale butchers. "Those will be gone soon. Somebody bought the building," he says. Latzky is wearing a white linen shirt, loose, untucked, and immaculately pressed, which seems like an unconscious compromise between the neighborhood's minimalist fashions and the meat guys' white coats. "It was a very rough-and-tumble, very male atmosphere in the Meat Market during the night," he recalls. "But they were like vampires. By the time the sun came up, everyone was gone, and they left this desolate urban beauty."

Latzky has known the area in every incarnation. In the seventies, he tagged along with his grandfather, Louie, who worked there for fifty-five years. In the eighties, he returned for the gay clubs, until AIDS ravaged the whole scene. In the nineties, when the art world started to trickle in, he worked at The Kitchen, the home of avant-garde performance culture on West Nineteenth Street. He moved to West Chelsea in 2006, just as it was evolving into a village of jillionaires, and was later appointed to the local community board. The changes have not lost their power to astonish him.

The skyline from the High Line

Today, the High Line, the old elevated freight track abandoned to the weeds in 1980, has turned into an airborne park, where nature and design simulate neglect. The walkway of concrete planks blurs into the grass. Sections of the original track materialize and peter out. Decommissioned switches sit by reclaimed rails, equipment repurposed as décor. As Latzky and I stroll uptown, the park narrows until it resembles the moving sidewalks in Chicago's O'Hare International Airport. Passengers with backpacks and water bottles shuffle purposefully along. Anyone who stops to take a picture creates an instant traffic jam. Once, the ruin connected nothing to

Loading and weighing beef at the West Washington Market, 1938

nowhere; now it runs from the new Whitney Museum of American Art to Hudson Yards, an immense future forest of skyscrapers, public spaces, and a shopping center five times the size of the Time Warner Center. Along the way, it threads through a crystal canyon of condos. Instead of flaking bricks, floor-to-ceiling windows now flank the park, like partitions in a zoo. Park visitors and apartment dwellers stare at one another through the glass, and it's never clear which of the two is on display.

No neighborhood in New York has changed identities so profoundly as this stretch of the West Side, from Gansevoort Street to West Thirtieth Street, even though so much of its physical fabric remains intact. The more things look the same, the more they have been completely transformed. To understand why, it helps to stand on the High Line just north of the Whitney and look toward the Hudson River, where a naked rusting arch rises mysteriously along this edge of Manhattan. This ruin, all that's left of the Cunard Line's Pier 54, is a relic of a brief period of grandeur between periods of decay.

From the mid-nineteenth century until the mid-twentieth, this was a tough waterfront area where hours were long, life was short, and the city's repertoire of injustices and corruption played out on an operatic scale. Before and after the Civil War, the waterfront was one of the only areas where whites and blacks lived side by side, but proximity did not lead to racial harmony. The all-white Longshoremen's Association complained that black dockworkers were driving down wages; shippers periodically hired them as strikebreakers. In March 1863, a rampaging white gang hunted down black porters, stevedores, and carters. When the Draft Riots broke out that summer, resentment spilled over into the waterfront's racial turf battles. Black longshoremen were beaten and lynched, their bodies hurled into the river. Intimidation worked. By the time the chaos abated, the Manhattan waterfront was almost totally white, as blacks fled to Brooklyn and New Jersey. Eventually, they returned. No horror was enough to weaken the magnetic power of trade, and the waterfront became ever more frightening, chaotic, and thrilling.

Physically on the city's extremities, the Meatpacking District was also its insalubrious heart, the embodiment of every ghoulish fantasy that outsiders nursed about a city of crime, sin, and blood. In E. L. Doctorow's novel *The Waterworks,* written in 1994 but set in 1871, Martin Pemberton, a rich man's son raised on a Hudson Valley estate, arrives in Manhattan and is walloped by the shocking stench of flesh:

> The hackney goes up the West Side along Eleventh Avenue, and the lungs of the young country boy fill for the first time with the sickening air of the meat district . . . the stockyards and slaughterhouses. Perhaps he thinks he has landed not in New York but on the chest of a monstrous carcass and is inhaling the odor of its huge bloody being.

As authorities tried vainly to bring order to the waterfront, shippers turned it into a jumble of makeshift, foul piers. Passengers and pickpockets milled among the horse-drawn carts that stood waiting for their loads. In the 1880s, when the Gansevoort Farmers' Market opened, ostensibly to ease crowding at the West Village markets, *Harper's Weekly* reported: "During the dark hours of early morning, as hundreds of wagons of all descriptions converge upon the market regions, pandemonium reigns as traffic chokes the thoroughfares for blocks around." Freight trains huffed slowly through the crowds along Tenth and Eleventh Avenues, preceded by an urban cowboy on horseback whose job it was to clear the tracks.

Even so, trains crushed so many pedestrians that Tenth came to be known as Avenue of Death. Those who risked their lives to frequent this area would

An urban cowboy precedes a train on Eleventh Avenue, 1910.

have scoffed at the notion that later generations would one day trot along the waterfront for their health and pleasure. The main leisure activity practiced on the nineteenth-century waterfront was drinking. Disembarking sailors had only to stumble a few yards into back-alley taverns that regularly changed sign and address but always pur-

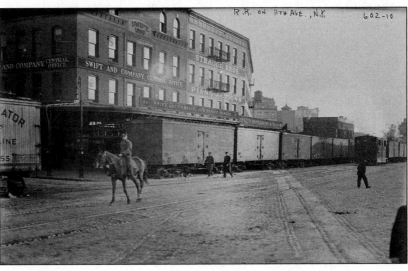

veyed the same fetid atmosphere and cheap rum. In his impressively morbid survey, *Low Life,* Luc Sante tells of Sadie the Goat, a two-bit Hudson River pirate who wore the ear she had lost in a bar fight as a pendant around her neck.

It was the ocean liner that finally brought some class to the West Side. The city, embarrassed that visitors who crossed in modern luxury disembarked in squalor, finally overhauled a stretch of shacks and rotting docks between Fifteenth and Twenty-third Streets. Houses, piers, factories, and gasworks were knocked down and replaced with a set of steel-framed sheds that jutted far into the river, making room for ever-bigger transatlantic liners. In 1910, the *Times* reported the project's cost at $25 million (more than $600 million today) and declared its completion "a matter for general congratulation." The new docks were miracles of transportation technology, the maritime equivalent of Europe's great train stations. Warren & Wetmore, the architects of Grand Central Terminal, designed a series of portals that proclaimed their expensive dignity. Pink granite façades, yawning arches, neoclassical pediments topped with terrestrial globes and adorned with statues of Neptune and Aphrodite—every architectural gesture was meant to dignify the industrial process of moving people and stuff quickly from deck to shore or vice versa. The new apparatus, crowed a journal of public engineering, could "get the passengers ashore with their baggage, finish the customs inspection and have the dock cleared of baggage, freight and other accessories in two hours. Under the old system this usually required nearer two days." It seemed safe to assume that glory days were coming to the neighborhood. The *Lusitania* and the *Mauretania* dropped anchor at the Chelsea Piers. The *Titanic* was supposed to do the same.

The docks proved almost immediately out of date. Bigger and bigger

The Cunard Pier in its heyday

All that's left of the Cunard Pier

ocean liners kept steaming over the horizon, and when those "queens of the sea" moored at the new piers, they left their rear ends sticking unceremoniously into the Hudson. The thousand-foot French liner *Normandie,* a glamorous Art Deco palace as long as the Chrysler Building is tall, made its maiden voyage in 1935 and the city scrambled to accommodate it with another row of piers farther uptown, between West Forty-fourth and Fifty-second Streets. The *Normandie*'s short career ended in sloppy calamity. In 1942, the liner was moored at Pier 88 (at West Forty-eighth Street), undergoing conversion to military use, when sparks from a welder's torch started a fire. A few hours later, she keeled over, settling into the river sludge. She lay rusting until the war ended, a vivid omen of New York's trajectory as a center of maritime transport.

Decline was fitful. World War II repurposed New York as a maritime metropolis. Convoys steamed through the harbor. Governors Island teemed with soldiers, who embarked for Europe at the Chelsea Piers. Seventy thousand people worked at the Brooklyn Navy Yard, producing battleships and aircraft carriers. When the war was over, New York was left with the world's busiest port and an industrial base on overdrive—a magnificent maritime machine that stretched from Red Hook in Brooklyn up to the West Fifties.

As the country demobilized, the working waterfront turned into a parallel universe run by a shadow government. In 1948, the *New York Sun* reporter Malcolm Johnson wrote a Pulitzer Prize–winning series that later inspired Elia Kazan's *On the Waterfront*. The movie focused on one gravel-mouthed young man (played by Marlon Brando), but Johnson was more impressed with the enterprise's imperial scale. "Here, in the world's busiest port, with its 906 piers, 100 ferry landings, 96 car-float landings and 57 ship buildings, drydock and repair plants, criminal gangs operate with apparent immunity from the law," he wrote. "These gangs are well organized and their control of the piers is absolute. Their greatest weapon is terror."

This outlaw apparatus worked with spectacular efficiency. To anyone in the business of moving goods, Chelsea was a dream. Cargo arrived by ship a few blocks away and by truck through both the Holland and Lincoln Tunnels. Freight cars that chugged into the rail yards, between Thirtieth and Thirty-fourth Streets, were shunted to the High Line viaduct, which ran right through buildings for easy unloading. A ground-level spur rolled through a tunnel inside the Chelsea Terminal at Twenty-seventh Street (later converted into the infamous Tunnel nightclub). Every day, pigs and cattle were carted in from the Midwest by train and marched to their deaths through underground passageways, mythic "cow tunnels" that may still survive somewhere in the Swiss cheese below the pavement. A network of underground cold pipes chilled warehouses all over the district. Virtually every pork tenderloin and T-bone steak that appeared on a Manhattan restaurant table passed within a few blocks of Gansevoort Street.

What finally killed the working waterfront was a banal but transformational invention: a stackable, standardized steel box, eight by eight by twenty feet. The shipping container could be hoisted from freighter to wharf by a crane, then dropped on a flatbed truck or train car without unpacking. The system needed fewer hands but much more maneuvering room than the old piers could offer. Shipping moved to New Jersey, jets displaced ocean liners, and, just like that, New York was finished as a port. It was a global phenomenon. Virtually every old urban port suffered the trauma of containerization and has been groping for some way to heal. Amsterdam has turned piers into the foundations for apartment buildings. Oslo perched an opera house above its fjord. Hamburg mounted a symphony hall on top of an old warehouse. Barcelona created a beachfront strip of outdoor leisure. What makes New York's waterfront unique is that it is so long, jagged, and varied. So is the story of its reclamation, which has lasted decades and taken innumerable forms.

Crime, container ports, plane travel, and neglect all conspired to turn the Lower West Side into a wasteland under an overpass. In December of 1973, a concrete-mixer truck drove onto an elevated portion of the West Side Highway near Gansevoort Street—and the roadway buckled. The highway was poorly designed to begin with, but to many its collapse seemed emblematic of a city in an advanced state of physical and moral putrefaction. The piers quickly devolved into a wilderness of rusting gantries and shattered concrete that nobody wanted—nobody, that is, except those who had nowhere else to go. In his novel *Nocturnes for the King of Naples,* Edmund White describes the piers in the seventies, abandoned except by a furtive night crew of gay men: "For me there was the deeper vastness of the enclosed, ruined cathedral I was entering. Soaring above me hung the pitched roof, wings on the downstroke, its windows broken and lying at my feet. . . . I smelled (or rather heard) the melancholy of an old, waterlogged industrial building." All that was left of Warren & Wetmore's 1910 piers was that skeletal entry to Pier 54, a weathered Arch of Failure. But the next rebirth was already under way.

In 1985, a French restaurateur named Florent Morellet opened a

Hanging out on the collapsing piers in the 1970s

bistro at 69 Gansevoort Street. He called it Florent, though he kept his predecessor's sign (R & L RESTAURANT), décor, and all-night tradition. The new establishment quickly became a magnet for transvestite hookers, local eccentrics, celebrities, suburban curiosity seekers, tourists, overstimulated clubbers, and old-time butchers. "We used to call it the Eat'em and Beat'em, because we used to go there at three o'clock in the morning, and eat our eggs and beat it out the door," a Gansevoort Market worker remembered. The restaurant's anarchic spirit, beautifully captured in the documentary *Florent: Queen of the Meat Market,* embodied the sense that the district was an urban frontier. Depending on the time of day, it could be difficult to tell whether the neighborhood was lively or desolate, burgeoning or dying out. A *Times* reporter paid a visit in 1995 and came away unimpressed: "It is 10:45 p.m. in the meatpacking district, a dreary patch between Hudson Street and 11th Avenue on the lower West Side, where nightspots lie scattered, often tucked away, among the frigid warehouses of beef, pork, veal and poultry."

< Exit the High Line back at Gansevoort Street and walk half a block east to **B,** No. 69.

By then the area was definitively changing—thanks in large part to Florent's fame. The butchers were being gradually evicted, art galleries were moving in, and real estate prices were rising. AIDS put a damper on the raucous gay nightlife that centered on sex clubs like Anvil and Manhole, so more wholesome daytime activities moved in. In 1995, Roland Betts, a co-owner (along with George W. Bush) of the Texas Rangers, converted the derelict old Chelsea Piers into a vast sports facility. It was a daring venture. At the time, just crossing to the river side of West Street felt risky; driving golf balls toward New Jersey from the *Lusitania's* old dock seemed like a fantasy.

Florent Morellet, who was an energetic activist for gay rights, fought to preserve the neighborhood, to protect its iron awnings and squat brick boxes from too many condos and shiny boutiques. In 2003, thanks in large part to his powers of persuasion, the Landmarks Preservation Commission designated the area as the Gansevoort Market Historic District. The irony is both delicious and tragic. Eighteen years after opening his antiestablishment establishment on the fringes of civilized Manhattan, with a middle finger grandly raised to convention, the restaurateur suddenly found himself wanting to slow down change. It's natural human behavior, this desire to upset the old order when you're young and then protect it as you age. It wasn't hard to see that enshrining the Meat Market as the Meatpacking District would only accelerate the change he had started and was now trying to stall. Florent closed his restaurant in 2008.

Around the same time, Apple opened a store at Ninth Avenue and Fourteenth Street; Google moved in a few blocks away, and the old brick warehouses quickly filled with boutiques and upscale chains. The area soon

< Continue along Gansevoort Street, turn left at Ninth Avenue, and go a block to **C,** the corner of West Thirteenth Street.

became an anthology of twenty-first-century architecture and inventive re-uses of old buildings.

>
Walk west along West Thirteenth Street one block, to **D**, the corner of Washington Street.

On Washington Street (No. 874), the firm WORKac slipped an entirely new building behind a pair of landmarked façades for the headquarters of Diane von Furstenberg. From the sidewalk, you can see the crystal tubercle on the roof, which scoops sunlight from the sky and funnels it into the masonry building, down a glittery hanging staircase. Half a block downtown (at No. 837), the architect Morris Adjmi erected a glass box on top of a two-story masonry depot, then wrapped it in a twisting exoskeleton of black steel. Past and present are entwined in these buildings, which is the way time in a city should work.

>
Walk one block north on Washington Street, turn left at West Fourteenth Street, and climb the stairs to the High Line at **E**.

The High Line crystallizes those chronological tensions, embodying both the persistence of industrial relics and the ferocious pace of change. Built in 1934, it saw plenty of unglamorous service and endured long past its usefulness. In 1980, a last train chuffed from the rail yards to a meat-market warehouse with a load of frozen turkeys. When it returned, the elevated freight line was taken out of service. Almost immediately, local property owners agitated to tear it down. A succession of mayors saw the structure as a hunk of rusting scrap iron and an obstacle to development. Demolishing such a sturdy apparatus proved cumbersome and expensive, though, so it lingered on, rescued by inertia. Urban adventurers clambered over the fence at night, leaving an archaeological sediment of drug paraphernalia, bottles, and soiled latex.

Then, in the late 1990s, Joshua David and Robert Hammond, two young enthusiasts who had only the faintest idea what forces they were about to unleash, thought it would be nice to turn the High Line into a park. By then it had become a strip of forgotten wilderness, pastoral and poetic. Tall grasses and wildflowers sprang from the toxin-laced gravel beds, obscuring the tracks.

With the blitheness of youth, they plunged into a multi-year financial and bureaucratic odyssey, from which they emerged both wiser and triumphant. They may have been naïve, but from the get-go the two understood the irony of their undertaking: that in order to preserve that strangely secluded place in the middle of New York, they would first have to destroy it.

David and Hammond had two important and connected insights that helped persuade doubters, enlist the support of then-mayor Michael Bloomberg, and attract top-drawer designers like the landscape firm Field Operations and the architects Diller Scofidio + Renfro. First, the High Line would become a unique public amenity right alongside new residential buildings and so would generate real estate value. Second, the structure had stifled development for so long that now it could unlock a new architectural world.

The green seam would stay the same, but the city would evolve around it.

The first freestanding buildings to push out of the rust evoked the area's history of brawn. The Standard Hotel straddles the High Line at Thirteenth Street like a Colossus of the Hudson, appearing to squeeze the old iron railway between its concrete knees. The building, designed by the firm Ennead, flaunts its musculature. Naked concrete piers ripple like a bodybuilder's legs, heaving the glass-walled structure sixty feet in the air. That's another way that a big new building can fit neatly in a historic neighborhood—not by donning antique-y cornices but by interpreting the spirit of a place. The slab bends at the center, like a thick volume opened to a matrix of private rooms. In the hotel's early days, some guests entertained the neighborhood by having sex against the glass walls. The hotel, which was still under construction, did nothing to

Morris Adjmi's 837 Washington Street

discourage the show. "We'll put up with your banging if you put up with ours," proposed one ad, which pictured a woman wearing nothing but a tool belt.

Even before it opened in 2009, the High Line provided a snapshot of a vanishing moment. The park threaded its way through a neighborhood that was famous for meat and sex but was well on the way to becoming something more decorous. By the time the second half mile opened two years later, the recession had come and was starting to ebb, tourists arrived by the millions, and new ultra-deluxe condos were hemming in the raised walkway. Now the High Line has reached its full length, swerving toward the sunset at Thirtieth Street, hooking around the rail yard and its cornfield of glinting train cars, and ramping down to meet the temporary nowheresville of Thirtyfourth Street. But the story isn't over, not by a long shot.

Walk north along the High Line to **F**, the bleachers at Tenth Avenue and Seventeenth Street.
<

Much of the park's appeal lies in the slight dislocation, the pleasing strangeness of walking through the city thirty feet above the street, beholding the city beyond and below. At Seventeenth Street, a section of the structure falls away to create a grandstand suspended vertiginously above Tenth

> Detour: Exit the High Line at West Eighteenth Street, walk one block west to Eleventh Avenue, then turn right and go one block to **G**, the corner with West Nineteenth Street. Read about Frank Gehry's IAC headquarters at 555 West Eighteenth Street and Jean Nouvel's 100 Eleventh Avenue in Interlude III, "City of Glass," p. 144. Then return to the High Line and continue north to **H**, West Twenty-first Street.

Avenue. The hanging space offers a gritty vista of uptown traffic on the erstwhile Avenue of Death, where cowboys once led freight trains on their slow, sometimes lethal march through the crowds.

The High Line is a watcher's Eden, a sequence of startling vantage points. This segment offers a look down a silent alley behind a former factory, where a pair of smokestacks looms. An outdoor parking lot with auto lifts puts its elevated cars just barely out of reach as traffic on Tenth Avenue lurches by below. Even now, Marty's Auto Body at 500 West Twenty-fifth Street endures, like a backdrop for a play about West Chelsea in the days before it turned chic.

Some neighbors embraced the dramatic spirit. As the first phase of the High Line was getting ready to open, a stray light shone directly on the fire escape of a woman named Patty Heffley, who lived at West Twentieth Street and had hung a license plate in her window reading AREA 51. Not one to waste the preciousness of a spotlight in New York City, Heffley turned herself into a fire-escape impresario. She hung paper lanterns, plugged in an amplifier, and invited over a cabaret singer, to the delight of the passing crowds. Heffley later hired a burlesque performer named Amber Ray to do a striptease show, a move that finally caused her landlord to shut the theatrics down.

Heffley had discovered that, as the industrial relic bloomed into a landscaped public amenity, it also reinvented the notion of home by the elevated tracks. Once, elevated subway lines rattled past tenements, yielding stroboscopic glimpses into households resigned to the noise and fleeting intrusion. Here pedestrians brush by luxury pieds-à-terre, taking pictures of wealthy residents who crave the attention.

The real estate market in West Chelsea didn't just heat up: It went from negligible to surreally expensive. On a soft late-summer afternoon, I climb a series of ladders to the top of a half-finished condo tower at 551 West Twenty-first Street, a block west of the High Line and visible from the park. From here I can see five buildings under construction within a few blocks. Designed by the British grandee Lord Norman Foster to satisfy the acquisitiveness of buyers with limitless resources, 551 has just "topped out"—reached its highest point—and the moment requires a ceremony. A corps of middle-aged men wearing hard hats and suits struggles up the sequence of stairs and ladders and more ladders and yet more ladders, until they're standing on a wobbly plywood platform 250 feet in the air. Workers gather, too. One of them affixes an American flag to a piece of steel. The rest snap selfies. Below is a double-height penthouse with a wraparound balcony and its own outdoor swimming pool.

With the ritual accomplished, the developer, Scott Resnick, pauses to consider the math that has moved staggeringly in his favor since he began the project. A square foot of Manhattan soil costs about $500. Add on construction costs, loan interest, legal fees, marketing, and so on, and Resnick estimates that a builder's break-even point is roughly $2,500 per square foot: $25 million for the ten-thousand-square-foot apartment we're standing above. He hopes to get double that figure for the penthouse. I suggest to Resnick that the market has the quality of tulip fever, the insane speculation that gripped the Netherlands in the seventeenth century.

"I wouldn't call it a bubble," he answers soberly. "More of a frenzy."

As the High Line moves north into the Twenties, it winds through West Chelsea, an area that has always defined the western edge of civilized Manhattan. In the late nineteenth century, Ladies' Mile—from Fifteenth Street north to Twenty-fourth Street, and west from Park Avenue South to Sixth Avenue—was the spine of the city's deluxe shopping district. The elegance petered out quickly west of Sixth Avenue. In Edith Wharton's *The Age of Innocence,* which takes place in the 1870s, the disreputable and lovely Countess Olenska arrives from Europe and rents a house in a dubious location "far down" West Twenty-third Street. "It was certainly a strange quarter to have settled in," Wharton writes:

Walk north along the High Line and pause at **I,** the West Twenty-third Street bleachers.

> Small dress-makers, bird-stuffers and "people who wrote" were her nearest neighbours; and further down the dishevelled street Archer [the novel's protagonist] recognised a dilapidated wooden house, at the end of a paved path, in which a writer and journalist called Winsett, whom he used to come across now and then, had mentioned that he lived. Winsett did not invite people to his house; but he had once pointed it out to Archer in the course of a nocturnal stroll, and the latter had asked himself, with a little shiver, if the humanities were so meanly housed in other capitals.

The Depression that battered the wealthiest neighborhoods pushed marginal ones into utter bleakness, and the largely industrial stretch of Chelsea between Sixth Avenue and the waterfront was among the deadest and most silent in Manhattan, especially after the sweatshops and small factories turned out the lights each evening. The few desperate souls who moved, illegally, into the unheated cold-water lofts were those who had no money and little choice: artists, for example. Willem de Kooning moved into 156 West Twenty-second Street, between Sixth and Seventh Avenues, in 1936. Rudy Burckhardt, a Swiss photographer with some family money and an omnivorous curiosity, and his partner, the dance critic Edwin Denby, joined him. In his photographs, Burckhardt captured the flinty glamour of the bohemian life in Depression-era New York. Here is de Kooning, handsome in an open-necked white shirt, standing in a corner of his sparsely furnished loft. And there's Denby, in tweed jacket, tie, and polished shoes, his forelock curling over his temple, sitting on the roof of their building. His sharply creased appearance contrasts with the street scene far below, a quasi-cubist gray jumble of fire escapes, stoops, trucks, and graceless buildings blurring into the smog.

For the rest of the twentieth century, Chelsea retained its air of windswept grayness, an inhospitable-looking frontier that became a gay haven and, eventually, a gallery district. If you ask new residents why they want to live in a neighborhood that lacks convenient subway service, grocery stores, and dry cleaners, they'll usually mumble something about wanting to be close to the art world. What they mean is the world of galleries and collectors, which doesn't necessarily include artists—or, rather, it trails them like a bioluminescent wake of money. When the dealer Matthew Marks opened a gallery on West Twenty-second Street, between Tenth and Eleventh Avenues, the artists were long gone, and his colleagues were hesitant to follow him. The area lacked restaurants, public transportation, and foot traffic. Why would anyone show up to buy?

Within two years, galleries were thick on the ground, and while the place still felt depopulated, dealers decided that they could do without passersby who popped in for a look-around but had no intention of buying. The real clients arrived by limousine; here they'd find plenty of parking.

Neil Denari's HL23

The High Line slices past freshly sprouting condos and old brick buildings that are suddenly tucked against the city's newest green bauble. Public park and private residence squeeze so closely together here that they literally overlap. HL23, Neil Denari's small but conspicuous apartment building at 515 West Twenty-third Street, reaches over the greenway like half of a ruined arch on an ancient road. The park's landscapers have fronted the building in a strip of lawn so incongruously lush that it looks like an ironic gesture: an airborne front yard for a post-industrial suburb. From the boardwalk, you can almost stroke the rippling steel skin of the façade. One apartment's glass wall sidles up so close that passersby can practically read a magazine over a resident's shoulder.

Just as the voyeur and the exhibitionist need each other, so the High Line and HL23 are joined in an intricate symbiosis. The park created the market and shaped the form of the building, which rises from a tiny plot and mushrooms asymmetrically as it goes up, held in balance by diagonal steel braces. The building is an attention-seeking container for attention-seeking people, and the park ensures a steady stream of spectators.

Continue along the High Line to J, West Thirtieth Street.
<

The High Line becomes more playful in its latest phase. The benches that peel up out of the paving seem to mutate, crossing, elongating, or morphing into picnic tables. Rails and ties remain embedded in the surface, and the switches still have movable levers (though they don't actually shift any tracks). A ramp lifts you like a gentle wave or drops beneath the rails into a playground, where kids clamber between the structure's exposed beams and pop up amid the plantings.

The Coach Tower rises over the soon-to-be-covered rail yards.

All this whimsy is framed by the original structure's serious brawn. The most stunning features are still the riveted metal plates and tough ornamental guardrails from the thirties—the industrial age's grudging nod to prettiness. Diller Scofidio + Renfro keep their interventions modest here, and after a block or two they practically peter out. A plain-vanilla macadam walkway flanks a curving strip of pristine grassland. This northernmost section, like an unrestored patch that sets off the brightness of a freshly cleaned painting, preserves the look of the High Line as it was during its years of abandonment. It can't stay this way forever, alas. Eventually, the beams will need to be shored up, the concrete replaced, lead paint banished, and poisoned soil carted away.

The High Line's architects knew they were designing a passageway through a fluid and unpredictable cityscape. That's in the nature of the original trestle, which railroad engineers drove through warehouses, over streets, and alongside tenements with supreme indifference to the urban context or aesthetics. The High Line began as a relic; it will end as a crowded approach to the city's most massive development, Hudson Yards. Already it winds beneath the immense Coach Tower, at Tenth Avenue and West Thirtieth Street.

The rail yard and its gleaming cars will vanish, and so will much of the sky. Instead of emptying out into open space and nothingness, it will sweep around Midtown's supercharged edge. The High Line may be almost done, but its story is far from over, because the city that changes around it is a show that never folds.

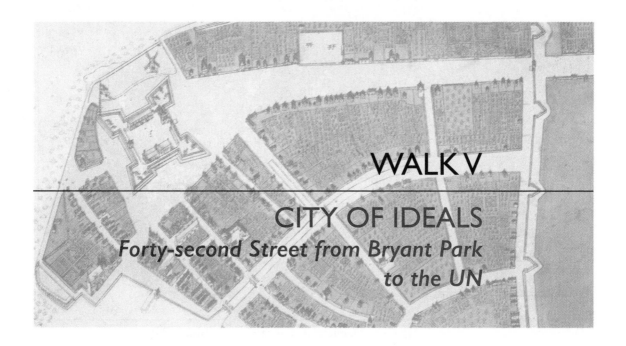

WALK V

CITY OF IDEALS
Forty-second Street from Bryant Park to the UN

Midwinter in Bryant Park: With year's end a few weeks away, I meander among the stalls that sell hot chocolate, fried dough, and alpaca mittens. The scents of sugar and cinnamon fill the cold air, and the stylish fuchsia hand warmers I have just bought from one of the booths are turning my coat pockets into little heated pouches. In the skating rink at the center of the block, gaggles of office workers and tourists wobble across the ice, parting occasionally to let an insouciant show-off glide by with one leg outstretched. Next to the rink, diners crowd into Celsius, the two-story temporary restaurant bolted together each fall like a giant erector set and taken down again a few months later. Every winter, the park becomes a festive village of miniature huts and adorable alleyways encircled by towers and the gracious bulk of the New York Public Library.

Forty-second Street runs along the park's northern flank, and in the midst of all this seasonal sparkle I think about the street's reputation as an artery of sordid drear. From the Civil War to the 1990s, from the slaughterhouses along the East River to the rail yards by the Hudson, this stretch of pavement, pounded by hookers, con men, addicts, and pickpockets, knitted together the most distasteful parts of urban life.

But for just as long this has also been New York's most idealistic street. Here fine instincts and modern technology fused into a boulevard of high-

< Begin at **A,** Bryant Park, near the corner of Avenue of the Americas— or Sixth Avenue, as New Yorkers call it—and Forty-second Street.

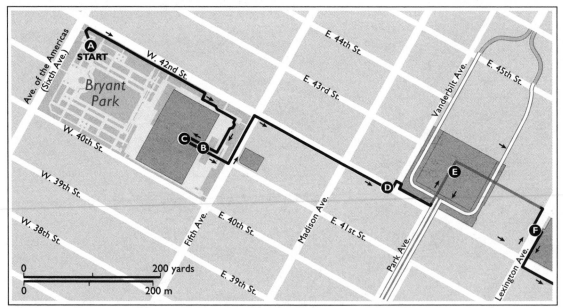

A Bryant Park

B New York Public Library Schwarzman Building

C New York Public Library, Rose Main Reading Room

D Grand Central Terminal

E Grand Central Terminal, Main Concourse

F Chrysler Building, 405 Lexington Ave.

G Daily News Building, 220 E. 42nd St.

H Staircase to Tudor City

I Tudor City

J E. 43rd St., plaza above First Ave.

K United Nations Headquarters

L Ford Foundation, 320 E. 43rd St.

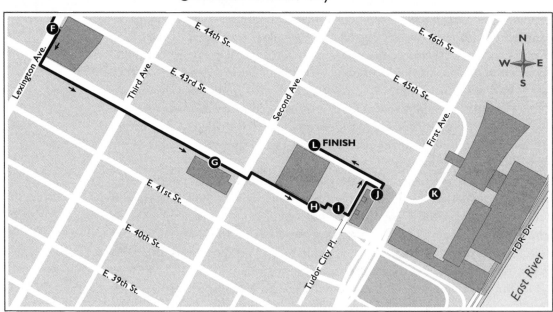

Fifth Avenue looking north toward Forty-second Street, 1912

minded civic aspiration. Manhattan's most visionary places and institutions line up along Forty-second Street: the United Nations, Tudor City, the Daily News Building, the Chrysler Building, Grand Central Terminal, the New York Public Library, Times Square, the New York Times Building. Even its roster of vanished landmarks is a testament to loftiness.

My thoughts wind back through the decades. The scene before me dissolves: Winter turns to summer, puffy parkas and cold-stiffened jeans metamorphose into coarse wool suits and calico cottons dampened by summer sweat. The traffic sounds change, too, from a motorized roar to the clatter of hooves and iron-rimmed wagon wheels on hard-packed dirt. Suddenly I am standing not in a geometrically laid-out park beneath naked, trembling trees but in a rough clearing, looking up not at the public library but at an even more formidable monument looming in the predawn haze. This is the Croton Distributing Reservoir, a perfectly square, battlemented perimeter guarding a four-acre enclosure.

Sunrise, July 4, 1842: A handful of early risers—not including the mayor,

The Croton Reservoir
just before
demolition, 1900

who's running late—have gathered to witness a miracle of engineering. This
island in a tidal estuary, laced with murky canals and surrounded by brackish
currents, has been in dire need of clean, drinkable water. Here it comes,
piped in from the Croton River, muddy at first, then clear and sweet. It
rushes through forty-five miles of tunnels that have been blasted and dug and
lined with brick, crosses the Harlem River atop High Bridge and into the
vast Eighty-sixth Street reservoir (in what will later become Central Park),
through more massive tubes, and flows into the great cistern at Murray Hill.
From here it will branch into narrower pipes and plash from public fountains
and newfangled fixtures in private homes. Croton Reservoir is really just a
holding tank, but it's the most visible juncture in an immense new aqua-
management system that will soon tip New York into a global metropolis.
Over the rest of the day, twenty-five thousand people will converge on the
reservoir to watch it fill and to line up for a free drink of ice water.

In the twenty-first century we take infrastructure for granted, except on
those occasions when a gas main blows or a bridge crumbles. We don't go on
outings to admire a highway interchange or visit an airport for the view.
We've lost our ability to marvel at great works. But in 1842 New Yorkers still
had some awe to spare for a plain stone wall plunked down in the rocky, uneven terrain at the edge of settled Manhattan. This guarantor of a city's most
basic necessity became an idler's destination, an elevated loop where people
strolled and enjoyed the panoramic view.

The Croton Reservoir took years of planning and the then-colossal sum
of $13 million to complete, and there was plenty of grumbling at the extrava-

gance and delays. After all, New Yorkers were not accustomed to receiving much in the way of municipal services. The city still lacked a police force, garbage collection, and electricity, and it had only the sketchiest form of public transit. Not everyone saw the need for those embellishments. But in July 1832 cholera attacked, killing thousands and inciting many more to flee. So many people left that by August, New York was eerily quiet and the air disturbingly free of smoke from factory furnaces. Three years later, fire decimated the mercantile core around Wall Street, destroying seven hundred buildings, including the supposedly indestructible Merchants' Exchange. On that frigid night in December 1835, firefighters could only stand helplessly by, water frozen in their pumps, until they were finally able to stop the destruction by dynamiting unburned buildings and creating a firewall of rubble. Suddenly an aqueduct looked like an instrument of survival.

In 1842, water was a promise and a balm, irrigating the city's ambitions and nourishing its future growth. The aqueduct was built for the ages: Its architecture invoked ancient Egypt, and its scale seemed eternal in a city destined for rapid change. Walt Whitman joined the throngs who clomped up the stone stairs for the view, and it roused in him enthusiastic fantasies of posterity and grandeur. He imagined strollers in the future looking out on a city that had expanded to enfold the reservoir, a megalopolis that had spread even into the Forties and beyond:

> The walks on the battlements of the Croton Reservoir, a hundred years hence! Then these immense stretches of vacant ground below will be covered with houses; the paved streets will clatter with innumerable carts and resound to deafening cries; and the promenaders here will look down upon them, perhaps, and away "up town," towards the quieter and more fashionable quarters, and see great changes—but off to the rivers and shores their eyes will go oftenest, and see not much difference from what we see now. Then New York will be more populous than London or Paris, and, it is to be hoped, as great a city as either of them—great in treasures of art and science, I mean, and in educational and charitable establishments. . . . Ages after ages, these Croton works will last, for they are more substantial than the old Roman aqueducts . . .

As it happened, Whitman's "ages after ages" would last only sixty years, by which time the irrigated city had outstripped even his grandiose projections, and a far more extensive web of pipes made the reservoir obsolete. That's the thing about New York: Today's unimaginable ambition becomes tomorrow's quaint relic. New York in the 1840s was a swaggering adolescent, a bit insecure but ready for great things. And Forty-second Street has always been where New Yorkers come to think big and to solve seemingly intractable problems by force of imagination.

This thick belt of a street is where the press (the *Daily News,* the *Herald Tribune,* the *Times,* and *The New Yorker*) have continuously tested the limits of the First Amendment, where pedestrians reclaimed civic space from cars and dereliction (in Times Square), where doctors tended to wounded veterans (the Hospital for the Ruptured and Crippled, which once existed between First and Second Avenues). Charity workers (at the Ford Foundation) tried to stanch the world's worst ills, and a global financial institution (Bank of America) erected what was then the world's greenest skyscraper. On Forty-second Street, even the destitute can enter one of the world's great research libraries, sit in its aristocratic reading room, and dive into virtually any published book (or simply nap in peace), without paying a dime. And half a dozen blocks east of the public library, diplomats from all over the world convene to hammer out intractable conflicts, not with weaponry but by sitting around a conference table and talking. When you think about it, Forty-second Street isn't just the epicenter of spectacle but also a boulevard of noble ambitions.

That's not an especially sexy reputation for a major thoroughfare, especially one with such a famously skanky past. But what makes this the quintessential New York street is that tinsel and marble coexist so naturally here. If you see an unkempt man shuffling along the sidewalk in a ragged jacket, the remains of breakfast still clinging to his beard, you might not be able to tell if he's a scholar heading for his assigned carrel in the library, a hobbyist seeking out the last remaining porn shops along Eighth Avenue, a Pulitzer Prize–winning *Times*man, or Mandy Patinkin on his way to a rehearsal for a Broadway show.

But let's imagine that he's Whitman again, having descended from the ramparts to confront a more dramatic and detailed version of the future. It's July of 1853 now, and in the field next to the reservoir rises the Crystal Palace, all airy cast-iron lacework, topped with a great glass dome—the largest building America has ever seen. The reason for its existence is the "Exhibition of the Industry of All Nations," and, although it has taken less than nine months of construction and portends a future of technological marvels, its builders are grateful to have gotten the thing up at all. The press is obsessed with its size, reverently enumerating every possible dimension. At a time when many Americans still sew their own clothes, visitors to the industrial fair wander through a cathedral of industry. According to the official catalog of the exhibition, experts demonstrate strange-smelling chemicals, woods destined for furniture, "specimens of New-Orleans long moss for upholstery purposes," immense, clanking steam engines, "an improved machine for breaking and dressing flax," maps, window dressings, pistols, scythes, and "philosophical instruments." The building shows off the new art of photography, and it also shows up well in photographs: A plethora of daguerreotypes at the fair is turning New York into the medium's effective capital. Several times a day during the Palace's second summer, Elisha Otis slices the cable on his demonstration elevator, proving over and over that his patented safety catch will keep passengers from plummeting to the ground.

The Crystal Palace

Whitman doesn't just visit the exposition—he haunts it. He returns again and again, as if trying to absorb its minutiae and revelations. The fair's encyclopedic hopefulness permeates his verse. Nearly two decades later, he will write "Song of the Exposition," which still quivers with the freshness of that first encounter with the industrial art:

> *Around a Palace,*
> *Loftier, fairer, ampler than any yet,*
> *Earth's modern Wonder, History's Seven outstripping,*
> *High rising tier on tier, with glass and iron façades.*

The fact that the Crystal Palace attracts so much attention makes some observers nervous that New York might embarrass itself in front of a skeptical world. *Scientific American,* which printed a lavish and moody rendering of the building on its cover before construction had even begun, takes umbrage at the condescending jibes being lobbed across the Atlantic. New York aches to be taken seriously, but the truth is that it can't quite keep up with London or Paris. Its grandeur is punier, its monuments less monumental, its extravaganzas less extravagant. The Crystal Palace is, reporters reluctantly admit, about one-eighth the size of London's.

And, in a remark that will soon become a refrain, the *Times* frets that crowds are being lured to a dicey part of town: "We warn the authorities against permitting this indiscriminate growth of taverns around the Crystal Palace. Half its attraction, half its beauty will vanish, if those poisonous fungi are allowed to grow undisturbed around its base."

If, more than a century and a half later, I linger on a building that collapsed in a quick and violent fire after just three years, it's because for me it represents the tension between materialistic ambition and the street's history of shabbiness. The industrial exposition heralded modernity's promise: a good life of speedy travel, well-tended health, well-lit leisure, and comfortable work. A few decades later, that promise devolved into the kind of urban ghastliness that sent millions skedaddling to the suburbs. Yet now, as I sit on one of the metal chairs scattered on the gravel walkways of Bryant Park, I'm amazed anew at how many thousands of people I could count in five minutes of sitting and how many different purposes propel them past this corner. Out on the sidewalks beyond the park's balustrades, New Yorkers move with a determined stride, bulling past slow-moving families of tourists and high-end shoppers clutching their branded cargo. The Bank of America Tower, a cream-white glass behemoth designed by Kohn Pedersen Fox, disgorges lunchers. Young men in suits steer blue Citi Bikes around cabs and plumbers' vans and double-decker tour buses. A woman in sunglasses talking into her headset steps blithely off the curb against the light and lopes through the inching traffic without a pause in her conversation. Two blocks west, the crowd in Times Square often seems to consist of unadulterated tourists; two blocks east, the UN's international army of diplomats fan out across several blocks. But right here, if you scooped up a shovelful of passersby at any given moment, you'd find that you'd collected specimens from most of the world's nations and the full economic spectrum from homeless person to plutocrat, with every gradation in between. I think of Harry Warren and Al Dubin's lyrics for the film musical *42nd Street:* "Where the underworld can meet the elite . . . Naughty, gaudy, bawdy, sporty / Forty-second Street."

It's not happenstance that in 1952 Ralph Ellison chose the street just outside Bryant Park as the setting for a viciously climactic moment in *Invisible Man.* Today, that scene reads like the overture to the grim roll call of unarmed black men killed by cops over minor infractions: Michael Brown, Eric Garner, Freddie Gray, Philando Castile, and so many others. Ellison's narrator comes across the once-proud Brother Tod Clifton selling Black Sambo dolls on the sidewalk, making them shimmy in a grotesque minstrel dance at the end of a thread. When a policeman bears down on him for lacking a vendor's permit, Clifton lashes out, effectively committing what we now call "suicide by cop." As the officer's pistol fires, Ellison registers the shock of a primal act on a crowded street, where tragedy and minutiae jangle in an urban freeze-frame:

> He fell forward on his knees, like a man saying his prayers just as a heavy-set man in a hat with a turned-down brim stepped from around the newsstand and yelled a protest. I couldn't move. The sun seemed

to scream an inch above my head. Someone shouted. A few men were starting into the street.

Or try watching *Midnight Cowboy,* a 1969 ode to sleaze. Joe Buck, a good-looking, buckskin-clad dishwasher from Texas (played by Jon Voight) arrives in the big city, eager to sell his body for, well, a buck. He counts out his change to pay for a room at the Hotel Claridge, which once upon a time had been equipped with red runners and gilt-trimmed settees. But when Buck arrives it's one step up from a flophouse, with a begrimed view onto Times Square, the universal magnet for hustlers. The movie portrays Manhattan as a ruthless isle: No matter how sordid your dreams, newcomer, you are still aiming too high.

That fiction was not a stretch in the seventies, when the merchants who frequented the leafy geometric plain of Bryant Park sold forms of joy more treacherous than today's hand warmers and hot chocolate. Happiness was a heated spoon with a dose of heroin bubbling away in it, and the paths were carpeted with needles. "It's a dangerous park," a groundskeeper told the *Times* in 1976. "There's a crew in this park, all they do is walk around and mug people. It goes on all day." A demoralized community board chairman suggested that the only way to disinfect the park of crime might be to close it completely. Forty-second Street from Sixth to Eighth Avenues—from Bryant Park to the Port Authority—was a frightening caricature of urban threat. "Times Square, which for generations had been understood to exemplify the freedom and the energy and the heedless pleasure-seeking of New York, now came to be seen as the emblem of a city deranged by those very attributes,"

Fifth Avenue at Forty-second Street, looking south toward the New York Public Library, 1917

wrote James Traub in his astute urban portrait of the area, *The Devil's Playground.*

Even at its grimmest, this area abutted some of the city's most high-minded civic institutions—the New York Public Library, for example, which sits right where the Croton Reservoir did. From where I sit on the Bryant Park side, the library seems forbidding, pinstriped by great vertical piers and narrow windows that look as if they were designed to repel a siege. Go

>

Walk to the front entrance of the New York Public Library's Schwarzman Building, **B,** on Fifth Avenue at Forty-first Street. Enter the library between the lions, Patience and Fortitude, and climb to the Rose Main Reading Room on the third floor, **C.**

around to the Fifth Avenue side and it is formidable in a different way, an august institution raised on its own temple mount. Actually, it's a genuinely inviting place, designed to welcome the masses.

Since the day the library opened in 1911, anyone, from the barely literate to the Nobel laureate, could pass between the friendly lions named Patience and Fortitude and climb the imperial-scaled stairs to the third-floor Rose Main Reading Room. With its profusion of sunlight and carved timber, and its great oak tables burnished by millions of elbows, the chamber expresses the democratization of earthly awe: Even people who live in joyless garrets have a right to grandeur.

At a time when electricity was still relatively novel and far from universally available, the architects John Carrère and Thomas Hastings offered readers a vast menu of illumination. There's the daylight that blazes in through one wall of great arched windows and passes to the other in the course of the day; the illusory radiance that suffuses the painted frescoes on the ceiling; the theatrical glow from two rows of hanging chandeliers; and the incandescent cone formed by the shaded desk lamp at each chair. Ironically, technology has made all that brilliance a hindrance instead of a help to reading. On sunny days, you can see researchers and scholars squinting at their laptops, shading the screen with one hand.

Frank Larson,
Lady and the Lion,
1955

In that image you can see the paradox of the great library in the digital age. While information increasingly lives in the ether, the New York Public Library's headquarters is an intensely physical place. This iron-and-stone storehouse was built to enshrine knowledge in ink-on-paper form. Its massiveness guaranteed that no word it contained would ever be lost and there would always be room for more. But temples grow brittle. In 2014, one of the rosettes on the reading room ceiling broke off, failing to kill any patrons only because it happened in the middle of the night. The room closed for renovations for two years.

That's not the only structural problem. Eventually, the library found that its overcrowded storage system was threatening its contents. The public isn't allowed into the stacks, but a few years ago I had the chance to explore the claustrophobic and endless honeycomb where four million volumes moldered away in a warm, damp fug. This is both the library's heart and its skeleton. Thickets of iron columns and seven levels of tightly gridded shelves, held in place by ornamental cast-iron plates, support the upper floors. For a century, the reading room rested on piles of books. Recently, though, the volumes have been moved for their safety, most of them to a newly renovated, climate-controlled vault deep beneath Bryant Park. The old retrieval system endures, albeit in updated form: Whenever a call number is dropped (electronically, now) into the building's bowels, library staffers—aptly called pages—unearth the requested titles and place them on a miniature train that hauls them up to the surface like hunks of coal from a mine. Meanwhile, the original stacks sit empty, patiently holding the architecture together and waiting for a fresh purpose.

The other great Beaux Arts monument of Forty-second Street did for travel what the library did for reading: surround the experience with splendor. A few years ago, I asked half a dozen renowned architects and urbanism experts to name their favorite building in New York. I expected an argument—perhaps an Art Deco skyscraper versus the Seagram Building. Instead, I got virtual unanimity: Grand Central Terminal. I agree.

< Exit the library. Walk to the south side of Forty-second Street and continue east to **D**, Vanderbilt Avenue. Look across to Grand Central Terminal. Then enter the Terminal and walk to **E**, the Main Concourse.

Every time I duck in from Forty-second Street, I'm struck again by how the building makes me wait a couple of beats for its great architectural climax. A ramp guides me toward the great waiting room, a place fit for a coronation or a conclave of gods but one that makes a puny commuter feel ennobled, too. It is a place I come with pleasure even when I have nowhere special to go.

Grand Central opened a century ago as a triumphant fusion of profit and public-spiritedness. Designed by the firms of Reed & Stern and Warren & Wetmore, it was the emblem of Cornelius Vanderbilt's New York Central Railroad and the endpoint of a transportation system that webbed the entire continent. (Today, it's where a handful of commuter lines converge; oh, how the mighty railroads have fallen.) The building's history begins with a horrific accident. In the morning rush hour of January 8, 1902, two trains collided just outside the old depot on the site, filling the tunnel with boiling spray and coal smoke. Fifteen people were killed. The New York Central Railroad decided to switch to electric trains, which didn't pump fumes into the air and so could run beneath the streets and enter the station from below. The company's chief engineer, William J. Wilgus, realized that it could pay for an underground station by selling the right to build in the air. Thanks to that insight, Grand Central Terminal became one of the world's most high-tech facilities, dedicated to the era's great mission: speeding people wherever they wanted to go. It also incubated a colossal real estate project, creating the concept of air rights, which has been a staple of New York development ever since. Burying the open tracks created Park Avenue and a grove of new towers.

In Europe, most train stations of that era consist of a huge anteroom facing toward the city and platforms leading away from it. Arriving passengers typically haul their luggage out of the station and onto a vast but confusing outdoor plaza, where they have to hunt for trolleys, buses, cabs, and information, and where they are easy marks for con artists waiting to rip them off. Grand Central stacks its transportation functions vertically: trains below, linked to the subway, with city streets on all four sides and an elevated roadway wrapping around the outside. People arrive on every level and from all directions, and they can rush in one side and out the other, converge on the focal point of the waiting-room clock, pause for a meal on the mezzanine, or pick up (extremely high-priced) groceries on the way to the train.

In the rationalistic spirit of the age, the building was engineered down to the minutest detail, merging efficiency with beauty. Hallelujah shafts of sunlight angle through vast double windows and glass-floored walkways, heating the interior and minimizing the need for electric lighting. Early visitors rhapsodized over the ramps from street to tunnel. "The idea," reported the *Times,* "was borrowed from the sloping roads that led the way for the chariots into the old Roman camps of Julius Caesar's army." To determine their precise angle, the architects made mock-ups and then recruited testers: "fat men and thin men, women with long skirts, women with their arms full of bundles." The result is a complex of gentle slopes through which people move in a counterpoint of varying tempos. Thanks to that attention to detail, Grand Central was—and remains—one of the modern world's most exquisitely complex and welcoming public palaces.

> Exit Grand Central at Lexington Avenue and look across to **F**, the Chrysler Building, at 405 Lexington Avenue. Then continue east along the south side of Forty-second Street to **G**, No. 220, the Daily News Building, between Second and Third Avenues.

Is there any human activity that architecture can't elevate? The Chrysler Building, an auto company's monument to itself that functioned as an urban-scale corporate logo, stamped the skyline with the glamour of driving. The original plan for the Daily News Building called for a low-rise home for a rumbling printing press that might rattle nerves in a newsroom above but had no sleeping neighbors to disturb.

Architect Raymond Hood reimagined it as a skyscraping tribute to the business of asking rude questions of powerful people. I spent a dozen years working at *Newsday,* a suburban tabloid whose headquarters was a sprawling two-story box encircled by parking lots and roadways that never saw a pedestrian. I felt deprived of architecture and yearned to work someplace like the News Building, which started construction in 1929 and opened in 1931 in a burst of delusional confidence, as if the Depression were just another journalistic opportunity.

The man who paid for it was Captain Joseph Medill Patterson, the left-leaning scion of the McCormick family, which owned the *Chicago Tribune*. (Patterson's daughter, Alicia, would later found *Newsday,* the paper I worked for.) Every great venture has its creation story, and the *News*'s is especially redolent: During World War I, Colonel Robert McCormick and his cousin, Captain Patterson, sat on a manure pile in the French village of Mareuil-en-Dôle and indulged in a drunken fantasy of life back home. Patterson, a populist idealist, had spent time in England on his way to the front and fallen in love with the

Daily Mirror, a cockney-flavored tabloid that kept Londoners supplied with salacious gossip, provocative pictures, and short, punchy stories. He decided to create, with McCormick's help and *Tribune* money, a similar publication for New York. The first years were brutal for the business, but by 1926 the *News* had won over the lunch-pail classes, and its circulation rose from ten thousand to well over a million, making it the largest daily in the country. After a few more years of success, Patterson knew where to place a new printing press—on Forty-second Street, close enough to the *Times* that he could beat the competition to the newsstand every day. He also knew who should design the building: Raymond Hood, who had won the famous 1922 competition to build the Tribune Tower in Chicago. If Hood was good enough for McCormick, why should Patterson use anybody else?

Lobby of the
Daily News Building,
1930

Patterson wanted a printing plant with a newsroom on top; Hood charmed him into building a thirty-six-story skyscraper. Negotiations were tense, until the moment when Patterson shrugged and surrendered: "Listen, Ray, if you want to build your goddamn tower, then do it," he said.

Hood insisted that his design was the product of calculation, not inspiration:

> When I say that in designing the News Building the first and almost dominant consideration was utility, I realize I am laying myself open to a variety of remarks and reflections from my fellow architects, such

as: "It looks it!," "What of it!" and so on. However that is my story . . .
In passing, I might remark that I do not feel that The News Building
is worse looking than some other buildings, where plans, sections, ex-
teriors and mass have been made to jump through hoops, turn somer-
saults, roll over, sit up and beg—all in the attempt to arrive at the goal
of architectural composition and beauty.

Hood, like Patterson, was an avowedly practical man for whom money
was—in theory, anyway—an infallible guide. Patterson demanded that arti-
cles be short and photos shocking, because that was what would sell papers;
Hood kept ornaments spare and proportions precise, because that would
please the client's accountant. In his mind, and in his rhetoric, the News
Building was the manifestation of virtuous slide-rule thinking, which held
that the most efficient way to design a building was inherently the most har-
monious as well. If that seems like an odd credo for an architect who had
beribboned the Tribune Tower in Gothic frippery, it was also the founding
doctrine of modernism, which later architects boiled down to an austere language of glass and steel.

High-end New York real estate has always been replete with symbols,
metaphors, and irrational desires. Letting arithmetic design a tower is like
using a protractor to plan out sex: It can probably be done, but it's not likely
to yield the best results. Despite his declared pragmatism, Hood produced an
artistic creation, a jazzy concoction of syncopated setbacks and white brick
stripes shooting toward the sky. In a city of flat façades, this was a sculpture
to be appreciated from all sides. Hood claimed that he simply stopped the
building when he ran out of floors, rather than capping it with some fancy
crown, but in truth the corrugated shell extends well past the roof, hiding the
mechanical equipment and defining the top with a straight, sharp horizontal
line. Simplicity is not usually simple to achieve.

Like all good architects, Hood knew how to deploy his budget for maximum effect, concentrating all the sumptuousness where people could see it.
The relief above the main entrance resonates with Patterson's fondness for
brief texts and telling illustrations. It teems with New Yorkers of all kinds—
flappers, construction workers, financiers, a young girl telling off an overen-
thusiastic dog—and an inscription abridges Lincoln's aphorism "God must
love the common man. He made so many of them." (The *News* version includes only the second sentence.)

>
Enter the
Daily News Building
lobby. The shiny black-and-brass lobby is even stagier, with its quartet of clocks
set to various time zones and its giant globe, symbolizing the paper's worldwide reach. As an example of journalism's public face, this was the anteced-
ent of the maps and screens and headline crawls in today's TV newsrooms—

a statement that going out into the field and coming back with a story is serious business, best left to the pros. The *News* eventually abandoned the building (and many of its global ambitions), but so completely did Hood's design capture the urban drama of journalism that his tower had a starring role in the 1978 film version of *Superman,* playing the headquarters of the *Daily Planet.*

I've already observed the various ways in which, in just a few blocks, architects and dreamers turned necessity into pleasure, often by merging public-spiritedness with unapologetic self-interest. Water, knowledge, manufacture, transportation, business, news—each of these aspects of culture produced a building that was better than it really needed to be, feeding a city's aspirations to greatness. What was missing was shelter. Whitman, gazing down on the district from the ramparts of the Croton Reservoir in the 1840s, imagined an orderly grid of private houses popping up as the city expanded, but the reality was more chaotic. To the east, squatters erected shantytowns of mud and planks. Before the Civil War, as workers laid the rigid street grid over rough terrain, they left houses clinging to mini-escarpments between the freshly graded roads. For a time, the nineteenth century's menu of modern improvements—streets, industry, and public transit—ruined the area. Affluent New York families had their country estates overlooking the rushing East River, but industry swallowed them up. Starting in 1878, the Third Avenue El clattered above the street all the way from the Bronx to South Ferry, dividing the genteel neighborhoods along Fifth and Madison Avenues from the stench and misery farther east. In the 1880s, Paddy Corcoran and his "Rag Gang" dominated the rocky bluffs of Prospect Hill, above First Avenue. A 1988 Landmarks Preservation Commission report, usually a dry research document, indulged in a vivid description of the zone's afflictions: "Bracketed to the west by the noisy Elevated Railroad and to the east by noxious abattoirs, meat-packing houses, gas works, and a glue factory, the area . . . had, by 1900, become a slum inhabited by ethnically diverse immigrants."

Enter Fred F. French, a brawny Bronx kid who had dropped out of college and had a knack for getting fired from low-paying jobs. French treated his own poverty as an excellent business opportunity. He enjoyed talking about the time he borrowed five hundred dollars from an acquaintance, blew ten dollars on a lavish meal, and then parlayed the rest into his first real estate deal: He bought his family's cramped house. Eventually he became a bona fide mogul, and his mantra was that he'd rather make a small profit on a large business than a large profit on a small one. And the biggest real estate business of them all was Tudor City.

Climbing the stairs to get there is like shinnying up Jack's beanstalk; I emerge into a serene and verdant world perched above the roar of traffic and the commercial jangle of the street. It aspires to the picturesque tranquility

< Continue walking east along Forty-second Street to Second Avenue, cross to the northeast corner, and continue halfway down the block toward First Avenue. Climb **H,** the staircase to Tudor City, **I,** which extends from Fortieth to Forty-third Street, between First and Second Avenues.

Samuel Gottscho,
Tudor City, 1930–33

of an Elizabethan village, amplified to urban scale. Launched in 1925, Tudor City was the largest residential complex in the country. It was also a control freak's fantasy, a hilltop enclave of eleven buildings with 2,800 apartments—practically a manufactured town. It boasted its own streets, hotel, a slightly cramped but fully operational eighteen-hole golf course, and two parks, each with a romantic gazebo. In building it, French placed the high-yield, high-risk bet that has enriched—or, often, impoverished—developers in every generation: He believed that middle-class people would choose to live in the city, rather than migrate out of town, so long as they could keep urban squalor and chaos at bay. He promised working stiffs an affordable bucolic refuge that didn't require a long commute.

French fitted out his buildings with modern efficiencies (like refrigerators) and architectural flourishes evoking the days of monarchs in wide collars and rich brocades. Carved griffins, stained-glass windows, and ornate lanterns turned the oversize brick boxes into middle-class castles. The strategy worked. The development was stupendously successful, despite tiny apartments with almost no eastward-facing windows. Enjoying a river view would have had a disconcerting downside: a vista of charnel houses and the stench of blood and offal drifting in from neighbors like the Butcher's Hide and Melting Association. (Today, the abattoirs, the el, and the slums are all gone.)

French's gamble extended the sphere of respectability eastward, and other developers followed. Ten blocks to the north, River House replaced a cigar factory at the end of East Fifty-second Street, staking out a position for ultra-deluxe waterfront living within spitting distance of some of the city's most troubled slums. (To read more about River House, see Interlude IV, "City of Apartments.") In the 1940s, the developer William Zeckendorf quietly accumulated seventeen acres of shoreline between Forty-second and Forty-ninth Streets—right below Tudor City's cliff-top position—and then noisily announced that he planned to build a gargantuan development there called X City. Zeckendorf had seen the future and it was his to build. With its chorus line of office and apartment towers, ranging from thirty to fifty-seven stories, its beams of light pointed at the heavens, and its domed opera house, X City was a megaproject that would make Tudor City look like a sand castle.

In New York, as in most places, the term "developer" carries a taint, precisely because of the land-eating, shadow-casting, sky-blocking grandiosity of projects like these. In the movies, real estate moguls are constantly paying off politicians, evicting the powerless, and despoiling pretty landscapes in their sinister drive to acquire, build, sell, and start all over again. One of the most comically nasty of all fictional developers is Lex Luthor in the 1978 *Superman* (the same version that showcased the News Building). Luthor, played by Gene Hackman, lives in a sumptuous lair two hundred feet below Park Avenue (in Metropolis, not Manhattan, but still . . .) and dreams of total world acquisition. "When I was six years old," he declaims, "my father said to me . . . son, stocks may rise and fall. Utilities and transportation systems may collapse. People are no damn good. But they will always need land, and they will pay through the nose to get it."

Real-life big-time developers lend themselves nicely to caricature. A certain amount of rapaciousness goes with the job. They do—they must—wheedle tax breaks out of City Hall, demand zoning tailored to their needs, schmooze with the powerful, and flick away those who are not. They are secretive and dynastic. The New York real estate world is a gilded bubble populated by a handful of multigenerational clans: the Dursts, the Zeckendorfs, the Roses, the Ratners (originally from Cleveland), the Rudins, the LeFraks, the Speyers—and, of course, the family currently headed by that most Luthoran of moguls, Donald Trump.

Yet despite all that, I have a deep reserve of admiration for the adventurers who built New York, block by visionary block. This city was a real estate venture from its earliest days, and developers created from scratch many of its most authentically charming quarters (Washington Square, Gramercy Square, Prospect Lefferts Gardens in Brooklyn, Forest Hills Gardens in Queens), as well as its most towering monuments. Rockefeller Center was named for the family that built it. It takes a lot of nerve to scrounge a billion dollars and erect a skyscraper in the hope that others will want to live and work there. The bets are huge, the market fickle, and the city is always threatening to fall apart. But, then, a New York developer is by definition an irrational optimist.

Zeckendorf never did build X City, which joined the pantheon of forgotten projects. Instead, his fellow tycoon and principal rival, John D. Rockefeller, Jr., bought him out in 1946—not so that he could add to his gajillions but because he was convinced that the right deal could save millions of lives. Rockefeller saw the X City site as the ideal home for the United Nations.

If you're looking for world peace, this is where they make it: the UN Sec-

Continue past the playground and small park, then turn left on Tudor City Place and walk one block. Turn right on East Forty-third Street and walk to **J**, the plaza at the end, which offers a good view onto **K**, the United Nations complex. The only way to visit the UN is on a guided tour through the visitor center. The tall slab directly in front of you is the Secretariat Building, with the Conference Building beyond (where the Security Council meets). The domed swoop to the left is the General Assembly. The long, low block to the right is the Dag Hammarskjöld Library.

<

retariat, a big glass brick standing upright on the edge of Manhattan. The UN occupies a cluster of structures, but the Secretariat, the hive of diplomacy's worker bees, is the international body's contribution to the New York skyline.

Among the United Nations' first tasks—before the partition of Palestine or the Universal Declaration of Human Rights—was to shop for real estate. A scouting party examined various other sites, including the suburbs of Philadelphia, the Presidio in San Francisco, Fairfield County, Connecticut, and the site of the 1939 World's Fair in Flushing, Queens. But it was eventually decided that only Manhattan embodied the UN's ideal of vigorous optimism. Besides, if thousands of diplomats from all over the world were going to converge in one place, it had better be somewhere with excellent restaurants. Rockefeller, in a supreme gesture of *noblesse oblige,* offered to buy Zeckendorf's reeking acres of riverfront for $8.5 million (roughly $103 million today—still a spectacular bargain) and donate it to the organization. Wallace Harrison, who was court architect to both developers—he had worked on Rockefeller Center, designed X City, and would later collaborate on Lincoln Center—helped broker the deal. With the clock counting down on the UN's deadline to select a location, Harrison grabbed a detailed site map, crashed Zeckendorf's birthday party at the Club Monte Carlo on Madison and East Fifty-fourth Street, and made his hurried pitch. The developer barked a quick yes, scribbled his promise to sell on Harrison's map, and returned to his party.

Having secured the money, the job, and the land, Harrison handpicked an international troupe of modernist architects and took on the role of ringmaster. Many contributed, but two squabbling geniuses could agree on almost nothing. The Swiss-French guru Le Corbusier and his Brazilian counterpart Oscar Niemeyer fought over the shape, number, and orientation of the buildings, whether the glass curtain wall should include a sun-shading grid of stone, and—most ferociously—who got credit for what. Le Corbusier complained to his mother of the "apparent kidnapping of [his] UN project by USA gangster Harrison." The cocktail of haste, diplomacy, vanity, and genius might have yielded an architectural hangover. Instead, it produced the first monument of postwar modernism.

One thing designers and clients could agree on was that a new world should adopt a new architecture. During World War II, various dictatorships had poisoned imperial neoclassicism and official sumptuousness. So the polyglot team agreed on an international language, composed of innocence, transparency, and logic. This cool aesthetic was not an easy sell when it banged against inherited notions of grandeur. The city's building czar, Robert Moses, wanted to link Midtown to the rest of the world by a suitably majestic boulevard, so he ripped out the Forty-second Street trolley tracks,

United Nations
General Assembly
and Secretariat

widened the roadbed and sidewalks, planted trees, and slung a new ornamental bridge between the two halves of Tudor City. Suddenly a city street
became the UN's driveway, suitable for limousines or chariots or whatever
form of dignified transport the world's diplomats would choose to adopt.
Meanwhile, Vermont senator Warren Austin warned that if the U.S. Congress was going to front the money for the General Assembly, the building
had better have a dome. Niemeyer responded, reluctantly, with a squashed,
shallow hump that looked as though it had been half-buried in the roof. He
dressed it in terne-coated copper, which had a subtle silvery sheen. Workers
later tried (unsuccessfully) to seal the roof by spraying on a crud-brown rub-
berized coating, making the cupola seem even more grudging.

    This majestic emblem of comity was also a monument to paper-shuffling.
The Secretariat is a vast receptacle of diplomatic industry, and it projects a
clear and simple message: *Peace takes work*. Many critics found the complex
soulless and its creators deluded in the idea that World War III could be
averted by orderly administration. "If the Secretariat Building will have anything to say as a symbol, it will be, I fear, that the managerial revolution has

taken place and that bureaucracy rules the world," wrote Lewis Mumford in *The New Yorker.*

I toured the UN complex exhaustively in 2010, by which time it had devolved into a decaying time machine. Rain seeped around ancient windows and leached asbestos from crumbling ducts. Cumbersome fire doors broke up the flowing hallways. The Secretariat Building lacked sprinklers and blast-proof windows. Traces of original detail spoke both to the building's elegance and to its obsolescence. The lobby's green marble walls sported the lovingly designed but now culturally unsuitable ashtrays. In the great public rooms, pairs of vinyl-covered chairs were yoked together by steel bowls that hadn't seen a cigarette butt in years but still gave off the bitter whiff of burned tobacco. Architecture that once promised a more perfect world had now seen better days.

A $2.1 billion overhaul restored the original spare elegance. As I look at the Secretariat from across First Avenue, the blue-green glass curtain wall sparkles like a Nordic waterfall, and the white concrete walls at either end gleam like sugar cubes. Everywhere you gaze, the refreshed campus looks like a period movie, the kind in which vintage cars shine. The Security Council's sixty-year-old chairs have been reupholstered in bright Naugahyde, water stains have been cleaned off limestone and marble panels, wall hangings have been revivified, and decades of nicotine have been scrubbed away from buffed terrazzo floors.

All the cosmetic improvements are icing on a high-risk rescue of a creaky modern landmark. When crews began removing the Secretariat's exterior glass curtain wall, they found that it was barely hanging on. Windows were just a bad storm away from popping off. And the surprises kept coming. Once demolition got under way, workers discovered that some concrete floor slabs were held together with wire mesh rather than reinforced with iron bars. Engineers tested the concrete's strength by building an enormous tank on one of the floors and filling it with water. After forty-eight hours, the slabs hadn't budged—which is fortunate, because if they had sagged at all, it would have meant tearing down the whole structure and starting from scratch.

Michael Adlerstein, the assistant secretary-general in charge of the renovation, had to contend with far more terrifying possibilities, too. After a car bomb blasted through the UN offices in Nigeria in 2011, security experts demanded that the Conference Building, which is cantilevered over the FDR Drive, be fortified with extra steel. Meeting halls were moved away from the vulnerable sections, creating new lounges—and fresh opportunities for décor. (One such space, paid for by Qatar, looks like the lobby of a luxury hotel in Doha.) Then, in October 2012, Hurricane Sandy pounded through New York, knocking out the brand-new air-conditioning system and causing $150 million in damage. It might have been easier—and possibly cheaper—to demolish everything and build anew. However, for an organization where precedent and symbolism govern every handshake, the historical meaning of the UN's architecture still resonates.

David Fixler, an architect at the Boston firm Einhorn Yaffee Prescott, led the UN renovation; he says that the best way to be faithful to advanced postwar architecture is to honor its principles and discard its physical components. In the General Assembly Building, chalky sunlight filters through a wall of translucent windows into an atrium lined by sinuous white balconies. The glass, etched with a now-defunct photographic process, had to be junked and replaced with a more or less faithful copy. "Modern architecture anticipates change and expresses progress," Fixler says. "Very few buildings of the modern era were designed for the ages."

But there is one postwar building that was built to last forever—or that at least looks eternal: the Ford Foundation.

< Walk west on Forty-third Street to L, No. 320: the Ford Foundation.

In 1968, just when permanence and idealism seemed like chimeras, Kevin Roche and John Dinkeloo provided the do-gooding Ford Foundation with a solid, deeply dreamy headquarters, just west of Tudor City. Like other midcentury office buildings, it is made mostly of glass. But with its sunset-colored granite piers and weathered steel beams, the Ford Foundation has an imposing look of perpetuity. The warm bulk of its stone is like a ghostly memory of the Croton Reservoir. The patina of rust on the great beams suggests not decay but antiquity. The foundation's mission is to battle the full panoply of timeless injustices around the world, and its home base is a see-through fortress, braced for an endless war. The building's materials, arranged with a collagist's sensitivity, create a dance of delicacy and brawn, permanence and fragility, stolidity and romance.

The Ford Foundation did for the office building what Tudor City had done for the apartment complex: smuggle nature into its heart. Today, green design is often a color-coded metaphor, a checklist of energy-saving features that soften a building's environmental blow. Roche, however, created a work of environmentally sensitive architecture before the term had much currency. The main staff entrance is on quiet Forty-third Street, but during business hours anyone can step out of the cacophony of Forty-second and into an indoor Eden. Walkways made of chocolate-brown glazed brick thread through an almost preposterously lush bower, where every leaf appears to have been polished by hand. This multi-story cloister, designed by the landscape architect Dan Kiley (and closed in 2016 for a two-year renovation), was meant to inculcate a sense of serene, almost monastic community in the foundation's pencil-wielding professionals. "It will be possible in this building to look across the court and see your fellow man or sit on a bench and discuss the problems of Southeast Asia. There will be a total awareness of the

*Ford Foundation
atrium*

foundation's activities," Roche predicted before construction had even begun, and he was right.

Achieving that effect meant sacrificing some of the real estate developer's vital essence: square footage. Ford gave up substantial floor area for the sake of trees, light, and air. That sacrifice made the building itself a magnanimous gesture, a gift of greenery to a city that has always been invited in to enjoy it; I stop in there virtually every time I walk past. Part Victorian greenhouse, part modernist Crystal Palace, part corporate plaza, the landscaped atrium was a powerfully original idea, even though it later became a cliché. What better place to end a tour of civic aspiration than in this humanistic gathering place that distills Forty-second Street's dewy idealism.

This avenue of institutions has a spotty record of saving the world from itself. The UN has allowed innumerable atrocities and wars to rage unchecked, including the latest Syrian calamity. The *Daily News* has spent much of the last half century threatening to go out of business. The national passenger-train system that fed Grand Central Terminal dried up years ago; today, millions of cars despoil the environment instead. And critics regularly accuse the New York Public Library of hastening a bookless future by forging blindly into the digital age. At the same time, the architectural legacy of massive purpose-built monuments has demonstrated an impressive ability to adapt. This is a city that can be pitiless toward age: west of Sixth Avenue, Forty-second Street has almost entirely remade itself in the last few decades, preserving a few token theaters wedged between towers of glass. East of Sixth, though, the stone metropolis has survived, partly because the landmarks law protects it, but also because buildings that were once advanced and daring have remained doggedly useful as they age. Not every monument to progress can do that: Fire doomed the Crystal Palace; the city's voracious need for water first created the Croton Reservoir and later made it obsolete. But taken together, the behemoths of Forty-second Street proclaim this city's nimbleness, its ability to navigate the chaotic present without jettisoning either its history or its dreams.

Interlude III
CITY OF GLASS

New York was once a city of fancy façades. Terra-cotta reliefs, brownstone fronds, granite gargoyles, and cast-iron pilasters all served to advertise someone's ability to pay for them, or else they veiled poverty beneath a richly filigreed curtain. I love that tactile quality of an old city, the way you can read a street by running your fingers over brick and stone.

Jean Nouvel's 100 Eleventh Avenue reflected in the façade of Frank Gehry's IAC headquarters

All over the world, opaque materials and artfully placed windows are what give a cityscape its sense of mystery and depth; they allow the sensuous dance of light, shadow, color, and texture. The mottled silhouette of a tree shatters against an uneven wall. Flashes of fanciful tile brighten up a slag-toned vista. In photographs from the 1940s, even Times Square's patchwork of hard surfaces and dazzling lights gives it a rough romance. Today, Times Square is ringed almost entirely in glass.

The tyranny of smoothness has asserted itself over the modern city. Where once we built and dressed our buildings in every practical material, now the palette has been scaled back to a primitive trio of concrete, steel, and glass, with the first two usually serving as supports for the third. Everything else is doled out in doses as trim or accent or interior fit-out.

Glass is an ancient material. The Romans made thick green bottles from it, and in the Middle Ages craftsmen assembled brightly colored pieces into

Woolworth Building façade

wall-size Gothic windows. But in the last century, the clearest, purest form of glass became the stuff of modern life, with all its pristine chill. In Julius Shulman's famous 1960 photograph of Pierre Koenig's Case Study House No. 22, two women in white flouncy skirts chat in the corner of a glass box that hangs over Los Angeles like a flying saucer. That imagery has endured, both in real estate ads and in movies. In Sofia Coppola's 2003 movie, *Lost in Translation,* a melancholy Scarlett Johansson gazes through the vast window of a high-rise hotel onto a sleepless Tokyo. In the credit sequence of the television series *Mad Men,* the shadow of a man in a suit plummets past a curtain wall that offers no handholds or sympathy.

Glass has plenty of virtues. It can be easily cut, transported, installed, cleaned, and replaced. It is cheap, durable, and versatile. It changes moods with the shifting light. High-tech coatings can make it clear or reflective, silvery or dark. In a mile-long factory in Germany that never shuts down, sand pours ceaselessly into one end and passes through hellish fires to emerge as a ten-foot-wide ribbon of molten glass floating on a layer of zinc. That liquid substance, allowed to harden and sliced into flawless sheets, gets assembled into curtain walls for skyscrapers. The thin membrane forms a selectively open border between outdoors and in, letting light through virtually unchallenged (and waving heat in pretty liberally, too, and then refusing to let it leave). Everyone inside gets a view and plenty of life-affirming daylight.

But glass has become so ubiquitous that its use goes far beyond what makes sense. It is, for starters, curiously ill-adapted to the modernity it represents. Floor-to-ceiling windows would make a lot more sense if we had eyes in our shins, or if we all lived without furniture, or if the skies were always cloudy and the weather cool, or if nobody in an office used a computer, or if city dwellers had no neighbors, or if everyone lived above the fiftieth floor. Yet each month the tide of glass advances, making New York ever shinier. New towers preen in one another's reflective surfaces, creating a metropolis of mirrors.

Glass has produced its share of masterpieces. Mies van der Rohe's 1958 Seagram Building was the sublime prototype of the prismatic office tower. Mid-century California modernists perched crystalline mansions above unpeopled ravines. Philip Johnson nestled his Glass House on the lush hillside of his Connecticut estate. In New York, the most recent tsunami of the stuff has produced some fine architecture, along with acres of dross. The Dakota of glass—the pioneer and apex of its use in a residential building—is Richard Meier's trio of condos along West Street.

When the first pair, 173 and 176 Perry Street, went up in 2002, they were defiantly different from everything else in the old-time West Village, and they instantly became the decade's most influential apartment buildings. Meier took Mies's pared-down, transparent workplace aesthetic and fused it with the sexy California aeries of Pierre Koenig, Richard Neutra, and John Lautner. Those classic modernists shared a worship of visibility, but there was a huge difference in the sights they framed. In Midtown, white-collar laborers toil in stacked modular units, glancing across the street at one another from time to time. In Los Angeles and Palm Springs, residents of modern mansions gaze out on vistas of desert, ocean, or distant city.

Richard Meier's 165 Charles Street, the third of his West Street triplets

Meier's Perry Street buildings attempt an odd compromise between proximity and panorama. They look out on drivers and joggers who gaze right back, enjoying high-definition views of the inhabitants and the backs of minimalist sofas. The style, apparently so advanced, seems oddly backward-looking. In the mid-twentieth century, glass was a modernist symbol of a clean and clear-eyed future, stripped of history's clutter. Today, it's a legacy of the past. Meier, now in his eighties, was once a fresh-faced heir to Mies; he, in turn, spawned schools of neo-modernists. With his two tours de force of transparency, Meier severed the urban glass structure from its office-building associations and made it stand for a new kind of lifestyle spectacle. Mies had already gestured in that direction in the late 1940s, with his pair of curtain-walled towers on Chicago's Lake Shore Drive. But whereas Mies segmented the exterior with a heavy black grid of steel, Meier frames his façade in a vanishing white matte that makes the curtain wall appear to float. The third building, at 165 Charles Street, seems even more evanescent, the structural elements mere wisps from a draftsman's pencil.

The effect of all this lightness is to draw the outsider's eye past the surface, into the exposed dwellings, and to allow someone standing inside a virtually uninterrupted vista. It hardly matters if there is nothing much to see; the constellation of podium, proscenium, and scenery fabricates its own illusions and projections. You might read the West Street façades as so many stacked storefronts, displaying the phantasmagoria of costly lives, or as a tower of vast computer screens—a display of displays.

I have mixed feelings about these apartments' watery cool. I'm attracted to their austere classical beauty but not to their look-at-me pose. Meier fashioned paradises for the wide-screen age. Even when there's nobody home or nothing much to see, they broadcast the sense that attention must be paid to the lives being led within. The new glass houses express our contemporary ambivalence toward privacy. Tracking software, email monitoring, identity theft, and NSA data-mining have raised alarms online—yet we voluntarily give away reams of personal information to corporations like Facebook and Google. At a time when everyone carries a camera, how can you tell the watchers from the watched? These buildings play their role in a culture of mutual surveillance and exhibitionism.

Peeping is an honorable metropolitan activity, and so is rewarding the watchful with an impromptu floor show. Some New Yorkers keep a pair of binoculars on the sill. Others prefer the oblique view from the sidewalk: a crammed bookshelf, an oil painting hanging high on the wall, perhaps the occasional flamboyant chandelier. Until recently, an unspoken pact governed the relationship between spy and spyee: The first watched at a distance, unobserved; the second pretended to believe that nobody could see. *Rear Window* depends on the conceit that what happens indoors goes unobserved by polite society; only Jimmy Stewart's aw-shucks earnestness saves him from being a creep.

But that premise seems increasingly antique. For years, *Lifestyles of the Rich and Famous, MTV Cribs,* and the *Real Housewives* franchise have led the curious into the domestic life of people whose crises are more operatic and customs more alluring than our own. The real estate business has tried to stimulate and satisfy the complementary desires of the show-off and the peeper. These days, it's almost rude not to stare.

The Standard, a hotel at 848 Washington Street, opened in 2009 with glass-walled rooms looking out onto the High Line and immediately started marketing itself as an exhibitionist's playground. A few blocks away, Shigeru Ban's Metal Shutter Houses face West Nineteenth Street demurely, receding behind balconies and veiling themselves with perforated metal screens. But at the back of the building, the bedrooms, walled in floor-to-ceiling glass, nuzzle the side of Frank Gehry's IAC headquarters, giving the staff some potentially exciting lunchtime entertainment.

Residents in glass-skinned apartments can always lower the shades, of course, turning a monolithic façade into an irregular checkerboard of clear and opaque panels. You could see that grid as a map of society's conflicted feelings about reticence and display. Some people encrypt their lives; others send pornographic self-portraits flitting from phone to phone.

The glamour of living under glass spread quickly, evolving from the modernist sparseness of Meier's designs into both more nuanced and more plebeian uses. The great glass wall has become an alternative to the ponderous luxuries of the pre-war *palais*. If New York has embraced the architecture of self-exposure, it's

The Standard straddles the High Line

partly because some city dwellers are already accustomed to broadcasting their lives from fire escapes and stoops and through flimsy walls. The soundtrack of the city has always been made up of scorching insults and loud sex, tender exchanges and screaming fights. At the same time, the shadow play of intimate life isn't always comprehensible from the outside. Every evening, my neighbors install themselves in their see-through boxes like the ladies of Amsterdam's red-light district, but they do not generally engage in public orgies and glamorous soirées. Instead, they spend hours cuddling their laptops. For all I know they could be praising terrorists, composing odes, or hacking my credit card. Their privacy is intact, in the physical world, at least.

Glass is a morally tricky material: It promises honesty but it can also misdirect, making it ideal for an architecture of theatrical illusion. In the 1990s, after a newly unified Germany moved its capital to Berlin, the architect Norman Foster rehabilitated the Reichstag, the burned-out old parliament building, and topped it with a spectacular glass dome. Transparency in design symbolized transparency in government. A mirrored cone gives citizens a glimpse into the workings of parliament (although mostly it allows visitors to take a good long look at themselves). Foster's equation couldn't be simpler: *democracy=glass.*

That trope travels well. In 2007, *The New York Times* moved into a new tower designed by Renzo Piano, with glass walls encircled by a screen of ceramic rods. Almost every modern office building has a see-through curtain wall, but Piano, following Foster, gave his a philosophical *raison d'être.* The *Times* promotes openness and fights opacity, and so, he reasoned, it should occupy a building that does the same. He placed the newsroom in a low-rise podium alongside the columnar tower, so that passersby could in theory gaze in on the operations. Visibility reigns within, too. Reporters throughout the three floors can look across the central court and spy on the page-one meeting in a central glass-walled office. But seeing is not the same as understanding. A view of heads bent over desks gives *Times* watchers on the side street no clues about what's going on inside. The ultra-clear walls and skylight let a gorgeously diffuse radiance into the newsroom, but the tower's shell of sunshade rods reads as forbiddingly opaque.

Passersby check their iPhones in front of Apple's Fifth Avenue glass cube.

If glass is supposed to reveal what a building's about, perhaps the most honest example in New York is the cube atop the Apple Store on Fifth Avenue at Fifty-ninth Street, because it shows off nothing but a dangling logo. Walls, ceiling, and floor are all glass, as are the spiral staircase and the elevator leading to the subterranean depths where actual products are sold. The cube, by the firm Bohlin Cywinski Jackson, is very nearly a work of invisible architecture, but it accomplishes a lot of tasks. It places a giant Apple logo in a display case, evokes the beloved old Power Mac G4, translates a corporate design aesthetic to huge scale, and redeems the GM Building's grim sunken plaza. In 2011, the pioneering assemblage of ninety sheets of glass was replaced by an even more transparent structure of only fifteen pieces.

Still, I think—I hope—that the wonder of a building that weighs millions of tons yet seems no more solid than a soap bubble is growing old. Some architects are becoming bored by the fetish of transparency. They have started to muddle glass, to endow it with some of the texture and density of plaster and stone. The fact that the rich crave the stuff is good for architecture, because it's becoming an ever more complex and flexible material. So long as clients will pay to live behind it, experts will keep finding new ways to bend it, toughen it, color it, coat it, cast it, etch it with acid, blast it with sand, fill it with light, and bake it full of glare-abating ceramic dots.

Winka Dubbeldam's 497 Greenwich Street

One superb example of deluxe textured glass is the fanciful fish tank that Winka Dubbeldam, the principal of Archi-Tectonics, bestowed on 497 Greenwich Street in 2004. The glass in Dubbeldam's condo has both the liquidity of water, which ripples down the inclined façade, and the roughness and depth of masonry, which links it to the muscular workhorse buildings all around. The interloper throws an arm over the old brick warehouse next door, making it a partner in the block's modernization.

Across town is 40 Bond Street, a touchably textured condominium in NoHo. Instead of using glass in diaphanous sheets, the Swiss architects Herzog & de Meuron have molded it into thick, viscous-looking, bottle-green tubes that frame the separate windows. By sculpting the surface in cast-glass relief, they have defied the blankness of the curtain wall. It's a gesture that makes itself felt on the inside, too, where the window frames give an aqueous halo to the view onto the street.

The ultimate in playful glass is a pair of buildings at the western end of

West Nineteenth Street: Frank Gehry's IAC headquarters, a milky-white tour de force of curving panes, and Jean Nouvel's 100 Eleventh Avenue, part of the architectural geyser touched off by the High Line.

Nouvel's condo turns its spangled skin toward the west in a burst of camera-ready glamour. A wall of slightly tinted windows, angled like mosaic tiles, sweeps around the corner. From the outside, the variously tilted panes fragment the sunset and give the curving façade a glittering, disco-ball effect. Crescent-shaped rooms get wraparound views, segmented like a jigsaw puzzle by irregularly sized windows that fit together, with no solid wall in between. It's as if the builders had removed the masonry, chunk by chunk, until there was nothing left but glass.

Texture and glass at Herzog & de Meuron's 40 Bond Street

The façade throws a reflection on the surfaces of Frank Gehry's IAC headquarters, across the street, which breaks and bends the image, turning that end of the block into a friendly funhouse game between architectural superstars.

"It's an interference—an intentional interference—that makes me happy," Nouvel once told me. "And it makes Frank happy, too."

Gehry's building reaches its apex of glamour in wretched weather. Fog and snow haze its edges and bleach its white skin whiter, so that it seems to be constantly evanescing and rematerializing. On such dim days, the ceiling lights inside make the building fluoresce, and the curved glass wrapper appears to liquefy. On a clear day, when the glass glistens and the edges look sharp enough to slice a finger on, the billowing form resembles a square-rigged schooner on a southwesterly course. The dialogue between Gehry's and Nouvel's buildings breaks up the uniform tedious sheen now stretching across the city. It would be nice to think that we could soon rediscover the textured beauties of other materials, too, before New York turns into a crystal forest. I believe that's starting to happen.

BEYOND
THIS POINT
YOU MAY
ENCOUNTER
NUDE
SUNBATHERS

West Nineteenth
Street seen from the
High Line

Builders have begun revisiting the historical menu of terra-cotta, brick, copper, stone, and even heavy timber, though these remain luxuries. Architects can also draw from a new repertoire of synthetic composites, perforated metal panels, fiber-reinforced concrete, and even cross-laminated timber—materials that can be tailored by computer and crafted on a factory floor. For example, the San Francisco Museum of Modern Art's new extension, designed by Snøhetta, is wrapped in a white rippled skin that looks as loose and alive as a walrus hide. As the cliché of glass becomes ever more apparent, surfaces like these will yield a new kind of streetscape—one that gratifies touch and rediscovers shadow, unevenness, idiosyncrasy, wrinkles, and the passage of time. Our newest buildings will once again age with pride.

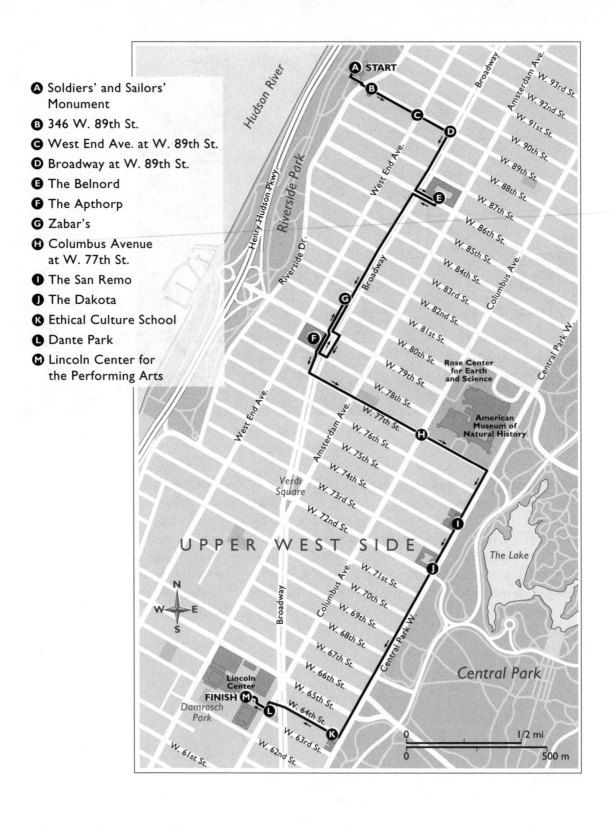

Ⓐ Soldiers' and Sailors'
Monument

Ⓑ 346 W. 89th St.

Ⓒ West End Ave. at W. 89th St.

Ⓓ Broadway at W. 89th St.

Ⓔ The Belnord

Ⓕ The Apthorp

Ⓖ Zabar's

Ⓗ Columbus Avenue
at W. 77th St.

Ⓘ The San Remo

Ⓙ The Dakota

Ⓚ Ethical Culture School

Ⓛ Dante Park

Ⓜ Lincoln Center for
the Performing Arts

WALK VI

CITY OF NOSTALGIA
The Upper West Side

On a spring morning so bright that the city seems lit from below the pavement's crust, I find myself at the end of West Eighty-ninth Street. Riverside Drive broadens here to make room for the Soldiers' and Sailors' Monument, a tall colonnaded cylinder with a cakelike crown, and Riverside Park falls away below, leaving waves of yellow-green pollen that roll along the sidewalk and fill my eyes with tears. It's an unusually tranquil spot. A bus pulls up and gives a bull-like snort as it kneels to let an elderly man lower himself to the curb. Down in the park a woman is hooting for her errant beagle, which answers with a hoarse yip. A toddler in the playground at the bottom of the escarpment is loudly demanding something. Suddenly a whir of bicycle tires pans past me and down along the steep path. Each distinct and identifiable sound reinforces the general feeling of tranquility.

This does not seem like the ideal place from which to launch

< Start at **A**, Soldiers' and Sailors' Monument, Riverside Drive at West Eighty-ninth Street.

Schwab Mansion, 1909

> Cross Riverside Drive to **B,** the freestanding house at the southeast corner, 346 West Eighty-ninth Street.

a fierce campaign against noise pollution, and yet in 1905, when Julia Barnett Rice moved into the handsome villa on the southeast corner of Riverside Drive and West Eighty-ninth Street with her husband and their six children, she found the noise level intolerable and unabating.

The Hudson, at the moment a silvery platter bearing a single kayak, was then black with tugboats and barges bellowing through the day and night. Each horn gave off a low, tubalike blast of warning or greeting or just because. Together they massed into a never-ending brass choir that lifted off the river and rumbled through the stone mansions on Riverside Drive. Every few minutes, another freight train pounded down the tracks that ran along Man-

Soldiers and Sailors Monument,
New York

Postcard of the Soldiers' and Sailors' Monument, 1903. The Rice Mansion appears on the right.

hattan's western flank, trailing a plume of oily smoke. Living at the top of this cliff at the turn of the century meant feeling the clangor as a buzzing in your bones. Like any good Upper West Sider, Julia Rice channeled her annoyance into activism: She hired Columbia students to count tugboat toots; she generalized the issue, turning herself into an advocate for ruckus-addled hospital patients; and she formed the Society for the Suppression of Unnecessary Noises, which for a while had real political clout.

Today, the yeshiva that inhabits Villa Julia, as her solicitous husband, Isaac, dubbed the house, has allowed it to subside into quiet dilapidation. The graceful hodgepodge of red brick and white marble, with its elaborate porte cochère and a weathered relief of a Julia-like mother and her six children on the Eighty-ninth Street façade, is an ever-deteriorating relic of the Gilded Age. It looks as though the owners couldn't make up their minds whether they wanted an austere Georgian mansion, a flamboyant Beaux Arts château, or a Renaissance palazzo, so the architects, Herts & Tallant, swirled them all together. In its some-of-this-and-some-of-that aesthetic, the house broadcast the habits of Julia and Isaac, who pursued a fantastically varied range of passions with expertise and élan.

Born into a Jewish family in New Orleans, Julia Barnett arrived in New York to attend Women's Medical College, where she graduated with an M.D. degree in 1885, and promptly married Isaac Rice, a gentle, German-born lawyer. They shared a love of music—he published a set of waltzes under the title *Wild-flowers* and found time to write a book called *What Is Music?*, which attempted in under one hundred pages to synthesize all the world's tradi-

Isaac and Julia Rice Mansion

tions into a "cosmical theory of music." If this sounds like an amateur crackpot's task, it's worth remembering that, nearly one hundred years later, another Upper West Side Jewish polymath, Leonard Bernstein, took a stab at the same topic in his Norton Lectures at Harvard.

Rice made and spent enormous quantities of money in idiosyncratic ways. He invested in railroads, started a prestigious political journal, and be-

came a defense contractor supplying the government with submarines. But his true passion and cause was chess. While Julia charged out into the deafening world to compel it to lower the volume, Isaac pursued tranquility by blasting a basement vault out of the rock. Down in his chess bunker, Rice developed a gambit, which he named after himself; it involved White sacrificing a knight in order to set up a stealth blitz by the rook. He was so taken with his innovation that he sponsored tournaments in which players had to use it, and he became such a benevolent figure that, on his death in 1915, the American Chess Bulletin devoted a supplement to his praise. (Later experts have felt less indebted: The 1996 edition of the *Oxford Companion to Chess* dismisses the gambit as "a grotesque monument to a rich man's vanity.")

The Rices were also unconventional parents. When their daughter Dorothy claimed she saw "no point in clogging my mind with things that everyone knew" and announced she was quitting school at twelve, her parents acquiesced. She went on to become a motorcycle racer, an aviatrix, and, echoing her father's chess obsession, a bridge virtuoso. Her younger sister Marion died in 1990, and the *Los Angeles Times* printed an obituary whose opening sentence intimated a movie-worthy life: "Marion Rice Hart, who sailed a 72-foot ketch around the world and flew solo across the Atlantic seven times between the ages of 74 and 83, has died. She was 98."

I linger on the Rices' story because I feel as if I know these restless engines of the Jewish bourgeoisie: passionate activists, idealistic eccentrics, earnest participants in the city's cultural life. Even in her concern for the precarious psyches of hospital patients, Julia Rice anticipated the torrents of mental-health professionals that later flooded the Upper West Side.

This is now a more moneyed area than it was thirty years ago, and in that sense it has come full circle, back to the enclave of affluence that the Rices settled. But, like them, the neighborhood still draws its energy from the arts and intellectual pursuits. A few random vignettes: Strolling along West End Avenue in warm weather, I stop to listen to some relentlessly practiced Brahms piano music crashing through an open window. In Zabar's Café, a man consults the Metropolitan Opera's season calendar on his iPad and tells anyone who will listen what shows they shouldn't miss. A book-club night at Symphony Space attracts an overflow crowd to hear three novelists discuss W. G. Sebald's sublimely arcane nonfiction novel *The Rings of Saturn*. Dog owners cluster in Riverside Park early in the morning, watching their pets tear around a hillside while they chat about Ibsen and canine psychology.

Novelists and musicians converged on Brooklyn in the early 2000s, making it the official epicenter of cultural hotness. But even after the influx of bankers, the Upper West Side still retains the foot soldiers of New York's creative economy: theorbo-playing lawyers, standing-room regulars, theater mavens entitled to cheap seats for union members, freelance editors who work from their kitchen offices, violinists who like the quick late-night subway ride home from a Broadway pit or Lincoln Center, actors who've spent decades playing eyewitnesses on cop shows, percussionists who've filled their living rooms with drums and marimbas, Columbia professors who support their ceilings with columns of books, plus a whole army of ad producers, sound techs, lighting designers, choreographers, book-jacket designers, animators . . . I could go on. Artistic genres, social consciousness, and religious pursuits coexist in an amiable jumble. Last year, I attended a Yom Kippur service that took place in the Church of St. Paul and St. Andrew, on the corner of West Eighty-sixth Street and West End Avenue: a thousand atoning Jews packed into a Christian sanctuary. When I slipped out for a bit and wandered around the building, I found a darkened theater on the second floor, where a handful of singers gathered around a piano and belted out

Christian tunes by candlelight. "I heard there's some kind of Jewish thing going on tonight, too," one of the participants said between numbers. Then I followed the sound of a jazz combo up the stairs and found the group jamming in a top-floor practice room. In the basement, a few homeless people were bedding down in the shelter. Back outside, a Black Lives Matter banner hung on the side of the church.

When Isaac Rice was scouting sites for his home, the area was a patchwork of promise and wilderness. Mansions popped up along Riverside Drive—the most sumptuous was Charles Schwab's seventy-five-room full-block château between Seventy-third and Seventy-fourth Streets—but they looked out over garbage-strewn ravines and industrial wastelands. In 1867, after decades of failed attempts to preserve various shoreline patches as parkland, property owners managed to get the cliffs beneath their houses set aside for Riverside Park and gave the job of designing it to Frederick Law Olmsted. But the residents' desire for scenery collided with the need for a flat zone where the city's dirty work could take place. The painter George Bellows captured that clash sensitively. In his turn-of-the-century views, elegantly dressed West Siders promenade along winding paths, gazing appreciatively at the ice-crusted Hudson and the far shore's snow-spangled cliffs. The leisure-seekers doggedly ignore the moorings and garbage dumps lining the river.

My favorite of his many New York winterscapes, *Snow-Capped River,* from 1911, takes in the sweep of the Hudson, bounded on the far side by the whipped-cream heights of the Palisades. Tugboats and barges slice through hunks of ice, trespassing on the snowy idyll. But the clouds of hot steam have a wispy white beauty all their own; these working vessels provide a picturesque touch for the gentry and their dogs ambling up Riverside Drive. We can't see the shiny new palaces on our side of the avenue, but we seem to be enjoying the view from one very expensive window. To Bellows, this genteel cliff-top trail provided a vantage point on the seasons. The spring scene, *Rain on the River,* sweeps from the romantic granite outcrop where Edgar Allan Poe rambled in search of inspiration, down past the pristine sod and gracefully corkscrewing pathways of Olmsted's fledgling park, to the sooty, clanking railroad tracks and sludge-hued Hudson beyond.

Away from the river, the side streets filled in with townhouses for the affluent, fantasias of carved polychrome brick and limestone trim that gave the neighborhood a reputation for architectural flamboyance. Whereas unremitting brownstone townhouses had given other parts of the city a reputation for mud-colored uniformity, here, the august critic Montgomery Schuyler enthused, "the wildest of the wild work of the new West Side had its uses in promoting the emancipation" of the row house.

< Walk east on West Eighty-ninth Street and pause at **C,** the corner of West End Avenue.

> Continue another block east to **D**, Broadway.

Bloomingdale Road (originally Bloemendaal, in Dutch), the meandering country road toward Albany, had been paved, straightened, and widened in 1868. Known as the Boulevard, it was as gracious a street as an American could imagine in the nineteenth century. Ample carriageways ran in both directions, flanking a median shaded by elms, and *le tout* Manhattan converged there of a Sunday to clop up and down in cabriolets. In 1899, the street was rechristened Broadway, one of the innumerable attempts to nudge along a real estate boom with nomenclature. Farther east still, the Ninth Avenue El, which opened in 1871 and ran steam-powered trains along a viaduct above what is today Columbus Avenue, linked the Upper West Side with the city proper, unstoppering new floods of money. All this new affluence, transit, and real estate—plus the construction of Central Park—was supposed to transform a rocky, rural area into a splendid precinct, set on a picturesque plateau and bounded by noble parks. "Assuredly this region will be the site of the future magnificence of this metropolis," wrote an early neighborhood champion in 1865. The boosters were right that the wealthy would reinvent the West Side in their image. It took a little longer than they thought, but by 2000 or so, the job was done.

The Dakota broods over frozen Central Park lake, circa 1900.

In the late nineteenth century, sumptuousness advanced slowly and unevenly. Squatters built huts between millionaires' residences, and the castlelike Dakota on Central Park West at Seventy-second Street looked out on a grid of stony fields and freshly painted townhouses. The building had its own power source; electricity came to the rest of the avenue only in 1896. When the area did begin to develop with dizzying speed in the 1890s, change was fueled by a transformative power that not all developers had fully understood: Jews.

From its earliest days as a strip of settlement along the Bloomingdale Road, the Upper West Side has had, and still has, a startlingly varied population. Turbulent eddies of history deposited Southern blacks, Puerto Ricans, Dominicans, Russians, and Ukrainians. The Jewish presence fluctuated, but ever since the Rices' days, it never stopped shaping the neighborhood's ethos: politically engaged, culturally aware, and slightly sanctimonious. The Rices lived in their mansion for less than the time it took to build it. In 1907, Isaac's travel schedule and his finances brought home the lunacy of maintaining a Manhattan villa. The family moved to the new Ansonia Hotel, on Broadway between Seventy-third and Seventy-fourth Streets, a hyper-modern marvel that offered residents luxuries they had never thought to crave, like air-conditioning and, for a few years, geese raised on the rooftop farm.

Even before the townhouse-ification of the Upper West Side was complete, it was already passé. The cost of maintaining a multi-story residence had become prohibitive for all but the hyper-wealthy, and developers saw the economic logic of tearing down a cluster of four-story homes and putting up a single eighteen-story apartment building instead. Photographs of the neighborhood from the early decades of the twentieth century show a skyline that looks like a bar graph: clumps of stubby columns interrupted by the occasional big jump. Some blocks have remained that way. But by the 1920s, the apartment building had become the norm. Especially along West End Avenue, rooflines and cornices more or less lined up to create uniform street fronts that were gray, noble, and formidable, resembling the residential quarters of Vienna and Berlin. The best addresses boasted archways and courtyards. Most made do with a few perfunctory signs of graciousness, lending a patina of delicacy to stolid structures and thick-walled rooms.

Those grave buildings proved to be the enduring backbone of the Upper West Side. Built for the affluent, with maids' rooms, dumbwaiters, and marbled lobbies, some eventually housed the out-of-work and underpaid. Many of these solid constructions survived neglect and eventually lent themselves to luxurious upgrades. Hitler's rise in Europe populated this American facsimile of a European city with refugees, survivors, and émigrés. The combination of sturdy architecture and traumatized lives gave the Upper West Side a wistful character that has never quite dissipated. More than most parts of the city, it is shadowed by memory.

The walk south brings me to Isaac Bashevis Singer territory. The Yiddish-language writer who bestrode the Old World and the New also trudged the length and breadth of the Upper West Side. He defined it as the stretch between Seventy-second Street and Ninety-sixth Street, flanked by the two parks, but he is construing the borders too narrowly. Some taxonomists would extend the area as far north as 110th Street; most would go as far south as Fifty-ninth Street, using the length of Central Park as the measuring stick, which would include the area of doomed tenements once known as San Juan Hill, and now called Lincoln Center. Singer made the rounds of his regular lunch spots, Eclair and Famous Dairy Restaurant, both on Seventy-second Street, and the American Restaurant, which was actually a Greek coffee shop, on West Eighty-fifth. All of them are now gone, like so much of what Singer

<
Walk south to West Eighty-sixth Street. Cross Broadway, and continue up the north side of West Eighty-sixth Street until you get to E, the mid-block gate, No. 225.

A ruined mansion on West Eighty-sixth Street between Broadway and Amsterdam Avenue, where the Belnord now stands, 1890

describes. Born out of the ashes of European Jewry, his work now reads as a necrology of the Upper West Side. "Almost every day on my walk after lunch, I pass the funeral parlor that waits for us and all our ambitions and illusions," he wrote. "Sometimes I imagine that the funeral parlor is also a kind of cafeteria where one gets a quick eulogy or Kaddish on the way to eternity."

Singer lived for decades in the Belnord, a massive limestone palazzo that was built in 1909 and occupies an entire block from Eighty-sixth to Eighty-seventh Street, and from Broadway to Amsterdam Avenue. In his day it sported a distinctly Old World air of decrepit grandeur; now it is the definition of deluxe. Singer described the area he patrolled in tender detail, and he distanced himself from his characters by means of a few blocks. He housed Boris Makaver, the protagonist of his novel *Shadows on the Hudson,* in a different courtyard château that seemed at once solidly anchored and capable of drifting across oceans of memory:

> The apartment building into which Boris had just moved reminded him of Warsaw. Built around an enormous courtyard, it faced Broadway on one side and West End Avenue on the other. The *cabinet de travail*—or study, as his daughter Anna called it—had a window overlooking the courtyard, and whenever Boris glanced out he could almost imagine he was back in Warsaw. Always quiet at its center, the courtyard enclosed a small garden surrounded by a picket fence. During the day the sun crept slowly up the wall opposite. Children ran around on the asphalt in play, smoke rose from the chimney, sparrows fluttered and chirped. All that seemed to be missing was a huckster carrying a sack of secondhand goods or a fortune-teller with a parrot and a barrel organ. Whenever Boris gazed into the courtyard and listened to its silence, the bustle of America evaporated and he thought European thoughts—leisurely, meandering, full of youthful longing. He had only to go into the *salon*—the living room—to hear the din of Broadway reverberating even here on the fourteenth floor. Standing there watching the noisy automobiles, buses, and trucks and catching the subway's roar from under the iron gratings, he was reminded of all

The Belnord, 225 West Eighty-sixth Street

his business affairs and thought of telephoning his broker and arranging to meet his accountant.

Singer can only be describing the Apthorp, a full-block colossus between Seventy-eighth and Seventy-ninth Streets that for decades housed both wealthy celebrities (like Al Pacino) and more modest professionals enchanted by the building's combination of grand spaces and regulated rents. Through the 1990s, more and more apartments were decontrolled and rents multiplied like a drug-resistant superbug. In 2008, new owners converted the building to condominiums, turning it into a bastion of the ultra-rich and also the object of an extravagant adieu by the writer Nora Ephron. "I lived in the Apthorp in a state of giddy delirium for about ten years," she wrote. "The tap water in the bathtub often ran brown, there was probably asbestos in the radiators, and the exterior of the building was encrusted with soot. Also, there were mice. Who cared?" What she did care about were the feverish rents and the courtyard full of "idling limousines waiting for the new tenants to be spirited away to their fabulous midtown careers." And so Ephron, one of the most privileged persons on the planet, was forced out of her apartment, and the Upper West Side, by an even more privileged cohort, the People Who Ruin Everything.

<
Walk downtown on the west side of Broadway to **F**, No. 2211, between Seventy-eighth and Seventy-ninth Streets.

Maybe because the neighborhood has such gravitas and yet contains such a multitude of agitated lives, change and permanence intensify each other here. Sift through old photographs, or through the memories of longtime residents, and you can make out the layered ghosts on every block. Even ca-

Courtyard of the Apthorp, 1905

sual conversation acquires an elegiac tone, and every observation that a new store is opening contains within it the recollection of all the ones it displaced. Is that a function of the West Side's ingrained Jewishness? Jewish sacred texts and prayers are cornucopias of lists: catalogs of ancestors, plagues, sins (both committed and hypothetical); forms of death (actual and potential); invocations of the past and terrors for the future. Children grow up to the hum of recited memory. Jews recall vanished towns in Europe, the witticisms of long-dead rabbis, the cus-

toms of communities that were extinguished generations ago. These are memories of trauma and dislocation, but the Jewish experience in the United States shows that wistfulness can thrive even during decades of peace and relative stability. The Upper West Side, the American Jerusalem, provides its own steady drip of loss. My wife grew up in two different apartments two blocks apart, and she can still itemize the businesses along the west side of Broadway between Eighty-sixth and Eighty-seventh, circa 1975: Barton's Chocolates, a tobacconist, Chock Full o' Nuts, Herman's stationery store, a shoe repair, and a lingerie shop. That collection of storefronts has been replaced by exactly two establishments: a Banana Republic and a bank.

> Cross Broadway to the east side and walk one block south to the corner of Seventy-eighth Street.

Railing against change is often an exercise in self-indulgent nostalgia, and we wind up mourning establishments we never patronized or buildings we never really liked. But there are also good reasons to kvetch. One day a few years ago I noticed that a new wound had opened on the east side of Broadway, across from the Apthorp, between Seventy-seventh and Seventy-eighth Streets. One of the last full blocks of low-rise buildings and small shops, it had suddenly acquired that familiar, ghost-town look that precedes obliteration. Shortly before, the restaurant Ruby Foo's, Manhattan Diner, a Così sandwich bar, a tae kwon do school, the Curl Up and Dye hair salon, a watch-repair service, a travel agency, a jewelry-making school, a pizza joint, a Subway, World of Nuts, and a jewelry shop crammed into two hundred feet of frontage. A dozen businesses in all, catering to vanity, hunger, creativity, and the pursuit of health, had vanished. It was a common enough tale that I knew how it would end: A teeming commercial ecosystem would give way to a pair of vast establishments, stretching from corner to mid-block.

Broadway's small businesses—bookstores, shoe-repair shops, florists, quirky clothiers, and so on—were being choked by the spread of a toxic commercial monoculture. That wasn't some inexorable Darwinian process but the desired result of landlords and developers, who always prefer to sign a long-term lease with a clean, quiet, stable, and heavily capitalized corporation rather than risk renting to an amateurishly managed boutique or an odoriferous diner. Sadly, cleansing the sidewalks of small establishments changes the rhythms that give Broadway its character. Businesses and residents pay fortunes to be immersed in the irregular, contrapuntal flow of foot traffic: people striding to work, pausing to scrutinize a restaurant menu, slowing down to covet a pretty pair of earrings, or herding kids in little white uniforms and color-coded belts to a session of martial arts. All this human activity so easily drains away. Who wants to walk along a boulevard where the shop windows offer nothing more tantalizing than mouthwash and free checking? The low Broadway building was—and is—an endangered species. Every sighting feels provisional, and coming across a full block of them is like glimpsing a whole pride of pumas. I believe in height and density—they are the sources of New York's strength—but not if they are evenly slathered across areas that were once more varied.

In Manhattan, where the value of land is multiplied by the value of the air above, low-rise structures are inherently wasteful. Developers look at a short building on a site where a tall one is permitted and they see hundred-dollar bills flapping away in the breeze. Yet those are the spots where the street lightens, the horizon opens, and the pace slows. The city suddenly seems a little more manageable and humane. The Broadway skyline on the Upper West Side is a jagged thing, a parade of elephantine apartment palaces and tiny, humble stores. That profile is the record of the avenue's piecemeal evolution, as a farm here and a shed there gradually gave way to the next temporary placeholder: a tenement, a tower, a supermarket. Conventional planning wisdom holds that tall buildings should line the avenues to leave the side streets low at mid-block, which is fine, except that not every boulevard is created equal. Park and West End Avenues were shaped by fell swoops of development that gave them their distinctively gracious uniformity; Broadway was not.

The architect and provocateur Rem Koolhaas once suggested, in a polemical exhibit called *Cronocaos,* that the world should routinely clear out the underbrush of junk architecture. The habit of preservation, he argued, is

< Walk back uptown on the west side of Broadway to **G,** Zabar's, on the corner of Eightieth Street.

keeping cities sluggish and out of date. Koolhaas was once a connoisseur of New York's contradictory quirks; these days, he has only to stroll up Broadway on the Upper West Side to observe the progressive erasure he advocates doing its baleful work. Here the preservationist impulse is needed not in order to cherish the past but to safeguard the vibrant present.

A few low buildings remain that way, for now, thanks to the Zabar family, which over the years bought up properties and left them alone. The four-story complex that houses Zabar's, the famous food emporium, displays practically archaic dimensions, like an old wooden house with doorways that force an adult man to duck. Christopher Gray, long the *Times*'s architectural historian, who knows every limestone lintel's backstory, outlined the history of the building in a 2002 column, and the tale brings out the threads that bound the whole area together in the first half of the twentieth century. In 1919, a Russian Jewish immigrant named Aaron Chinitz leased the row of derelict tenements, gave it some class and a Tudor makeover, and reopened it in 1920 as the irreproachably un-Jewish-sounding Calvin Apartments. The renovated complex, Gray wrote, was "entered through a one-story cottage-like structure that faced 80th Street and had leaded casement windows, Gothic decoration, a beamed ceiling and decorative downspouts. Advertisements promised 'dining service on premises' and offered two-room apartments for up to $165 a month, 'all bright cheerful rooms' with radiators set in alcoves and built-in oak settees." Chinitz was the impresario of Singer's Upper West Side: He, too, lived in the Belnord, and he had opened the Tip Toe Inn, a delicatessen at the corner of Broadway and West Eighty-sixth Street that closed in the sixties and still today makes Jews of a certain age sigh at the memory of its apple pancakes. In 1941, Saul Zabar, a Jewish immigrant from Ukraine, opened a one-window grocery on the ground floor of Chinitz's Calvin Apartments, founding a food dynasty. His sons eventually bought the whole building, preserving its English-village façade and growing the business into the neighborhood's gastronomic nerve center, even now supplying the intelligentsia (and everybody else) with smoked sable and pickled herring in cream sauce.

Walk down Broadway to West Seventy-seventh Street, turn left, and continue to Columbus Avenue at H. A bench in front of the American Museum of Natural History is a good place to stop and continue reading.

Over the years, the Upper West Side's identity shifted this way and that between coexisting poles: bohemian and stolid, comfortable and marginal, crime-ridden and somehow serene. I have lived on the Upper West Side for most of my adult life, and whenever I return from a trip out of town, especially at the end of a summer weekend, the neighborhood seems to pulsate and judder. Eddies of heat and music and talk ricochet off the asphalt, and if sanitation crews haven't come through for a while, homeless people have rifled through the piled trash bags, coating the sidewalks in reeking household debris. But if I come home from an expedition to Midtown or Lower Manhattan, I almost feel like I'm hopping off a commuter train in some verdant Hudson Valley suburb, where the decibel level is lower (thanks, Julia Rice!), the side streets greener, the air cooled by its flanking parks.

I treasure the sense that my slice of Manhattan keeps heading in multiple directions at once. The oil spill of money that has washed over Manhattan has made it among the city's—and therefore the world's—priciest zip codes, but along Columbus Avenue, wealthy co-ops coexist with middle-income towers, low-income housing projects, and rambling rent-controlled pads. In 1969, Nicholas Pileggi, who was then cranking out magazine pieces for hire but went on to write the screenplay for *Goodfellas* (and to marry Nora Ephron and live in the Apthorp), profiled the Upper West Side for *New York* magazine. His article described a neighborhood that threatened simultaneously to collapse into anarchy and also to become as manicured and dull as the Upper East Side. Crime was high, but so were prices. (Both would later shoot much higher.) During the postwar housing shortage, landlords had chopped single-family brownstones into miniature apartments. Some would erect a Sheetrock partition down the middle of a prewar "classic six" (two bedrooms, formal dining room, living room, a kitchen large enough to eat most meals in, and a maid's room, plus a couple of bathrooms), turning it into two cramped threes, and then would vie to see how little they could spend on maintaining the bastardized result. Consequently, the wealthy and the practically indigent shared the same blocks, coffee shops, and subway stations, living apparently incompatible lives within inches of one another. "The residents of Manhattan's Upper West Side make a yeasty polyglot society that is as ethnically diverse and economically varied as any area in the United States, with the possible exception of Honolulu," Pileggi wrote.

It is a neighborhood, or series of neighborhoods, where certain recently renovated brownstone blocks have already taken on the hushed tone of affluence, while around the corner young Puerto Rican men, wearing sleeveless underwear and religious medals, spend most of their Saturdays rubbing Simoniz wax into six-year-old automobiles. It is an area in which Mrs. Jacqueline Onassis sends her son to a school that is within a block and a half of a Japanese supermarket, an Israeli coffee house with a floor show, a gypsy palmist, a hardware store specializing in "Bueno Bargains," an excellent Jewish delicatessen (Gitlitz), a pizzeria, a Lebanese restaurant (Uncle Tonoose) and a religious-articles store that sells evil-eye repellents, love potions and numerology books. . . . It is an area that houses, besides many Russian, German, Polish, black and Puerto Rican residents, substantial numbers of Japanese, Chinese, Mexicans, Haitians, Irish, English, Dominicans, Norwegians, Swedes, Czechoslovaks, Austrians, Italians, Canadians and Midwestern Americans.

Pileggi's article expressed the anxiety that unstoppable market forces were wiping out all this variety—that the neighborhood was too inherently wonderful to remain acceptably crappy. And yet for a long time it remained one of the city's most dangerous neighborhoods. The year his story appeared, 986 people were murdered in New York, nearly double the number five years before. Still, that number would soon come to seem quaintly low, as the city's population dropped and crime leaped. By 1989, when I moved to Morningside Heights as a Columbia graduate student, drugs and violence were strangling the city, and the next year the number of murders peaked at 2,245—dozens of corpses hauled off sidewalks and out of blood-spattered apartments, week after week after week. That airborne murder rate left a contrail of other crimes. New Yorkers were being raped, beaten, mugged, and robbed, their apartments burgled, their cars stolen, their lives hemmed in by fear. Those two decades of decline have become mythologized in the story of New York as a frontier of liberty, when punk music and graffiti art thrived and the coffee wasn't worth spending money on anyway. I, too, fell in love with the city during my first, impoverished years here, and I don't want to overstate its miseries or shortchange its pleasures, which were plentiful. But I also remember headlines like this one, from July 27, 1990: STRAY BULLET CLAIMS ANOTHER NEW YORK CHILD—the third that week.

While crime rose unflaggingly, economic fluctuations whipped the neighborhood back and forth so quickly that residents weren't sure whether to fear gentrification or decline, so they worried about both at once. Yuppie boutiques opened, then closed. In the 1980s, Columbus Avenue briefly turned into a strip of loud-music and high-priced restaurants and bars, which shut down when the money ran out.

> Walk east along West Seventy-seventh Street, turn right on Central Park West, and stop at I, No. 145, between West Seventy-fourth and Seventy-fifth Streets: the San Remo.

The Upper West Side has always contained extremes of wealth and poverty. Julia Rice could look out of her bedroom window at the shanties that lined the railroad tracks along the Hudson. Today, the shortest route to Central Park from a pair of luxury towers on Broadway at Ninety-ninth Street runs through a public-housing project; heading for Riverside Park means jogging down a block of single-room-occupancy buildings that take overflow from the city's shelter system. My route brings me to the historic epicenter of those contrasts: the San Remo, Emery Roth's twin-towered Xanadu on Central Park West at Seventy-fourth Street. In a case of spectacularly bad timing, the San Remo began construction in 1929, part of the last climactic burst of luxury building before the Depression barreled into the neighborhood.

Successful Jews, unwelcome on the East Side, migrated to the West Side, where their freshly made fortunes took a while to dwindle. In 1930 there were still enough affluent Jewish families to constitute a market for the fanciest residences. Only a generation removed from Lower East Side peddler's carts, the textile merchants and fashion moguls who converged on Central Park West could afford not just comfort and leisure but a glittering life. They furnished their living rooms with Steinways and Victrolas. They bought concert subscriptions and paid for music lessons and contributed to progressive causes, though not necessarily to synagogues. Like the Rice kids, the offspring of these affluent families were brought up according to the most enlightened science of child-rearing, usually more by nannies than parents, who were busy with their own work and social lives. Two of these gilded children of the garment trade moved into the brand-new San Remo in 1930: Diane Arbus, who grew up to be a photographer of urban eccentrics, and Stephen Sondheim, whose musicals explored the discontents and neuroses of the upper middle class. Arbus's parents owned the fancy Fifth Avenue fur store Russeks and lived in a fourteen-room apartment facing the park. Diane used it as a launching pad for water balloons that would soak passersby. Sondheim's family had slightly more modest resources, and they made do with fewer rooms and a less verdant view.

The San Remo, 145 Central Park West

The Jews who settled the Promised Land of Central Park West found that their wealth never sufficed to buy entrée into Knickerbocker society or the most prestigious clubs. So they created their own parallel institutions, their own channels of secular prestige. These included societies, schools, and summer camps that were not overtly Jewish but were patronized almost exclusively by Jews. Among them were Camp Androscoggin, in Maine, where Sondheim spent his summers (and so, some years later, did my father), and the Ethical Culture School on West Sixty-fourth Street, which Sondheim and Arbus both attended in the 1930s. Founded by a German-born rabbi's son, Felix Adler, in 1878, the Ethical Culture School was a pillar of non-religious Jewry. As a teenager, Adler was already being groomed to succeed his father as rabbi of the ultimate establishment synagogue, Temple Emanu-El, on Fifth Avenue. But then he went off to study at the University of Heidelberg and came back imbued with Kantian ideals and the conviction that ethics were best kept separate from religion. Adler devoted his life to instilling values of tolerance, universal dignity, and social justice, without resorting to ancient texts or rabbinic precedent. That made his school the perfect institution for a social group that treasured Jewish values but weren't so crazy about being Jews.

"I never knew I was Jewish when I was growing up," Arbus recalled, many years later. "I didn't know it was an unfortunate thing to be! Because I grew up in a Jewish city in a Jewish family and my father was a rich Jew and I went to a Jewish school, I was confirmed in a sense of unreality."

At that time, the Central Park that Arbus looked over from her windows was not the landscape of manicured wilderness and jade-green lawns it is

A squatter's encampment in Central Park during the Depression

today but an urban dust bowl. Until 1930, a pair of adjoining reservoirs had stretched from Seventy-ninth to Ninety-seventh Street. Modern conduits made them obsolete, and the lower section was drained and partially filled in with construction debris. In that great rectangular pit (where the Great

Lawn is today), the Depression's victims erected an encampment of lean-tos, an enclave of wretchedness equidistant from Fifth Avenue and Central Park West. For Arbus, that weird no-man's land in her vast front yard offered her virtually the only childhood glimpse of poverty she had, and it dramatized the isolation of the fur-lined cocoon that was her life. Later, she told Studs Terkel:

> I remember going with this governess that I loved . . . to the park to the site of the reservoir which had been drained; it was just a cavity and there was this shanty town there. . . . This image wasn't concrete, but for me it was a potent memory. Seeing the other side of the tracks holding the hand of one's governess. For years I felt exempt. I grew up exempt and immune from circumstance. That idea that I couldn't wander down . . . and that there is such a gulf.

Arbus once again found herself wandering in Central Park in 1962, with her camera this time, when she came across a skinny seven-year-old boy dressed in a sailor suit and playing with a toy hand grenade. Then nearly forty, she hung around watching the kid, annoying him with her camera, until he made an exasperated face, his eyes zombie-like, his mouth stretching into a froglike grimace, the fingers of one hand clutching the realistic little bomb, the others curled into a horrible rictus. That shot, selected from among a contact sheet's worth of goofy poses, turned the scrawny boy into a symbol of the country's crazed militaristic obsession and made Arbus the poet laureate of American weirdness. Central Park plays its role, too. Irradiated with bleached light all around the kid's circle of stippled shade, the park could almost be a landscape caught in the last moment before it's blasted away. In the middle distance, a darkly dressed woman holds the hand of a little girl in a white frock, who balances on a curb; another grown-up pushes a smaller child in a pram. Those children could all be Arbus in the Depression years—blithe, careless, unaware of the catastrophic wind rushing through the trees.

Sondheim grew up similarly insulated from his Jewishness and from the knowledge of want. The family apartment was a place of glamorous self-invention, where his parents, Herbert and Janet, known as "Foxy," acted out a carefree marriage that ended abruptly when Stephen was ten. According to Sondheim's biographer Meryle Secrest, Herbert learned to play seven or eight basic chords at the piano, enough to entertain their frequent guests by banging out a stream of pop songs. Sondheim's mother held court. She "had a knack for gathering people around her, and a staggering amount of chutzpah," Secrest writes, "the kind of person who could talk a jeweler like Van Cleef and Arpels into lending her a priceless necklace and matching earrings to wear for the evening. . . . One can easily see why Foxy Sondheim had decided that the San Remo was the perfect background for the sophisticated life she wanted to have." The pampered boy's beat took him to Central Park, to Ethical Culture, and to his friends' homes. It certainly did *not* take him a ten-minute walk from the San Remo to an area in the West Sixties called San Juan Hill, whose destruction helped launch his career.

>

Walk south along Central Park West. The route goes past J, the Dakota, at the corner of West Seventy-second Street. You can read about the Dakota in the next chapter, Interlude IV, "City of Apartments," pp. 177–78. Continue on Central Park West, then turn right on West Sixty-fourth Street. Pass K, the Ethical Culture School at No. 2, and continue west to Broadway, L, the triangular Dante Park.

Herbert Sondheim walked out of his marriage in 1940, and Foxy and her two boys abandoned the San Remo. Seventeen years later, Stephen Sondheim wrote the lyrics for *West Side Story,* which was set in the tumbledown violent streets just blocks from where he spent his cushioned childhood. In the extended dance sequence that opens the movie version, rival gangs sprint and leap through vacant tenement-lined streets, into high-walled dead ends, and over mountains of debris. Between the time the show opened on Broadway in 1957 and when the movie was shot on location, San Juan Hill had been condemned to mass demolition.

In later years, Sondheim admitted to some sheepishness about the lyrics he had contributed to *West Side Story,* which in retrospect didn't feel gritty enough. "I had two street kids singing, 'Today the world was just an address, a place for me to live in,'" Sondheim marveled. It's hard to imagine that even if he had opted for rougher prosody he would have gotten terribly close to the idioms of San Juan Hill, where Puerto Rican Spanish merged with African American dialect. There's rich irony in the fact that Leonard Bernstein paid tribute to the neighborhood's Latino roots in his hip-shaking score and then in 1962 conducted the inaugural concert at Philharmonic Hall, which was built on the rubble of Riff and Tony's turf.

Until the 1930s, the neighborhood west of Amsterdam Avenue, between Fifty-ninth and Sixty-fifth Streets, contained the city's largest black population, along with a significant minority of whites, and it was famed for its street fighting and race riots. If the Central Park shantytown was a symptom of a country temporarily in free fall, San Juan Hill seemed to concentrate the city's perpetual discontents. When right-thinking reformers came to inspect, they found thousands of desperately poor families jammed together in conditions that shamed a modern city: rats galloping through airless tenements made of brittle brick. "Old-law tenements stand, blowsy and run-down, in silent shoulder-to-shoulder misery, full of filth and vermin," the *Times*'s music critic Harold Schonberg wrote in 1958, making the case for the construction of Lincoln Center. What those shocked outsiders missed, of course, was the intricate network of economic and human relationships that made the squalor tolerable and made the area feel like home. In any case, Schonberg was castigating a neighborhood that was already doomed. A cadre of planners, led by the master builder and slum-clearance lord Robert Moses and cheered on by much of the mainstream press, had decided to raze the area and start from scratch.

"Why Lincoln Square?" Moses rhetorically asked a banquet room full of construction executives in 1956. "Because these sixty-odd central, diseased and rapidly deteriorating acres can be rebuilt and made healthy only by condemning land and selling it to sponsors. . . . No plasters, nostrums and palliatives will save this part of town. It calls for bold and aseptic surgery."

Lincoln Square may have been a slum, but it was a slum full of bohemians and distinguished artists, some of whom mobilized to block the destruction and mourned the area once it was lost. The neighborhood looked thrillingly scary to visitors—and did indeed have plenty of actual horrors—but it also incubated a complicated cultural life. Thelonious Monk grew up at 234 West Sixty-third Street, and his biographer, Robin Kelley, writes: "Stories of crime and violence dominated newspaper accounts of San Juan Hill. The neighborhood made great copy for voyeuristic whites fascinated by popular images of razor-toting, dice-tossing, happy-go-lucky Negroes. What the papers rarely covered was San Juan Hill's rich musical culture." Until the Harlem Renaissance, the area "boasted the largest concentration of black musicians in the city."

As Moses saw it, the people who lived on the West Side were merely inconveniences. Their homes were "worthless structures," their turf a blank canvas on which to paint the gleaming future. Culture was what took place onstage, not in the street. Monk didn't see it that way: He kept returning to his old home after each tour, even once the demolition got going and parts of the neighborhood resembled Berlin in 1945. Finally, when walking those blocks felt too much like camping out in a war zone and breathing in the dust of destruction, he gave up. Only in 1987 did his music manage to wriggle back into the old neighborhood, with the founding of Jazz at Lincoln Center.

After twenty-five years of hanging around Lincoln Center, I still savor its lingering magic. Half an hour before curtain, as dusk falls on the travertine village levitating just above the street, the great white boxes glimmer, the fountain's spray creates an illuminated corona, and crosscurrents of humanity flow across the plaza. Defiantly rumpled students lope to discounted seats. Women stab the pavement with sharpened heels. Europeans make entrances under the impression that gowns and tuxes are still de rigueur at the opera. I haven't lost my jolt of delight in the way the Met's showy staircase gives the arriving audience its moment on a stage, or the way the costume-jewelry chandeliers get sucked up into the ceiling of the auditorium as the house lights dim.

It used to be that as soon as the performance started, the plaza cleared out. But these days there's always something happening—someone taking selfies

< Cross Broadway to M, Lincoln Center's Josie Robertson Plaza. As you climb the stairs and approach the fountain, David Geffen Hall is on your right, David H. Koch Theater to your left, and the Metropolitan Opera straight ahead.

or irritating the security guards by balancing on the lip of the fountain. This sixteen-acre round-the-clock arts compound keeps churning out culture. More than twelve thousand people use its basement rehearsal rooms and dingy offices and Juilliard classrooms, and on a busy Saturday, thirty thousand ticket-buyers come and go. There are few more effective fusions of indoors and out—or of classical and popular arts—than a summertime inter-

Lincoln Center

mission, when audiences drift out onto the balconies of the various halls and look down on dancers honing their merengue, backed by a live band, at Midsummer Night Swing.

What affects me most about Lincoln Center is the phenomenal aspiration it represents. Its scale speaks as much of America's mid-century cultural insecurity as of its pride. In the fifties, New York was still getting used to being a world capital of culture, and its leaders were anxious to show that the city could value the stuff as much as money or military might. Lincoln Center was, among other things, a move in the Cold War prestige game. In today's cultural climate, where land is precious and the arts have to fend for themselves, it's hard to imagine clearing so much Manhattan real estate for people to dance and sing.

It began as the brainchild of John D. Rockefeller III in 1955, at a time when the New York Philharmonic was about to be evicted from a dilapidated Carnegie Hall and the Metropolitan Opera had outgrown its creaky West Thirty-ninth Street home. Erecting a sleek new enclave for the arts and inserting it into the teeming West Side tenderloin would solve a barrage of problems at once. It would provide a home for the orchestra; it would allow the Metropolitan Opera to modernize and expand; and it would gather the city's major performing-arts institutions in a monumental space, appropriate to the cultural capital of a growing American empire. Lincoln Center was conceived to be selectively democratic: sealed off from the low-income neighborhood around it, but welcoming to any citizen with the inclination to climb an actual and metaphoric stairway and partake in the finer performing arts. The hope among arts leaders, planners, and philanthropists was that the benighted mass of Americans might eventually be made less philistine and that a new performing-arts center would serve as an elevating beacon. "Many of the little men and women have still to be sold on culture," Moses scoffed. Lincoln Center was built to close the deal.

As the idea was taking shape, the conclave of architects and consultants who were called upon to imagine it were unanimous in seeing it as a cloister of sorts: "For the arts and for music one needs to get out of the maelstrom and into a quiet place," they believed. What was required was "an area isolated from the hubbub of New York City." The center would be a special place, "concentrated upon an inward space and inward-looking." That did not please the urbanist Jane Jacobs, who thought such an acropolis would quarantine culture in a cold citadel. In a landmark 1958 article for *Fortune* magazine, "Downtown Is for People," she wrote:

> This cultural superblock is intended to be very grand and the focus of the whole music and dance world of New York. But its streets will be able to give it no support whatever. Its eastern street is a major trucking artery where the cargo trailers, on their way to the industrial districts and tunnels, roar so loudly that sidewalk conversation must be shouted. . . .
>
> And what of the new Metropolitan Opera, to be the crowning glory of the project? The old opera has long suffered from the fact that it has been out of context amid the garment district streets, with their overpowering loft buildings and huge cafeterias. There was a lesson here for the project planners. If the published plans are followed,

however, the opera will again have neighbor trouble . . . the towers of one of New York's bleakest public-housing projects.

The architect Wallace Harrison convened the leading lights of American modernism: Harrison's partner, Max Abramovitz, for Philharmonic Hall, Eero Saarinen for the Vivian Beaumont Theater, and Philip Johnson for the New York State Theater. They were determined to make Lincoln Center a democratic stronghold of the arts. Those were years when culture and mass media reinforced each other's power, and classical-music record sales were booming. At the old Met, the social register dominated the "golden horse-shoe" of private boxes; the new house had more mid-priced seats, and the other theaters did away with private family boxes altogether. And nearly half of Lincoln Center was open to the sky, creating a civic space for which no tickets were required.

At the same time, planners did have to deal with "neighbor trouble," as Jacobs called it, the holdouts who had survived Moses's bout of slum clearance. In early drawings, Wallace Harrison dreamed up imperial compounds. One version by the magnificent renderer Hugh Ferriss shows a domed Pantheon facing onto a circular, colonnaded piazza reminiscent of St. Peter's: ancient and papal Rome, fused on Columbus Avenue.

An early, rather imperial vision of Lincoln Center, as rendered by Hugh Ferriss

Harrison and his team of architects used an ancient technique to reassure the bluestockings that they wouldn't cross paths with the wrong sort of people: An unstormable travertine barrier blocks off the temple mount from the housing project to its west. As a space devoted to the classical performing arts, Lincoln Center was clearly an institution that would have to exist in constant dialogue with the past as well as nourish the future. So the architects threw out the modernist tradition of throwing out the history books and turned instead to a range of models. They considered the Paris Opera, with its broad avenue of approach; Piazza San Marco in Venice, a startlingly vast clearing reached from a skein of narrow alleyways; and the sixteenth-century Piazza del Campidoglio in Rome.

You can read the tug-of-war between openness and aloof monumentality in the architecture. Johnson made his State Theater (now the David H. Koch Theater) practically sarcophagal, turning it inward, focusing attention on the ample promenade and the auditorium's gilded ceiling and fronting the avenue with a featureless slab. Abramovitz conceived of Philharmonic Hall (later Avery Fisher, now David Geffen Hall) as a luminous box inside a cage of slender columns. For the Met, Harrison was forced to tamp down his desire for an exotic arrangement of barrel vaults and sweeping forms and instead produced a simpler structure with a spare arcade and a cramped lobby. The years have cloaked Lincoln Center's disparate parts in the illusion of harmony, but beneath the patina is an enforced collision of aesthetics, glued together by budget cuts and compromise.

With its white stone façades and noble arcades, Lincoln Center looks as though it's always been there and always will be, a 1960s acropolis that glows afresh each night, constantly rejuvenated by daily infusions of the performing arts. But in 2002 the campus looked older, sadder, and lonelier. The travertine was streaked, the pavers pocked, and the air conditioners creaky. On rainy nights, audiences exiting the halls picked their way around lagoons that leaked into the garage below the plaza. West Sixty-fifth Street might have been the back end of a big-box store. In the old days, attending a concert in Alice Tully Hall at Lincoln Center required a certain determination. The sign was easy to miss, but you could recognize the place by the clutch of smokers perched on the planters out front—nobody else would linger in such a hostile, amorphous plaza. To enter, you slunk beneath a forbidding slab, inched past a tiny box-office anteroom, and descended a short flight of stairs into a long and loveless lobby, where daylight trickled in through grudging slits. Another level down, in the buried auditorium, noise from an ancient ventilation system masked the sound of passing subway trains—and deadened the music. The procession suggested a highbrow speakeasy, as if there were something furtive about all that chamber music going on inside.

The Lincoln Center we see today is the result of a $1.2 billion renovation. The task of rejuvenating the aging complex went to Diller Scofidio + Renfro, a firm that is now among the most prestigious in the world but at that time

Alice Tully Hall at Lincoln Center, post-renovation

had yet to complete an actual building. They got the job because they weren't itching to tear the whole thing down and start from scratch. Instead, they treated the buildings with clarity, tenderness, and, when it was needed, unsentimental rigor. Tully Hall now announces its presence with a sharp prow that steers toward Broadway, riding a spray of light. West Sixty-fifth Street has become a festive thoroughfare, lined with marquees, theater lobbies, and a series of freestanding video screens parading down the newly generous sidewalk. The oppressive viaduct over the street has vanished, replaced by a graceful, twisting glass-and-steel footbridge. And on the main plaza, the dancing jets of water in the sleek round fountain were choreographed by WET Design, which built the aquatic spectacular at the Bellagio in Las Vegas.

The change is embodied, for me, by the new staircase that rises gently from Columbus Avenue. The old drop-off lane, a treacherous river of traffic that cut between stairs and plaza, vanished, to reopen safely underground. The subtle alteration shows the care with which the architects stitched the campus to the city and at the same time preserved its separateness. Now, once I cross the threshold, I find myself slowing down rather than rushing to my seat. The rhythm of the stairs imposes a stateliness of pace. You can't easily bound up them on the way to the box office or thunder down to grab a cab. The staircase acts as an anteroom, separating the fantastical realm of the stage from the reality lurking at the curb. When Lincoln Center opened, critics accused it of dowdy design, backward-looking values, and diluted modernism. Ah, but it was so much older then; it's younger than that now.

This area encapsulates how impossible it is to evaluate whether the transformation of a neighborhood is good or bad. To the thousands whose homes in San Juan Hill were razed, whose neighbors were dispersed and lifetime habits undone, the construction of Lincoln Center was a calamity. To all those who trained there for a life in music, opera, theater, and dance, or the millions who had transcendent artistic experiences there, it's been a boon. Like the areas around it, Lincoln Center draws people from all over the world who organize their lives around their love of music, theater, opera, and dance. Born of rupture, idealism, and injustice, Lincoln Center has gradually fused with the nervous system of the Upper West Side, permeating its spirit and imagination.

Interlude IV
CITY OF APARTMENTS

New York didn't invent the apartment. Shopkeepers in ancient Rome lived above the store, Chinese clans crowded into multi-story circular *tulou,* and sixteenth-century Yemenites inhabited (and their descendants still inhabit) the mud-brick skyscrapers of Shibam. But New York *re*invented the apartment many times over, transforming airborne slices of real estate into symbols of exquisite urbanity. Sure, we still have our brownstones and single-family homes. But in the popular imagination, today's New Yorker occupies a glassed-in aerie, a shared walk-up, a rambling prewar with thick walls thickened further by layers of paint, or a pristine white loft.

The story of the New York apartment is a tale of need elevated into virtue. Over and over, the desire for better, cheaper housing has become the engine of urban destiny. When the city was running out of land, developers built up. When we couldn't climb any more stairs, inventors refined the elevator. When we needed even more room, planners raised herds of towers. And when tall buildings obscured our views, engineers took us higher still.

This architectural evolution has roughly tracked the city's financial fortunes and economic priorities. The early-twentieth-century Park Avenue duplex represented the triumph of the plutocrat; massive postwar projects like Stuyvesant Town embodied the national mid-century drive to consolidate the

The baronial library of William Randolph Hearst on Riverside Drive at West Eighty-sixth Street, 1929

middle class; and the thin-air penthouses of Fifty-seventh Street capture the resurgence of buccaneering capitalism. You can almost chart income inequality over the years by measuring the height of New York's ceilings.

The apartment was not always the basic unit of Manhattan life. To the refined nineteenth-century New Yorker, the idea of being confined to a single floor, with strangers stomping above and lurking below, was an intolerable horror, fit for greenhorns and laborers. Living adequately meant living in a house, even if it stood shoulder to shoulder with other identical houses, each one propping up its weak-walled neighbor. The most vivid way to conjure up what it meant to be comfortable in those pre-comfort days is to visit the Merchant's House Museum on East Fourth Street, where Gertrude Seabury Tredwell was born in 1840 and died ninety-three years later.

After that, it was opened to the public. We tend to think of apartment buildings as vertical and houses as low to the ground, but the young Irish maids who tramped up and down the Seabury Tredwells' mahogany staircases dozens of times a day would probably have disagreed. The Merchant's House management has helpfully placed a bucket of coal in the basement

kitchen so that visitors can feel its heft and imagine what it was like to schlep the thing up to the fourth-floor stove.

The front parlor at the Merchant's House Museum

The house was not just a dwelling; it also functioned as hospital, maternity ward, funeral parlor, social club, workplace, dance hall, theater, auditorium, and school. It incubated elaborate social rituals that participants loathed but clung to fervently. The formal dinner party, for instance, depended on the existence of a formal dining room, a parlor to retire to afterward, servants with back-of-the-house access to the public rooms, and a kitchen just far enough away that it wouldn't pollute the guests with its odors—all so that hosts and guests might join together in festive somnolence and mutter about nothing over processionals of mediocre food. "Is there anything in this world more wearisome, more dismal, more intolerable, more reckless, more sumptuous, more unbearable, anything more calculated to kill both soul and body, than a big dinner in New York?" demanded the Swedish writer Fredrika Bremer in the 1850s. Much further along on the tedium scale, however, was the ladies' round of visits, another ritual that depended for its minutiae on the architecture of the private urban house. Women trotted around the city on the appointed afternoons, presenting visiting cards at one another's residences and making deadly conversation that avoided impermissible topics— which is to say, almost all of them. Sometimes they didn't come to talk at all but just left their cards, annotated with the nineteenth-century version of generic text messages, French phrases compressed into a terse code: *p.c.* meant "condolences," *p.p.c.* was "good-bye" (*pour prendre congé*).

The Merchant's House Museum evokes a stiff-collared time when the domestic architecture of the well-to-do functioned as both shelter and prison, especially for women. Even circa 1900, Edith Wharton's socially sensitive anti-heroine Lily Bart in *The House of Mirth* has strong opinions about what sort of female belongs in a flat instead of a proper house: not the good kind. Invited into the apartment of her male friend Selden, she reacts to his exotic habitat with a mixture of distaste and almost erotic envy:

> A breeze had sprung up, swaying inward the muslin curtains, and bringing a fresh scent of mignonette and petunias from the flowerbox on the balcony.
>
> Lily sank with a sigh into one of the shabby leather chairs.
>
> "How delicious to have a place like this all to one's self! What a miserable thing it is to be a woman." She leaned back in a luxury of discontent.
>
> Selden was rummaging in a cupboard for the cake.
>
> "Even women," he said, "have been known to enjoy the privileges of a flat."
>
> "Oh, governesses—or widows. But not girls—not poor, miserable, marriageable girls!"

For the likes of Lily, the apartment had only recently distinguished itself from the tenement, that dank and rickety brick structure that existed to pack the poor together as cheaply and efficiently as possible. My ancestors lived in them, and yours may have, too: The urban tenement rivals the prairie log cabin and the Southern tarpaper shack as this country's ur-dwelling, the humble place where our American story began. The Lower East Side Tenement Museum at 103 Orchard Street helps visitors envision what it was like to live in one: the half tub in the kitchen, the beds that slept children by the half dozen. Being a museum, though, it is also inauthentically clean and quiet and climate-controlled. What's missing is the smell of cooking cabbage pluming up the stairs, the furious family fights ricocheting through the narrow air shaft, the crowded rooms choked with coal smoke in winter and thick with heat in summer, the windows open to the marketplace ruckus and the stench of horse manure, the relentless crush of human bodies.

The middle class feared that sort of proximity, and for them apartments, tenements, and boardinghouses were essentially interchangeable concepts. Especially after the activist photographer Jacob Riis brought extreme pov-

Family room in a tenement

erty to public attention in 1890 with the publication of *How the Other Half Lives,* a squalor safari was a popular adventure for journalists and reformers.

The bourgeoisie had plenty of opportunity to learn the colorful details of living in disease-ridden firetraps. Some were moved to help; most were simply glad of their own good fortune and terrified that it might slip away. Respectability was a crucial issue in a society as fluid as New York's, where those who had achieved preeminence kept it only by erecting rigid social distinctions. In *The House of Mirth,* Wharton charts Lily's decline by plotting her narrowing real estate choices: She moves from a relative's house to a spare, lonely apartment, and then, after a brief stint as a social climber's paid companion in a decadently luxurious hotel, she drifts even further downward to a shared one-room flat. She finally winds up in a boardinghouse, one step from the gutter.

It took decades to cajole respectable New Yorkers out of their single-family homes, despite the arrival of a life-changing technology: the passenger elevator. Elisha Otis gave his famous demonstration of his patented safety catch at New York's Crystal Palace in 1854, but the previous year *Harper's New Monthly Magazine* was already making fun of it. The magazine foresaw that residential life would be changed, not necessarily for the better, by "the introduction of a steam elevator, by which an indolent, or fatigued, or aristo-

"A 100 percent cooperative apartment," 1924

cratic person may deposit himself in a species of dumb waiter at the hall-door, and by whistle, or the jingling of a bell, be borne up, like so much roast-goose with gravy, to the third, fourth, or fifth floor." The article goes on to imagine the indignity of getting stuck in such an infernal gizmo.

In 1857, Calvert Vaux, who later became Frederick Law Olmsted's partner in the design of Central Park, proposed a four-story, wide-windowed, thoughtfully designed set of "Parisian Buildings." His drawing included an elegantly dressed couple entering the lobby, but that was wishful thinking. While the city's population surged after the Civil War, and newcomers jammed into tenements, the affluent clung to increasingly exorbitant houses, even as they could hardly afford to build more of them. "Nothing denotes more greatly a nation's advancement in civilization than the ornate and improved style of its architecture and the erection of private palatial residences," the *Times* noted wistfully in 1869. With real estate values spinning out of control, the editorial concluded that the only realistic way to beautify the city was to erect more mansions for sharing: "the house built on the French apartment plan." If such a dubiously Continental innovation could be made to seem palatable, even splendid, to the upper crust, the bourgeoisie would surely follow.

The first building to overcome these sensitivities was Richard Morris Hunt's Stuyvesant Apartments at 142 East Eighteenth Street, a luxurious behemoth by 1870 standards. This structure defeated doubters with a two-pronged argument of aesthetics and pragmatism. The architecture oozed dignity: Five stories high and four lots wide, it had an imposing mass, an overweening mansard roof with yawning dormers, wrought-iron balconies, and ornamental columns. Even more persuasive, compared with the cost of building, furnishing, cleaning, and repairing a private home, all this respectability came as a bargain. Within a few years, the *Times* announced that a "domiciliary revolution" had taken place: A happy epidemic of flats had beaten back a plague of sinister boardinghouses. Young couples could now afford a bright new place in town; families no longer needed to fan out to the villages that lay miles from Union Square. The change represented the triumph of pragmatism over prejudice. "Anglo Saxons," the *Times* reported in 1878, "are instinctively opposed to living under the same roof with other people, and it is doubtful if [that resistance] would have been overcome had not the earliest flats been of an elegant kind, in the best quarters of the town, and therefore, expensive and fashionable." The rich made the apartment safe for the middle class.

Yet the first generation of buildings merely replaced old anxieties with new ones. Total aversion to apartment living gave way to practical puzzlements. Genteel New Yorkers saw the new architecture as an assault on moral rectitude. Visiting a lady in her Washington Square townhouse was a public, social act: You parked your carriage on the street and knocked on the big front door. But an apartment dweller could sneak downstairs to nuzzle a neighbor's spouse without anyone having to know. Apartments also couldn't always reproduce the strict segregation between sleeping quarters and public rooms, or between residents and servants. In the earliest, Paris-style layouts, a master bedroom connected to the parlor by a French door, but Americans were unsettled by the notion of allowing visitors a glimpse of a bed.

For people afraid that the new architecture would chip away at propriety, the list of worries was long and obsessive: that neighbors would have to make physical contact when passing each other in a shared hallway (a greater concern in an age of ample crinolines); that cooking smells could not be confined; that employers might inadvertently lay eyes on their servants—or, worse, on someone else's; that children would not be properly policed. Not all these embarrassments have gone away (one of my neighbors opens her front door whenever she's been frying fish, to clear the smell from her apartment), but developers faced them squarely. Builders adopted an assortment of strategies to dispel qualms about apartments' suitability. In 1884, the Chelsea opened on West Twenty-third Street as one of the city's first luxury co-ops, sparing residents the indignity of living in hired quarters. (Having evolved from an owner-occupied enclave of the well-to-do into the storied and famously shabby Hotel Chelsea, it has now gone condo.) That same year, the Dakota, on West Seventy-second Street, offered crowd-shy burghers access to Central Park just outside their gate and, inside, a quiet courtyard enclosed by a mock château replete with peaked gables, bays, and wrought-iron railings. These lavish touches effectively collectivized social status: Whereas the one-family mansion declared its owner's separate prominence, the Dakota's bulk and ornamental façade signaled that everyone who lived there was, by definition, Our Sort.

Wealthy, powerful people attract plenty of unwanted attention, and the Dakota's extremes of neo-Gothic sumptuousness have made it the setting for a whole festival's worth of real and fictional dramas over the years. John Lennon moved in in 1973 and in 1980 was murdered on the sidewalk out front. Mia Farrow drifted down its spooky hallways in the 1968 movie *Rosemary's Baby,* which treated it like a haunted castle dropped into the middle of Manhattan. Leonard Bernstein, Judy Garland, Lauren Bacall, and Rudolf Nureyev all lived there, giving the building the air of a celebrity clubhouse.

In 2011, Alphonse "Buddy" Fletcher, a black Harvard graduate, hedge-fund manager, philanthropist, and two-time board president of the Dakota, tried to buy an apartment in the building for his mother to live in (he already owned multiple Dakota residences). The co-op board refused, and Fletcher sued, describing the building in court papers as a bastion of old-fashioned racism. The whole thing might have remained an internecine dispute, except that Fletcher's lawsuit rebounded on him, focusing attention on his finances, which suddenly appeared to be tottering. Adding to the tabloid fodder was the fact that, after a long relationship with a gay man, Fletcher had switched allegiances and married Ellen Pao, another Ivy League overachiever—who filed (and lost) a discrimination suit against the Silicon Valley venture-capital firm where she worked. This litigious whirl of sexuality and race, respectability and disgrace, sudden sums and extravagant real estate made the story irresistible. *Vanity Fair* published a long feature article about the affair and headlined it SEX, LIES, AND LAWSUITS. The Dakota's unified front of snobbery cracked, revealing a small town's worth of squabbles, resentments, and payback, only with more zeroes.

What eventually assured the success of apartment living was the same fundamental element that has always shaped New York: money. The building's most persuasive asset was that it allowed the affluent to live better than ever while still downsizing the household staff. There were savings in numbers: In a large building, the cost of steam heat, electricity, and elevators could be shared. Instead of each family employing a laundress, one or two building employees manned huge machines in the basement. Residents of the finer addresses took their meals in vast and elegant central dining rooms, like passengers on a perpetual cruise. Those who preferred to eat at home but lacked a cook could have boxed meals prepared by the building staff and sent up by dumbwaiter. (New Yorkers have always been addicted to takeout.)

By the turn of the century, the mansion had become an albatross, not just expensive but primitive compared with a giant technological wonderland like the Ansonia Hotel at Broadway and Seventy-fourth Street, which opened in 1904. This was the bourgeois pleasure dome of early-twentieth-century New York. The young single man who installed himself in one of the

1,400 rooms and 340 suites could choose whether to move in his own bed and chest or select from the hotel's catalog of paintings, furniture, carpets, and hand towels. He could scrutinize the other transient and permanent guests by the dazzle of electric lights, dine in a restaurant that served five hundred, take a postprandial stroll past the live seals cavorting in the lobby fountain, and ride the quiet, exposed elevators just for the pleasure of seeing the seventeen stories scroll by. A few blocks over, the Hotel des Artistes on Central Park West at Sixty-seventh Street opened in 1917 as live-work space for gentleman artists, who required a northern exposure and high ceilings, even though some residents never touched a palette.

Aaron Naumburg, a rabbi's son from Pittsburgh and a fur magnate, lived in the grandest of the double-height dwellings. There, Persian rugs hung from the carved wood balcony that looked out over a vast living room encased in seventeenth-century English panels. The place resembled a period room and eventually became one: After Naumburg and his wife died, the interiors were disassembled and brought to the Fogg Museum at Harvard.

The immigrant architect Emery Roth erected the apotheosis of early-twentieth-century domestic grandeur on Central Park West at Eighty-first Street: the Beresford, a fairy-tale confection of towers, wrought-iron grillwork, terra-cotta cherubs, pediments, and balustrades. Each apartment pinwheeled around an entrance foyer, so that the sleeping quarters, public rooms, and servants' wing could be simultaneously separate and close at hand. Only New York could produce a monument to Jewish home life as imposing as the Beresford, and perhaps only in the late 1920s, in the exultant moment before the stock-market crash.

The Depression slammed the portcullis down on the era of residential magnificence. The Ansonia was chopped up into cubbies. The Beresford was sold off for a pittance. The Majestic, on Seventy-second Street, and the San Remo, planned in flush times, were completed in miserable ones and faced immediate financial trouble. Hundreds of other Upper West Side buildings, more modest but still genteel, adapted to less easeful times. Maids' rooms were repurposed as bedrooms. Bell boxes for summoning servants were disconnected. Stained-glass windows broke and were replaced with ordinary panes.

Savage as it was, the Depression thinned but did not extinguish the ranks of the wealthy, and some sumptuousness did slip through the closing gates. In 1931, the River House materialized on East Fifty-second Street, and its twenty-seven-story tower, flanked by fifteen-story wings, rose over the East River like an ocean liner. Inserted into a neighborhood of slums and slaughterhouses, River House retreated behind its gated court, a citadel reaching far above the gloom. The luckiest residents never needed to dirty a shoe on the cobblestones: They could, if they wished, commute by boat to Lower Manhattan or their Westchester estates from the private marina (an amenity later obliterated by the FDR Drive). I spent two college summers staying in a large River House apartment by myself, mystified that the absent owners—or anyone, really—could feel at ease in so much space. I had no use, of course, for the immense formal dining room with the foot-activated buzzer beneath the vast mahogany table to signal that the cook should bring the next course. The narrow balcony that once protruded over the private marina now hung above the thunderous FDR Drive, giving dinner al fresco the feel of a picnic on a highway median. I avoided the long *Shining*-like hallways and instead snuck from my bedroom through a back landing to the kitchen like a furtive maid, letting the rest of the apartment stretch out in unmapped darkness. The place creeped me out, which is odd, really, because when the building opened it represented the quintessence of open, spacious living.

Samuel Gottscho took photos from the higher floors and captured the thrill of living at those rarefied altitudes, when street level contained so much squalor. The haloed skyline, the chrome-plated water spreading out beyond the great bay windows, the airy apartments washed in morning light—all made River House the Valhalla of New York.

In that first phase in the saga of the New York apartment, the middle class emulated the prosperous in order to separate themselves from the poor. In the next chapter, plain but modern housing for the poor became the standard for everyone else. Widespread hardship, followed by a world war and a housing shortage, plus a multi-decade campaign to flatten differences in income, meant that New Yorkers of all strata were moving into streamlined homes, with lower ceilings and restrained rents.

Affordability and dignity had always been a goal of apartment advocates. In 1867, 1879, and 1901, progressives had pushed through laws requiring small increases in the standards of ventilation, light, and sanitation in tenements. In the 1870s, the Brooklyn philanthropist Alfred Tredway White built handsome complexes of worker houses like the Tower Buildings in Cobble Hill, which featured a toilet in each apartment, outdoor staircases, meticulous brickwork, and wrought-iron railings. But it was the Depression that brought the issue of how to house the have-nots into the realm of public policy. "Down with rotten, antiquated ratholes! Down with hovels! Down with disease! Down with crime!" proclaimed Mayor Fiorello La Guardia, ushering in a new bureaucracy charged with providing decent shelter: the New York City Housing Authority, known forevermore as NYCHA (pronounced NYE-tcha). In 1935, NYCHA rehabilitated a neighborhood of crumbling Lower East Side tenements by tearing down every third house, to maximize light and air, and renovating or rebuilding the rest. In the end, the First Houses project required near-total reconstruction, but the result inaugurated the public-housing era and remains an emblem of the promise, as La Guardia put it, "to give the people of my city, in place of their tenements, decent, modern cheerful housing, with a window in every room and a bit of sunshine in every window."

Providing apartments to those who needed them proved such a massive undertaking that all levels of government had to get involved. Rent control arrived in 1943, and a smorgasbord of federal, state, and city agencies floated bonds, granted tax breaks, wrote checks, evicted citizens, and redrew maps, all in an effort to eliminate putrid slums and erect stands of thick, solid towers instead. Private developers got in on the action, too. The Metropolitan Life Insurance Company opened Stuyvesant Town as a middle-class gated community around a series of verdant courts. One irony of that contradiction-laced period is that in order to save the decaying city, densely populated towers cut themselves off from the noise and mess of urban life. Residents didn't necessarily demand distance from the street, but planners did. "The growing antimetropolitanism of most housing architects [was] matched by the new suburban bias of the bankers, lawyers, and bureaucrats who wrote the programs and administered the policies," write Robert A. M. Stern, Gregory Gilmartin, and Thomas Mellins in *New York 1930*.

The story of mass housing is an intricate epic of idealism, destruction, and partial successes. Public projects obliterated neighborhoods, boosted the crime and segregation they hoped to alleviate, killed miles of street life, and vivisected vibrant communities—but they also redeemed a lot of grimly constricted lives. Look out over the Lower East Side from the Williamsburg Bridge, and instead of the chaotic ground cover of moldy tenements from a century ago, you see an orderly pattern of X-shaped high-rises, separated by greenery. From this altitude, you can almost recapture the mid-century optimism about public housing, the belief that erecting enough modern apartments could if not cure inequality at least mitigate its effects. In many cities, that experiment in social engineering has gone down in history as an abject, abusive failure. Pruitt-Igoe in St. Louis, Cabrini-Green in Chicago, Lafayette Courts in Baltimore—all over the country, mayors dynamited degraded brick towers in the belief that architecture had aggravated problems it was meant to address. New York has by far the nation's largest public-housing program, with an unofficial population of six hundred thousand—almost exactly that of the city of Baltimore—and it has had a different experience. The towers have endured, frequently decrepit and ravaged by drugs and crime but filled with people who are fiercely protective of their status as NYCHA residents. These high-rises were usually located in the least desirable parts of the city;

now some find themselves encircled by creeping luxury. Once, the nearest supermarket was a grim hike away. Now there's an organic-food store across the street, but the beautiful produce is still out of reach. A moat of bitterness encircles some of these projects: Residents feel abandoned, isolated, and threatened, while neighbors feel that the towers mar otherwise-golden enclaves of privilege. But anyone who looks on these hulks and wishes them away might remember the words of an early resident, a garment worker who said: "Before, I lived in the jungle. Now I live in New York."

"I live in New York." The pride buzzing through that phrase brought people here in search of whatever damp, dim, cramped digs they could find. Even as the authorities were condemning acres of cold-water walk-ups in East Harlem and the Lower East Side, Abstract Expressionist painters were renting similar apartments in Greenwich Village. If for Wharton's Lily Bart a poky flat represented the last rung before indigence and an early death, for the siblings in Ruth McKenney's 1940 play *My Sister Eileen* (and its 1953 spin-off, *Wonderful Town*), a basement pad in the Village had a raffish, stage-worthy glamour. "It is a large room and far from cheerful, but there is an air of dank good nature about it that may grow on you," read the stage directions for the opening scene. Like the garret in *La Bohème*, it's the sort of place that makes penury cool.

So powerful was the ideal of the apartment for the masses that luxury buildings aspired to it, too. Postwar architects embraced the austerities of modernism, which they applied to bourgeois quarters as rigorously as they did to public housing. The most bracing high-end apartment building was Manhattan House, an immense 1951 complex; architect Gordon Bunshaft clad it in glazed brick that everyone called white but was actually pale gray and has always looked slightly unwashed. Stretching along East Sixty-sixth Street between Second and Third Avenues, Manhattan House adapted the grand apartment to the stripped-down modern era persuasively enough to attract Grace Kelly as a resident, and Bunshaft chose to live there, too. Its huge scale, stark design, and chain of slabs sitting back from the sidewalk evoked Stuyvesant Town more than the prewar palazzi like the Beresford. Half a century earlier, New Yorkers had hoped to live fabulously. Now it was stylish to live just well enough.

It soon became difficult to distinguish Manhattan House from the knock-offs that developers churned out for less discerning clientele. For a while in the fifties and sixties, it seemed as though every new residential building, whether it contained compact studios or assembly-line "luxury" pods, wore a uniform of glossy white brick. An aesthetic of conspicuous sameness, developed for the poor and taken up by the affluent, trickled back to the middle class.

The charms of standardization eventually wore thin, and the New York apartment soon experienced a transformation almost as fundamental as it had at the turn of the century. In the sixties and seventies, many of the industries that had fueled the city's growth a century earlier failed, leaving acres of fallow real estate south of Houston Street. At first, nobody was permitted to live in those abandoned factories, but the rents were low and the spaces vast, and artists were no more deterred by legal niceties than they were by rodents and flaking paint. They arrived with their drafting tables and movie cameras and gloried in the absence of fussy neighbors. They would demarcate a bedroom by hanging an old sheet, or turn one end of the long space into an impromptu stage, with the audience sprawled on the paint-speckled floor.

The music critic John Rockwell later recalled the casually ecstatic atmosphere that surrounded the loft concerts of Philip Glass in the early seventies, before he began churning out operas and soundtracks for pretentious movies. "The music danced and pulsed with a special life," Rockwell wrote of a 1973 performance of *Music with Changing Parts,* "its motoric rhythms, burbling, highly amplified figurations and mournful sustained notes booming out through the huge black windows and filling up the bleak industrial neighborhood. It was so loud that the dancers Douglas Dunn and Sara Rudner, who were strolling down Wooster Street, sat on a stoop and enjoyed the concert together from afar. A pack of teenagers kept up an ecstatic dance of their own. And across the street, silhouetted high up in a window, a lone saxophone player improvised in silent accompaniment like some faded postcard of fifties' Greenwich Village Bohemia. It was a good night to be in New York City."

At a time when urban populations everywhere were dispersing to the suburbs, this artists' colonization had a profound and invigorating effect not just on SoHo but on the entire city. The traditional remedy for decay was demolition, but artists demanded the right to stay. Their presence attracted art galleries, and a treasury of cast-iron buildings acquired a new purpose. Artists didn't think of themselves as creating real estate value, but they did. Few events illustrate the maxim "Be careful what you wish for" better than the Loft Law of 1982, which forced owners to make SoHo's industrial buildings fully habitable without charging the tenants for improvements.

It was a triumph and a defeat. Legal clarity brought another wave of tenants, with more money and higher standards of comfort. As working artists drifted on to cheaper pastures in Long Island City, Williamsburg, and Bushwick—or out of the city altogether—SoHo's post-pioneers renovated their lofts, hiring architects to reinterpret the neighborhood's industrial rawness, or merge it with cool pop minimalism, or carve the ballroom-size spaces into simulacra of uptown apartments.

Once everyone wanted to be a tycoon; then everyone wanted to be middle class. Now everyone wanted to be an artist, or to live like one. SoHo filled up quickly, and the idea of the loft spread, reinterpreted as a marketable token of the unconventional life. The loft promised to lift the curse of the bourgeoisie through the powers of renovation. Realtors began pointing out partition walls that could easily be torn out. Lawyers, dentists, and academics eliminated hallways and dining rooms, folding them into unified, flowing spaces. Happily for those with mixed feelings about the counterculture, loft-like expansiveness overlapped with the open-plan aesthetic of new suburban houses. Whether in imitation of SoHo or Scarsdale, the apartment kitchen migrated from the servants' area to the center of the household, shed its confining walls, and put on display its arsenal of appliances. Cooking became a social performance, one that in practice many apartment dwellers routinely skipped in favor of ordering in, going out, or defrosting a package—but at least the theater stood ready.

Starting in the eighties, when the country more or less abandoned the pursuit of greater equality, and fresh college graduates coaxed the financial system into dumping sudden millions in their laps, the apartment took yet another turn. Triumphant traders—"Masters of the Universe," in Tom Wolfe's phrase—didn't spend much time at home, but in their few moments of leisure they wanted to gaze down on the city they had conquered.

For the next two decades, developers treated the apartment less as a private retreat than as a belvedere—a platform for a vista. For a time, the ultimate expressions of the panoramic apartment, which required vertiginous height, very fast elevators, and a perimeter of glass, were the penthouses atop Trump World Tower. This dark bronze totem that Costas Kondylis designed for Donald Trump at 845 United Nations Plaza (First Avenue between East Forty-Seventh and Forty-eighth Streets) was the planet's tallest residential building (and the one most loathed by its neighbors) when it opened in 2001. It was not shy about its stature. The ceilings got higher near the top, so that the tower appeared to be craning its neck, and, with vintage Trumpian hyperbole, the seventy-two floors were deceptively numbered up to ninety. The payoff was an IMAX view of the skyline below and the weird sensation that the closest neighbors were gulls, planes, and clouds. Of course, that sort of solitude only lasts until the next neighbor climbs the mast. The push to refine the apartment began with assurances that a fifteenth-floor home could rival a house set on a fifteen-foot stoop; today, a one-hundred-fiftieth-floor penthouse is not unthinkable.

Vertical living has behaved as promised: It multiplied the value of limited land, streamlined the machinery of leisure, sheltered the masses, and concentrated entrepreneurial energy into a compact urban zone. But the price of

Bjarke Ingels's VIA57

height is lightweight construction: glass walls, thin floors, and plasterboard walls. The original barons of the Beresford would have found today's condo towers pretty flimsy castles in the sky. New York has done such a thorough job of glamorizing the high-rise apartment that a Manhattan *pied en l'air* has become a billionaire's accessory and an eternal object of desire. Developers have searched for ways to leverage that lust—to reconcile the assembly-line efficiencies of the construction business with the quest for ever-greater heights of pampering. Enter the preposterous amenity. Today, the most extreme buildings compete to provide a Gilded Age menu of extras. If you want your dog to get his treadmill workout while you practice climbing a rock wall, then snuggle up together by the rooftop fire pit, you can do all that without ever leaving home.

In theory, the ultra-high-rise should not be simply an instrument of extravagant living but a path back to the egalitarian policies of the mid-twentieth century. In his book *Triumph of the City,* the Harvard professor Edward Glaeser argues that New York's vitality depends on people being able to live here and that the only way to make apartments affordable is to erect more of them. Mayor Bill de Blasio staked his mayoralty on just such a push, and the Department of Buildings authorized the construction of more than fifty thousand apartments in 2015—enough to house an entire new (small) city. But while builders keep cranking out the same few sizes and layouts, residents come in a dizzying and changing variety of configurations. Post-college roommates, groups of immigrants sleeping in shifts, multigenerational families, single-parent families, single business travelers who spend virtually no time at home, seniors who want to stay put but need less space than they once did, entrepreneurs who run businesses out of their homes— all their different needs challenge the construction industry's craving for standardization. Architects have offered an elaborate menu of ideas to address a changing urban society, including gerbil-scaled apartments and dorm-style shares. Mostly what they boil down to is charging more money for less space.

In every growth spurt, rental towers pop up all over the city like architectural acne, a pox of large, unsightly blocks whose creators claim it's the best they can do. But one architect who flicked away excuses to create something really fresh is the Danish superstar Bjarke Ingels, whom I met in 2011, when he was trying to explain what he had in mind for the desolate juncture of West Fifty-seventh Street and the West Side Highway.

His first New York building, he said, would fuse two apparently incompatible types: a European-style, low-rise apartment block encircling a courtyard, and a Manhattan tower-on-a-podium, yielding something that looked like neither and behaved like both. New York was ready to embrace such a griffin, he insisted: "This is the country that invented surf 'n' turf! To put a lobster on a steak: Any French chef would tell you that's a crime."

Five years later, Ingels walked me around the finished work (now called VIA 57 West), a gracefully asymmetrical peak with a landscaped bower in its hollowed core. The façade does double duty as the roof, swooping up from the shoreline to the mountainous ridge of Midtown. It follows a hyperbolic paraboloid, the curving, mathematically precise surface that gives us the Pringle and the saddle roof. In the early sixties, swooshes and upturned canopies captured the era's youthful eagerness, its faith in a limitless economy, in capitalism, technology, and the lure of space travel. Ingels taps into this Kennedy-era moment of futuristic self-confidence, not for its nostalgia value but to recover the geometry's forgotten potential. The crosshatched lines formed by the thousands of steel sheets make visible the curving grid of a mathematical diagram. Each panel is unique, cut and bent by an infinitely patient computer and assembled by workers who had to figure out what they were doing along the way.

The result resembles an aircraft wing, a ski slope, or a wave. It's tempting to see this as a celebrity architect's theatrical flourish, but consider all that the shape achieves: It maximizes river views and covered balconies, protects even low apartments from the noise of the highway, pierces the skyline with a jaunty top, and leaves room for a courtyard that even in winter basks in sunlight most of the day. The building looks wild, but it's born of logic; true originality flows from rigorous thinking. Ingels's inventiveness suggests that maybe all the contradictory forces of New York's real estate history can somehow be brought into equilibrium and the next generation of apartment buildings can combine affordability with vintage grandeur, great height, and the relentless pursuit of ease. That may seem like an implausible quartet of attributes, but it's precisely what the first middle-class alternatives to the tenement and the boardinghouse offered 150 years ago.

My first New York apartment was a one-bedroom on West 120th Street near Morningside Drive that I shared with my girlfriend (now wife). A grim security gate over one window gave the bedroom a certain cellblock chic, and one wall of the living room doubled as kitchen. Daylight paid a brief morning visit, dispensing a small, glowing square on the floor that lasted about an hour. The rest of the place was so dim that our cat spent his days sunning himself under a desk lamp, resting up after his nocturnal cockroach hunt. I was a graduate student at Columbia, which had bought the dilapidated building and was patiently waiting out the motley collection of tenants whose leases were part of the deal. Next door lived an elderly, impeccably gracious Japanese woman whose sole self-indulgence was a pair of Ferragamo shoes. Down the hall was Al, a tall and skeletal crack addict who might have been around thirty, or possibly sixty-five, with a nonchalant attitude about garbage disposal; he frequently carpeted the stairwell with chicken bones. Al periodically dropped by to "make a local call" to his dealer. Eventually we started responding to his signature knock—three slow, deathly thumps—by holding our breath until we heard him shuffling away. From time to time, we heard gunfire crackling a few blocks away.

In search of less excitement and more square footage for the same rent, we moved to a comparatively palatial apartment in Sunnyside, Queens. There the kitchen could accommodate a breakfast table, and the cat could position himself on the second-floor windowsill and parley with the squirrels in the tree outside. Later, we lived in a Manhattan high-rise built in the eighties, recently enough that some in the neighborhood still think of it as a monstrous interloper.

Thinking back over that trajectory, I am struck that almost the entire history of the New York apartment remains on the menu today, albeit at preposterous prices. Each listing is a potential location for the drama of someone's life. The crowds who troop around to open houses every Sunday are never just counting bathrooms and closets or calculating mortgage payments. They're wondering whether a refurbished tenement speaks of hoary miseries or new excitement, whether the view out each window is one they want to see every day, or whether they can see in their prospective neighbors the people they want to become. To hunt for an apartment is to decide which New York you belong in.

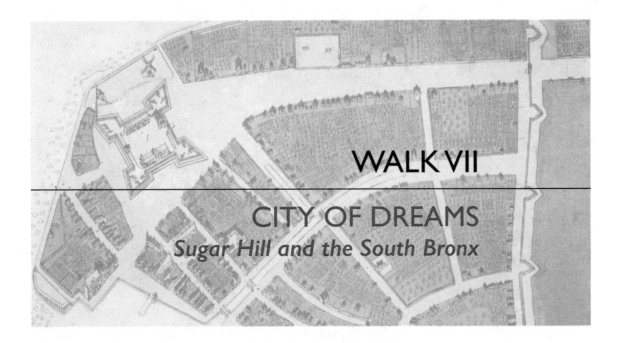

WALK VII

CITY OF DREAMS
Sugar Hill and the South Bronx

The most romantic bridge in New York reaches from cliff top to cliff top, joining two neighborhoods forged by dreams and disappointment. On a damp, tropical day, I've ridden my bike to High Bridge, a disused aqueduct in Washington Heights, dominated on its Manhattan side by a stone water tower that looks out over the Harlem River like a medieval fortification. A festive outdoor pool and a set of basketball courts stretch across the crown of the hill. Tinny radios emit competing soundtracks of salsa. From here, Highbridge Park, a picturesque wilderness of weeds and rusted stairs, tumbles down a steep escarpment toward the Harlem River Drive. Topography matters little in most of New York, where straight streets march up hills, trains burrow beneath them, and the roughest terrain was long ago flattened into gentle inclines. Here, though, a great ravine defined the area's destiny. Once, altitude meant affluence.

On the Manhattan side, the park follows the bluff south along Edgecombe Avenue to the Sugar Hill neighborhood, where for a glorious couple of decades African Americans seemed poised to overcome injustice by force of talent. On the Bronx side, the bridge hits a precipitous, village-like neighborhood, also called Highbridge, which dips and rolls and climbs to another great, hopeful ridge crested by the Grand Concourse. At different times and to different people, these two high points on opposite sides of the canyon

< This itinerary can be done on foot, but a few of the distances between stops are great enough that a bicycle—or a couple of very brief cab rides—would help. Enter Highbridge Park from **A**, Amsterdam Avenue at West 172nd Street, and follow the path to **B**, High Bridge.

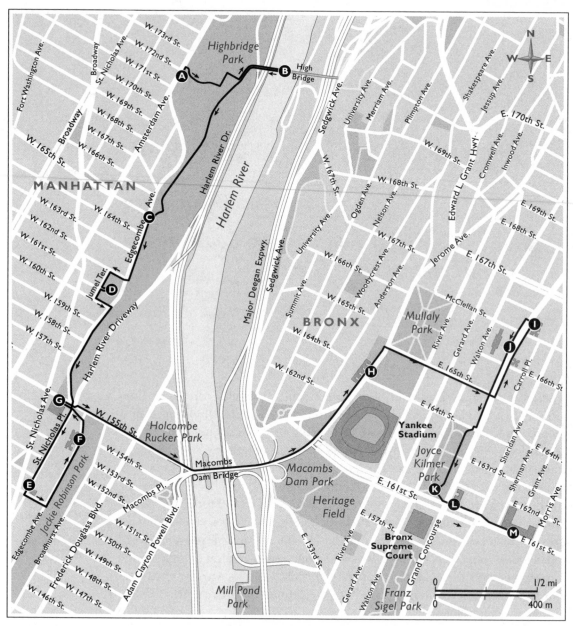

ⓐ Amsterdam Ave.
and W. 172nd St.

ⓑ High Bridge

ⓒ Edgecombe Ave. at W. 165th St.

ⓓ Morris-Jumel Mansion,
Jumel Terrace

ⓔ 10 St. Nicholas Pl.

ⓕ 409 Edgecombe Ave.

ⓖ 898 St. Nicholas Ave.

ⓗ 1005 Jerome Ave.

ⓘ 1150 Grand Concourse

ⓙ 1125 Grand Concourse

ⓚ Heinrich Heine Memorial

ⓛ Concourse Plaza Hotel,
900 Grand Concourse

ⓜ Bronx County Hall of Justice

represented the apex of the American dream, which has nothing to do with owning a private house with a white picket fence and everything to do with transcending the limitations of one's birth. On both sides of the river, that dream died violently and is now flickering back to life. High Bridge links two tragic and inspiring parts of the city that had to rescue themselves from decades of abandonment, racial hostility, and other forms of urban misery. Edgecombe Avenue and the Grand Concourse, two roughly parallel ridge roads on opposite sides of the river, were both nobly built; both saw their populations turn over and their architecture degrade. Both have now started to recover their old prosperity, though at dramatically different rates, and always at a cost.

High Bridge and water tower

I wheel my bike onto the span's handsomely restored brickwork, grateful that it's open again after years of neglect and closure. The view is majestically industrial, a panorama of mid-twentieth-century big thinking in the form of highways and housing projects. From here we can gaze onto the ambitions of New York's master builder Robert Moses, who from the early thirties to the early sixties put into practice his belief that if he could move enough cars quickly enough, demolish enough slums, and pack enough poor people into enough plain brown towers, the city could be manageable again. The bridge itself comes to us from the previous mid-century, another great industrial age, when it seemed as if society's ills were primarily problems of engineering.

Built in 1848 as an aqueduct to channel fresh water toward the Croton Reservoir at Forty-second Street (see Walk V, "City of Ideals"), High Bridge marched across the Harlem River in a stone parade of fifteen Roman arches, recalling the majesty of the ancient aqueducts in Segovia and Nîmes. In the nineteenth century, New Yorkers who enjoyed at least a day of leisure came to stroll back and forth between rural Upper Manhattan and the even more rural Bronx. Down below, within spitting and tossing range of the bridge, swells raced their carriages along the Harlem Speedway. Edgar Allan Poe is said to have hiked to this spot over the Bronx's rocky terrain from his cottage on the Kingsbridge Road, where his wife was slowly expiring of tuberculosis. The route became part of his mythology, thanks to a lithograph by B. J. Rosenmeyer that shows the writer trudging through the snow over a wind-whipped viaduct, the cliffs behind him plunging to the river below.

Shippers hated High Bridge, as they resented anything that slowed the smooth passage of their freight. Though the tall arches allowed sloops and ferries to pass between them, property owners and shippers needed clearance for ever-bigger boats. In 1928 they finally persuaded the city to rip out five arched segments and replace them with a broad steel span, splitting the bridge's personality in two. (On the walkway, the two sections are demarcated by different patterns of pavers.) The water was rerouted, the tower decommissioned. In the seventies, when

Fishing at Macombs Dam Bridge, with High Bridge in the background, 1869

the unlit bridge became a drug dealer's haven, the city handled it with the despairing shrug that was typical of the time: The gate was locked and High Bridge left to decay. The bridge spent forty-five years derelict and abandoned, a bit of nineteenth-century glory that had outlived its use. Then, in the spring of 2015, after a $61 million renovation, it reopened to pedestrians and bikes.

> Return to the Manhattan side, walk up a short ramp, and bear left along the park path that leads to **C**, Edgecombe Avenue at West 165th Street. Continue downtown on Edgecombe Avenue, turn right on West 162nd Street and left on Jumel Terrace. **D**, the Morris-Jumel Mansion, is open to visitors.

Height always conferred privilege. The British colonel Roger Morris, whose 130-acre estate was draped over the headlands, built his farmhouse on the loftiest point in 1765, and it still stands as the Morris-Jumel Mansion on Jumel Terrace, an evocative enclave of the eighteenth century. After the loyalist Morris family decamped to England during the Revolution, George Washington moved in for a month in 1776 and his forces won a short-lived military victory, the Battle of Harlem Heights.

As the country aged, it was entertainers, rather than soldiers, who earned the right to occupy the summits, and few addresses represent the aristocracy of showmanship better than the white-stone château at 10 St. Nicholas Place. With its deliberately roughened stone, carved vines, turrets, corbels, and stumpy cone-roofed knockoff of High Bridge Tower at the corner, the freshly restored 1887 house is a picture-book fantasy of a medieval strong-hold plunked down on a Manhattan hilltop. The late nineteenth century abounded with these Romanesque Revival spectaculars, but it somehow doesn't come as a surprise that its builder was a circus tycoon.

< Return to Edge-combe Avenue, turn right, and go to West 155th Street. Continue downtown on St. Nicholas Place to E, No. 10.

The outlines of the owner's life might have been plagiarized from a collec-tion of fairy tales. Jimmy McGinnis was born in Detroit in 1847 and grew up a penniless orphan. He ran away with the circus at thirteen, working his way up from the kid who ran ahead of the wagon train and slapped posters on clapboard walls to the head of a massive entertainment company. Early on, he attached himself to father figures and even took the name of one: Little Jimmy became James A. Bailey, the peevish behind-the-scenes workaholic who allowed his partner, P. T. Barnum, to soak up all the fame. It was Bailey who decided that their joint venture, Barnum & Bailey, had to have London's

James Bailey's mansion, 10 St. Nicholas Place

largest live attraction, Jumbo the elephant, and in 1882 sent a man over with ten thousand dollars to bring him back. It was Bailey, *The New York Times* re-ported years later, who had the idea of marching the star and twenty of his fellow pachyderms back and forth across the brand-new Brooklyn Bridge to trumpet the structure's strength (and the circus's delights). "It was Jumbo here, Jumbo there, and Jumbo everywhere," the paper recalled in 1891.

The circus eventually squeezed so much energy from the joyless autocrat that he suffered a nervous breakdown, decided to quit the business, and built himself a retirement home on top of Harlem's hill. His retirement lasted barely longer than construction. With his castle finished, he was soon back at work.

By the time Bailey died in 1906, a businessman named Philip Payton had formed the Afro-American Realty Company and begun renting apartments exclusively to black tenants, starting near the corner of West 135th Street and Lenox Avenue. Within a couple of decades, black Harlem belted Manhattan from river to river, from 110th Street north. The boundaries were debatable, but the epicenter of power was not: That sat on Edgecombe Avenue, atop the cliff known as Coogan's Bluff. Doctors, lawyers, writers, and celebrities dwelled in airy apartments overlooking the huddled tenements below, and the sweet life they lived up there cemented the name of Sugar Hill. It was an easy situation to mock, and even Adam Clayton Powell, Jr., the fair-skinned son of a famous pastor, described it with sneering admiration in 1935: "On Sugar Hill . . . Harlem's would-be 'sassiety' goes to town. 'Midst paneled walls, parquet floors, electric refrigeration, colored tile baths, luxurious lobbies, elevators and doormen resplendent in uniforms, they cavort and disport themselves in what is called the best *ofay* manner." The tinge of venom in Powell's tone makes it clear how tenuous and contradictory the position of the Sugar Hill elite was. Its members embodied racial pride yet sought the approval of whites, who embraced the small fellowship of talent and ignored Harlem's masses.

> Turn left on West 150th Street, walk one block to Edgecombe Avenue, turn left, and continue the equivalent of about four blocks, to F, No. 409.

Nearly half a century after Bailey built his mansion, another poor but ambitious Midwesterner introduced himself to an older man, who became his employer and adopted father and led him to a magnificent residence on Harlem's highest hill. In 1938, the young pianist and composer Billy Strayhorn showed up in Duke Ellington's dressing room at the Stanley Hotel in Pittsburgh, while the master was getting his hair styled, and wowed him by playing "Sophisticated Lady." In his biography of Strayhorn, *Lush Life,* David Hajdu quotes the two musicians' mutual friend George Greenlee, who set up the meeting:

> "Billy played it *exactly* like Duke had just played it on stage. He copied him to perfection." Ellington stayed silent and prone, though his hair work was over. "Now this is the way *I* would play it," continued Strayhorn. Changing keys and upping the tempo slightly, he shifted into an adaptation Greenlee described as "pretty hip-sounding and further and further 'out there' as he went on."

Impressed but unsure what to do with the kid, Ellington told Strayhorn to look him up if he came to New York and jotted down directions to his home at 409 Edgecombe Avenue. Strayhorn, eager to dazzle Ellington again, turned the instructions into a song: "Take the 'A' Train." A few months later, when he did in fact take the A subway line to the 155th Street stop, Strayhorn moved into Ellington's apartment at the top of the tallest building on Sugar Hill. There he found an Olympus of black America that was astonishingly pale—in skin color, in customs, and even in décor. He immediately called his friend Greenlee to report on its snowy color scheme. "You won't believe it," he said, "this place is completely white, even the rugs! I'm talking to you on a white telephone!"

From the street, 409 Edgecombe Avenue is architecturally undistinguished, except for its bulk. More than twice as tall as its six-story neighbors, it rises high enough that, until the late fifties, some residents could watch a Giants game in the Polo Grounds from their bedrooms.

More important, the building had inner beauty. A liveried doorman watched over a marble-lined lobby, and the spacious, high-ceilinged apartments sported luxurious touches like crown moldings and hardwood floors. Thurgood Marshall lived there, and so did W.E.B. Du Bois and much of the leadership of the NAACP.

Ellington's downstairs neighbor was Walter White, the pale, blond, blue-eyed black man who led the NAACP. His apartment, 13A, always abuzz with New York's integrated intelligentsia, was known as the "White House of Harlem."

"We had a full-sized grand piano at one time, because almost everybody had a piano at one time," White's daughter, the actress Jane White, recalled many years later.

> George Gershwin played "Rhapsody in Blue" on our piano soon after he wrote it. . . . Another person who was there, at some of our parties, was Sergei Eisenstein, the great Russian director. He was heard to say that my mother was one of the most beautiful women he had ever seen. I saw Claude McKay, Langston Hughes, Countee Cullen, Harold Jackman coming to our parties. . . . It was only by hindsight that I realized I was moving in Harlem society.

Even during the Depression, Sugar Hill was the setting for a vivid dream, one that took some time to dissipate. "There was a sense that if you *kept* your nose clean, and if you *went* to school, and you *held* a good job, and you *made* a little money, and you washed and ironed your clothes—that it was going to turn out all right," Jane White said. "This turned out to be a fallacy."

In August 1943, a white cop shot and wounded an unarmed black veteran in the course of a botched arrest in Harlem—such a depressingly familiar scenario, even all these decades later. Rumors that the soldier had been killed triggered a riot. Within minutes, Mayor Fiorello La Guardia called Walter White, who in turn grabbed his neighbor and fellow NAACP member Roy

Wilkins. Together, White and Wilkins hopped in a cab and rushed to the epicenter of violence, outside the Twenty-eighth Precinct on West 123rd Street at Eighth Avenue (Frederick Douglass Boulevard, today). For hours the mayor, along with White and other black leaders drove around, shouting at looters and exhorting them to get off the streets. "Don't destroy in one night the reputation as good citizens you have taken a lifetime to build," White pleaded with a megaphone. "Go home—now!" He might as well have been nagging a hurricane. The police killed five African Americans that night. A sixth died in the melee, and seven hundred people were injured.

A year later, the great poet Langston Hughes, a frequent visitor to White's home, pointed out that the physical separation between the cliff and the lowlands was also a social gulf. The privileges of the few did nothing to attenuate the misery of the many:

> It is, I should imagine, nice to be smart enough and lucky enough to be among Dr. Du Bois' "talented tenth" and be a race leader and go to the symphony concerts and live on that attractive rise of bluff and parkway along upper Edgecombe Avenue overlooking the Polo Grounds, where the plumbing really works and the ceilings are high and airy. For just a few thousands a year one can live very well on Sugar Hill in a house with a white-tiled hall.

> But under the hill on Eighth Avenue, on Lenox, and on Fifth there are places like this—dark, unpleasant houses, with steep stairs and narrow halls, where the rooms are too small, the ceilings too low and the rents too high. There are apartments with a dozen names over each bell. The house is full of roomers. Papa and mama sleep in the living room, the kids in the dining room, lodgers in every alcove, and everything but the kitchen is rented out for sleeping. Cooking and meals are rotated in the kitchen.

By the 1950s, Sugar Hill had lost its magic. Edgecombe Avenue remained a high and pretty street, but the black elite scattered to the Upper West Side or to the semi-suburban Queens community of St. Albans. As federal redlining made it harder and harder to invest in, borrow on, or insure property in African American neighborhoods, the owners of 409 Edgecombe Avenue allowed the building to slide into genteel decrepitude, though it still kept bleeding money. Down below, the Polo Grounds began falling apart, the Giants moved to San Francisco, and the baseball field eventually gave way to a forest of public housing. The Harlem Speedway, a scenic strip where horses and, later, cars raced beneath High Bridge, turned into a multi-lane highway. In 1979, the city took over the building at 409, adding it to the heap of municipal property on which landlords had stopped paying taxes.

On the highest point around stands the latest incarnation of the neighborhood's distinction, 898 St. Nicholas Avenue, designed by the African-born British architect David Adjaye.

If the Bronx ever invaded Harlem, its forces might hesitate at the sight of Adjaye's gloomy, fortress-like affordable-apartment complex. The medieval-looking structure looms like a ruined bastion, a pair of great squared-off boulders stacked slightly askew, as if a defending army had readied it for toppling. The west façade is pitted with small square windows that glint like mica in the granitic mass.

It's hard to fathom why Adjaye would evoke a hilltop citadel or clad it in storm cloud–colored concrete so that even on a perfect summer day it glowers forbiddingly against the sky—after all, the building's intentions are exactly the opposite. This castle is a home—124 of them, actually, built by a nonprofit developer to provide a struggling neighborhood with desperately needed affordable housing. Below the apartments are two institutions geared to kids: an early-childhood center and a children's museum, separated by a narrow court. It's a shame that the building turned out so grim, because it could have been a model for the kind of high-design, low-cost homes that the city needs. Adjaye rightly rejects the brick-box model of public housing and public schools. Why, then, replace it with a dead-eyed guard tower?

It's time to cross the Harlem River to the western edge of the South Bronx, which is, in a way, Sugar Hill's fraternal twin. On one side were the Giants and the Polo Grounds; on the other is Yankee Stadium. Harlem had its speedway in the lowlands; the builders of the Bronx planned to lay a new one out along the ridge. Where African Americans found temporary bliss along Edgecombe Avenue, Jews established their heavenly beachhead on the Grand Concourse. Both neighborhoods declined; Sugar Hill started first, but the Bronx fell faster and harder.

< Continue on Edgecombe Avenue a half block to West 155th Street, turn left, and walk to **G**, the corner of St. Nicholas Avenue (not to be confused with St. Nicholas Place).

David Adjaye's Sugar Hill housing, 898 St. Nicholas Avenue

> This is where transportation might come in handy, though it's not essential. Walk, bike, or drive over the Macombs Dam Bridge into the Bronx. Cross East 161st Street and continue on Jerome Avenue, with Yankee Stadium on your right, to **H**, No. 1005 Jerome Avenue.

The Park Plaza Apartments, designed by the architect Marvin Fine in 1929—and then redesigned when the new building burned suspiciously to the ground shortly before completion—was the first of the Bronx's Art Deco residential buildings. Brick piers shoot up between the window bays. In Midtown skyscrapers of that period, such vertical lines, like airstreams, made it look as though an immense rocket ship were tearing itself from the earth. Here the building's mass sits closer to the ground, an eight-story community of families located in the hollow between the Grand Concourse and the Highbridge bluff. Marvin Fine encrusted the exterior with polychrome terracotta reliefs and adorable gargoyles, turning the façade into a celebration of ornament and architecture. In several panels, a Beaux Arts turret rises into the sky from an Italianate apartment building—not the Park Plaza—crowned by the sun's rays. In other panels, ropes of water from a tall, slender fountain braid together on their way back to the basin. Beneath one corner window, a relief depicts an architect kneeling humbly before the Pantheon, offering a scale model of a skyscraper as modernity's paltry tribute to the past.

The Park Plaza Apartments expressed in solid materials its residents' flickering, anxious pride. As on Sugar Hill, comfort and social status were hard-won and tenuous; Marvin Fine literally set them in stone. While the world economy turned to ash, architects and developers studded the neighborhood with brightly colored emblems of good spirits. In medieval Europe, Gothic cathedrals had promised spiritual redemption by telling symbolic stories in stained glass; in the twentieth-century Bronx, modern apartment buildings promised material prosperity by telling symbolic stories in mosaic, limestone, and terra-cotta.

> Turn right on East 165th Street, go four blocks to the Grand Concourse, turn left, and continue to **I**, No. 1150, on the east side of the avenue.

I pedal over to the Grand Concourse and north to 1150, a phantasmagorical Art Deco palace known as the Fish Building. It's an architectural essay on happiness. The wavy façade ripples up the block. Near the entryway, an aquatic-themed mosaic, as bright and cheery as a coral reef, wraps a corner and ducks beneath a shiny metal awning. In the lobby, circles, triangles, and thin metallic lines turn the polychrome floors into a Kandinsky-like fantasia. A mural portrays a robed musician bowing a double bass while a chorus line of naked nymphs scamper by. Not many buildings in New York express such random joy.

Art Deco design indulged a craving for gratuitous dollops of merriment. There was still plenty of physical space in the Bronx of the late 1920s, and the combination of airiness and architectural icing had a special appeal for a generation of Jews who still remembered the congested alleys of the Lower East Side. The Concourse became for them what Sugar Hill was to African Americans, a place where the sunlit present mattered more than the shad-

Fish Building entryway, 1150 Grand Concourse

owed past. Here was a corridor of doctors' offices, synagogues, and rental palazzos, where poorly educated but successful entrepreneurs cushioned their families from prejudice and misfortune. By 1930, Jews made up 82 percent of some neighborhoods along the Concourse.

They had Louis Aloys Risse to thank for their coveted addresses. Born in Alsace, France, in 1850, he emigrated at seventeen. Arriving in the United States with a talent for drawing and not a word of English, he settled in the countryside outside New York: the Bronx. In her history of the Grand Concourse, *Boulevard of Dreams,* Constance Rosenblum describes a young man intoxicated by a wild green landscape freckled with tiny towns. Risse became a civil engineer, gripped by the belief that a well-designed road could shape an ideal city, or at least guide the growth of an imperfect one. He looked out over the craggy hills and saw that the inclined streets on the slope above the Harlem River would quickly fill in, and a multi-lane tree-lined boulevard would provide a dignified link between Manhattan, the new precincts, and the chain of parks beyond.

To today's urban dweller, the idea of a long, wide road built for the pleasure of driving it, or walking along it, seems staggeringly naïve. The twentieth century taught us to judge our urban roadways by how quickly we can get off them and how well they handle the monoculture of motor vehicles. But what Risse had in mind was a completely different beast. A century earlier, in

Washington, D.C., the civil engineer Pierre Charles L'Enfant had envisioned a grand avenue unfurling from the Capitol: That became the National Mall. In Paris, successive sovereigns, starting with Marie de Medici in 1616, extended an *allée* of trees from the royal gardens, which evolved into the Avenue des Champs-Élysées. In Berlin, a similar combination of vast palaces and martial rows of trees yielded Unter den Linden. As Rosenblum points out, this was the company Risse wanted his Concourse to keep, except that he would have to do without governments, palaces, or royal processions. Instead, ordinary renters would perambulate with princely dignity.

The American habit of emulating the appurtenances of European nobility has often produced awkward results: great knight's halls in elevator buildings, battlements without enemies to repel, ersatz coats of arms. Risse envisioned the Grand Concourse as a promenade, not a thoroughfare, a place where pleasure trumped efficiency. "[T]he endless procession of the family parties, enjoying the air, beaux and belles, the long array of children in charge of solicitous nurses and anxious mamas, and the other boulevard travelers, do not take kindly to trucks and freight traffic," he wrote. He began working on his design in the 1890s, when ladies and gentlemen on foot took precedence over commercial traffic. By the time the Concourse opened in 1909, the predominating philosophy had begun to flip, privileging the automobile. Today, the Grand Concourse is a thick cable of eleven car lanes, plus a pair of thin medians and a scraggly line of pollution-resistant trees. Even after a pedestrian-friendly redesign near 161st Street, crossing it remains a trek, and walking along it can feel like a solitary trudge. It's hard to imagine Risse's "long array of children" voluntarily coming anywhere near the place.

> Cross the Grand Concourse and walk half a block south to J, No. 1125, the Andrew Freedman Home. The front yard is generally open to the public, and the Home hosts events and art exhibits.

Diagonally across the street from the Fish Building is the Andrew Freedman Home, a wildly incongruous Italianate palazzo set back from the street in a lush garden, where the living seem out of place among the ghosts. Freedman, a blustering moneyman, subway builder, and owner of the Giants baseball team (not to mention a creature of Tammany Hall) had "an astonishing faculty for making enemies," according to the long-defunct newspaper the *New York World*. He also had an idiosyncratic approach to charity. When he died in 1915, his will revealed a tender spot for the elderly and indigent whose misfortune was made more painful by the fact that they had once been rich. Freedman left $5 million (about $119 million in 2016 dollars) to establish a home for the formerly privileged, ensuring that they would be pampered in the style to which they were no longer accustomed. Residents—or "members," as they were called, to preserve the illusion of a private club—paid no rent or board, took their meals together, and were waited on by white-gloved servants, whom they were not allowed to tip. A few were the kind of down-on-their-luck millionaires that Freedman had envisioned; most had acquired

The sitting room of the Andrew Freedman Home, 1938

more refinement than money. Opera singers, journalists, teachers, engineers, and, later, cultivated Jewish refugees from Nazi Europe lived there in an atmosphere of doddering luxury.

The press treated the place with condescending amusement. An article published in *The New Yorker* in 1933 may capture the eccentric atmosphere but also suggests that in those days the magazine's famous fact-checking department allowed for some imaginative fabrication:

> Meals at the home are sometimes trying, what with socially ambitious members continually attempting to get shifted to what they consider more desirable tables. One old gentleman discovered that whenever he shrieked "Pig! Swine!" at his dinner companion, he was shifted to another table. He kept this up at various tables until he reached the desirable couple who constituted his goal, only to have them shriek "Pig! Swine!" at him until they were moved away.

As the cost of maintenance escalated, conditions in the neighborhood became more dire, and Freedman's bequest bled away, the home struggled along, its heyday becoming ever more distant. The writer Vivian Gornick and the photographer Sylvia Plachy visited the Andrew Freedman Home in 1980, on assignment from *The Village Voice,* and found it a dovecote of cooing snobs, each marooned in memories and an inviolable sense of superiority. The great but forgotten artist, the historian of Belle Époque Berlin, the retired advertising execs, the octogenarian political scientist still working on his magnum opus—all these ancient, decorous people were living their last days behind the comfort of a chain-link fence topped with barbed wire. "The Andrew Freedman Home is the most civilized institution in New York in which to be old," Gornick concluded—before adding: "There is no such thing as a civilized institution in which to be old."

In 2007, it finally closed. I toured the place a few years later, when its members had all moved on to other, more permanent clubs and the rooms had been cleared of furniture and filled with freshly made art. The organization No Longer Empty installed a show called *This Side of Paradise,* a mournful celebration of a building that had outlived even its days of faded glory. In one room, the artist Nicky Enright had arranged a collection of beat-up typewriters on a ruined piano. Eerie typewriter-and-keyboard music clanked from the wracked assemblage as if some long-dead resident were still furiously entertaining his fellow shades. Elsewhere, Sylvia Plachy re-created the faded Viennese coziness of a room she had photographed more than thirty years before. When I slapped the tufted upholstery, clouds of loneliness puffed out into the room.

Continue south along Grand Concourse, enter Joyce Kilmer Park, and stop at **K,** the Heinrich Heine statue—also known as the Lorelei Fountain—near the corner of 161st Street.

These days, it's both shabbier and livelier than it was in its heyday. Every morning, children pack noisily into a basement daycare center. From time to time, the home's personable director, Walter Puryear, produces African American and Latino–themed plays in the wood-paneled library. On the second floor, where fibers of faded hallway carpeting are slowly merging with plaster dust, a rotating roster of resident artists crams the rooms. Behind one door is a cornucopia of painted sneakers, brightly spray-painted canvases, skateboards, and stacks of hand-decorated leather hats.

I pause at the monument to the German Jewish poet Heinrich Heine, an eloquent emblem of the area's shifting identities. After being rejected by Heine's hometown of Düsseldorf and turned away from sites in Manhattan and Brooklyn, the poor statue of the water sprite Lorelei landed in the Bronx in 1899, where many residents could probably quote the poet's work by heart (*Und das hat mit ihrem Singen, / Die Loreley getan*). Heine's mythological creature immediately became a victim of violence. Someone lopped off her arms in 1900, five years later her head blew off, and in the seventies the statue became a favorite target of vandals and graffiti artists.

Seeing the restored monument now, it seems to me that the entire avenue was built to preserve disappointed memories in the aspic of decaying elegance. Even during the worst periods, residents of Risse's promenade continued to raise children, go to work, and spare a smile for a fanciful façade. Today, the buildings are being fitfully renovated, the terra-cotta colors are brightening, and the brick façades are regaining their crispness. This is more than just a cosmetic freshening-up; it's evidence of a neighborhood slowly recovering from trauma. New York still harbors plenty of horrific poverty. Walls collapse, bullets go astray, homeless people too mentally ill to care for themselves freeze to death in parks. Drugs, vandalism, homelessness, cruelty, and crime—these urban scourges never disappear. But what this corner of the Bronx experienced from the late 1960s through the early 1980s was not garden-variety decline or the orderly replacement of one class by another. It was disaster.

In *Boulevard of Dreams,* Rosenblum describes how quickly and thoroughly a building that had aged gracefully for a generation could suddenly degrade into a dangerous, waterlogged shell: "In the lobby, leaks left holes in the ceiling, crumbling plaster carpeted the marble floor, and nests of shredded plaster remained where slabs of marble had been stripped from the walls." All through the area, vacant apartments filled with garbage and elevators died, leaving their shafts as terrifying voids. Vandals methodically ripped out wires and plumbing. Arson and abandonment competed to see which could ravage the Bronx more thoroughly.

I look back on those years with horrified awe. When observers remarked that the Bronx of the seventies looked like a war zone, they were not merely using a figure of speech. It would be easy, at this remove, to confuse photos of the South Bronx in 1978 with views of Aleppo, Syria, today: an inhuman landscape of scorched concrete and naked rebar. There is something surreal and apocalyptic about the degradation visited on all these buildings, about the desperate people who kept living in them. Standing here now, it's hard to understand how the lung-filling expectations that built this area gave way, only thirty years later, to a time when New Yorkers wrote off large sections of their city as a toxic wasteland—or how vigorously, if gradually, it is coming back.

Even as it collapsed, the South Bronx nurtured a hardy cultural ecosystem. Graffiti and hip-hop, the two exuberantly confrontational art forms that came out of this period of deprivation, were resilient and tough, like the trees growing along the Grand Concourse. Young men boasted in rat-tat-tat rhymes over an implacable beat or asserted their cockiness in oversize coded signatures. The story of hip-hop has been baked into a mythology of the block party that begat a billion-dollar business. But it wasn't the entertainment industry that healed the Bronx or cleared the rubble and rebuilt. That unglamorous task fell not to the people who made money and moved away but to the activists, neighbors, and do-gooders who stayed and battled decay one stoop at a time. They found a powerful partner in Mayor Ed Koch.

On October 5, 1977, President Jimmy Carter visited Charlotte Street in the South Bronx (a couple of miles from where I'm standing) and strolled dolefully onto a rubble-strewn field to contemplate the ruins of the American urban dream. "See which areas can be salvaged," Carter told his housing secretary, with a hint of hopelessness. He could just as easily have been referring to the rest of New York, where lots lay fallow, office towers sat unfinished, and nobody was building a thing. By the mid-eighties, with Carter evicted from the White House and Koch in his second term as mayor, Charlotte Street sported a row of trim suburban houses—some with white fences, even!—and the city was in the throes of a construction spree that was practically choking the skyline. The Koch administration (1978–1989) took over fully a third of the buildings along the Grand Concourse, parceled them out to nonprofit developers, and watched the Art Deco dowagers reincarnated as decent, if basic, affordable housing.

> Exit the park and cross the intersection to the northeast corner of Grand Concourse and East 161st Street. The twelve-story brick building with a limestone base is **L**, the former Concourse Plaza Hotel.

In 1982, the *Times* columnist Anna Quindlen visited the Concourse Plaza Hotel, famous in the 1930s as the spot where Yankees, gangsters, and politicians held court and where prosperous furriers vied to hold the most magnificent bar mitzvahs. Like most other epicenters of glamour, the hotel had had a rough couple of decades, and the bands had fallen silent long ago. But Quindlen found poetic justice in the building's new life as housing for senior citizens:

> There are no vacancies, and the lobby is full, and some of the same people who danced in the ballroom in their best clothes have returned. . . . It seems right that Edna Mandelbaum, who shook hands with John F. Kennedy in the lobby and lived in one of the hotel's suites with her husband, should now have a studio apartment on the top floor, overlooking Yankee Stadium. It seems right that Mary Markowski, who spent her wedding night at the Concourse Plaza, a great extravagance in 1939, should have a neat one-bedroom apartment there.

Quindlen's glowing report didn't mean that the borough had fully recovered—or even reached bottom. The crack epidemic was just getting going, and with it came a wave of crime that made the previous decade seem quaint. Even as painters and electricians were getting the Concourse Plaza ready for its new/old guests, popular culture was getting a thrill by dramatizing the Bronx's slide into savagery. Paul Newman starred as the last good cop in *Fort Apache, The Bronx*, a movie that portrayed the black and Latino population of the area as an undifferentiated sea of hookers and thugs. In *Bonfire of the*

Vanities, Tom Wolfe's ruthless vivisection of New York in the mid-eighties, the Bronx County Courthouse (the big gray cube on the west side of Grand Concourse, just across from the Concourse Plaza) stands as an emblem of a soured civic pride:

Bronx County Courthouse, 1930

> The building was a prodigious limestone parthenon done in the early thirties in the Civic Moderne style. It was nine stories high and covered three city blocks, from 161st Street to 158th Street. Such open-faced optimism, they had, whoever dreamed up that building back then! ... Its four great façades were absolute jubilations of sculpture and bas-relief. ... Noble Romans wearing togas in the Bronx! Such a golden dream of an Apollonian future!
>
> Today, if one of those lovely classical lads ever came down from up there, he wouldn't survive long enough to make it to 162nd Street to get a Choc-o-pop or a blue Shark. They'd whack him out just to get his toga.

And yet here I am, twenty years later, unmolested astride my bike, surveying a landscape of tenuous recovery.

The new county courthouse, which was designed by Rafael Viñoly Architects and opened in 2008, evinces a different kind of positivity. It appears at first too fragile to be a criminal courthouse. Greenish glass panes form its corrugated outer walls, and the grand glass curtain wall at the entrance leads to an open sunlit lobby. Inside, too, there's a profusion of glass. The place looks like no match for an irritated juror, let alone a repeat offender.

< Walk two blocks east along East 161st Street to **M**, No. 265, the Bronx County Hall of Justice.

But just as we recognize the protective value of transparency in government and in the justice system, literal transparency can be a security feature, too. In the eighteenth century, the philosopher Jeremy Bentham envisioned a prison—the panopticon—in which inmates could be under constant, surreptitious observation. Viñoly's courthouse is a collective panopticon: It allows everyone to observe everyone else. This doesn't obviate the need for cameras or guards, but it limits the possibility of nasty surprises.

Everybody knows what impregnability looks like: massive stone walls, slits for windows, and a single gate, preferably behind a moat. But safety is partly a matter of perception. After 9/11, when New York was suddenly pocked with bollards and barriers, every security measure reignited nervousness. Such fortifications intimidate the very people they are meant to protect. But Vinõly's Bronx courthouse suggests that we can plan for worst-case scenarios without living in their grip, that we can build public places where citizens know they're being watched over yet don't have the feeling that they're on parole.

Two unanswered questions hang like banners across the Grand Concourse: Why did the neighborhood slide so quickly from comfort to total ruin? And can it happen again? The answers to the first question have multiplied in the last forty years: racism, suburbanization, redlining, drugs, the deindustrialization of the economy, fiscal collapse, black and Latino migration, slum clearance and public housing, profiteering landlords, gangs, the trauma left by the Cross-Bronx Expressway, the allure of the new Co-op City in the borough's northern reaches—each of these separate forces whirled together into a terrifying tornado of hopelessness. And none of them quite explains why, when a middle-class family packed up its overstuffed sofas and moved out of a gracious building in, say, 1965, a few years later that same structure should have turned into a blackened shell filled with garbage and despair.

In a sense, there's comfort in a phenomenon whose very complexity makes it unlikely to reoccur. New York proved sturdier than other devastated cities, like Newark or Detroit, just as Sugar Hill fared better than the Bronx. But the seventies haunt a generation of New Yorkers who see dysfunction as a submerged monster ready to pull us all back down again at the slightest show of weakness. Whenever a budget shortfall leads to diminished library hours, whenever a homeless man paws through the garbage or a subway car's air-conditioning fails, whenever a backyard party ends in a shoot-out, the savage city reappears.

The story of the South Bronx offers no neat parable of redemption. The Grand Concourse never became as splendid as Risse intended it to be, and now it's neither as grand nor as bleak as it once was. The same is true of Sugar Hill. Both struggle on: Privilege makes inroads against deprivation on one block and is beaten back on the next. Here and there, the hard, boring work of activism and social justice gets traction, and suddenly a family has a kitchen and a bathroom and a safe walk to school, where all those things were out of reach before. At the same time, thousands more families live imprisoned within high walls of circumstance. They speak little English, know only other immigrants from their own town back home, and face futures foretold by grim statistics. The Bronx remains the nation's poorest county, where nearly a third of its residents live below the poverty line. The borough's residents get sicker, die earlier, lose more infants, and struggle harder than most other Americans.

Even such a frail and troubled place has New York's unfathomable resilience. Someone is always complaining that the city is dying or dead, someone is always willing to write it off as too poor or too rich to matter anymore. But the South Bronx today still stands, ready for its old beauties and ambition to be rediscovered. It's already happening, and when newly inducted members of the bourgeoisie find their way back in large numbers, putting pressure on long-standing Latino communities who see no reason to leave, then a new kind of conflict will open up, one of real estate prices and chain stores. And then New Yorkers with selective memories will start to complain that the Bronx is losing its character. Of course it is; it always has been and always will be. All over this city, some dreams blare while others fade to a quiet mutter. On block after block, if you listen for a moment, you can hear one group's aspirations rub up against another's in a constant bleat of yearning.

Albert Ledner's
O'Toole Building, or
"overbite building,"
originally the
National Maritime
Union headquarters

FINALE
City of Memory

To live in New York is to watch yourself getting older. As pieces of the city disappear, they carry our memories off with them. You take the same walk you always take, and one day a sign appears in an empty shop window thanking you for forty years of patronage. For a moment you can't remember what was there, until, suddenly, it wasn't. The coffee shop with every table taken by a klatch of grizzled men? The health-food store that smelled vaguely of wheat germ and ammonia? Another few months, and there's another awning with freshly printed lettering, and soon a new routine overlays the old. You even start buying coffee in the bright new place.

Chronic amnesia is part of the New York condition. Here even colossal towers are merely placeholders, temporary arrangements of future debris. Consider the fate of the Singer Building, which became the world's tallest in 1908 and, still beautiful but no longer cost-effective in 1961, became the tallest building ever demolished. (That record has only been surpassed by the destruction of the World Trade Center, which stood a few blocks from the site of the Singer Building.) And yet at the same time, the vast majority of buildings in the five boroughs have outlived their predicted life span, and so have pipes, bridges, and subway tracks. At times, the decrepitude asserts itself with violent drama: A manhole cover rockets into the air; a two-hundred-year-old building finally gives way; a cracked water main floods an entire zip code. After a falling hunk of terra-cotta killed a college student in 1979, the city enacted a law requiring regular façade inspections, effectively making scaffolding a permanent feature of the cityscape. Sometimes it feels as if the only thing preventing Manhattan from turning into rubble is chance.

It's often said that the one constant in New York's history is change, but that's not quite right. There is also nostalgia. Together the two form a distinctively New York emulsion of restlessness and regret. Change and nostalgia are the sweet and sour of life here, complementary opposites that New Yorkers unthinkingly keep in equilibrium. You can see them in the way new skyscrapers and relics live together, in the faded signs for shirt collars or castor oil that emerge on the side of a building when a neighbor is torn down, in the graciously rusting skeletons of ancient piers doing a slow-motion swan dive off a new bike path into the Hudson River, in the grocery store or cobbler that endures long past actuarial expectations as it gets hemmed in by banks. The past doesn't always disappear gracefully when it's supposed to. This is a city of tenacious ghosts.

All great cities incubate their distinctive forms of wistfulness; New Yorkers who came of age in the seventies and eighties have refined the fond recollection of Lower Manhattan in its late bedraggled period. When the city crackled with danger, the timid fled (taking their money with them), leaving plenty of cheap space for hardy, creative pioneers.

The photographer Zoe Leonard moved from Morningside Heights to the Lower East Side in the late seventies, then waited another twenty years to start documenting her city's disappearance. She took pictures of stores, often after hours, like portents of the final closure that awaits all small businesses. She noted their battered signs and faded lettering, the patterns and wounds on the metal gates that dropped down every night, turning streets into steel-sided corridors. Her photographs are full of the language of low-end retail and storefront services, hand-lettered or crudely printed: TAX DIVORCE BKRUPTCY; SUCKLING PIGS SOLD HERE; MEAT; SHOES; CREDIT; and even INFINITY, 99 CENTS.

Leonard's litany of old or doomed businesses recalls Eugène Atget's obsessive catalog of Vieux Paris from the turn of the twentieth century. There is a crucial difference, though. Atget's alleys were already being bulldozed; Leonard's Lower East Side was merely trading one population for another, as it had for decades. Jews, Italians, Puerto Ricans, Ukrainians, hippies, and drug dealers moved in and out of the same derelict tenements, leaving sediments of memory. What bothered Leonard was that the next influx was whiter and more middle class, turning tiny, dingy apartments into efficiently designed, freshly renovated cubbyholes. The people who followed her to the ever-welcoming slice of Manhattan were more like her than the poor immigrants she replaced.

The writer Luc Sante, too, reached adulthood in the 1970s and glorified the neglected, downward spiral of New York in those years:

> It was a ruin in the making, and my friends and I were camped out amid its potsherds and tumuli. This did not distress me—quite the contrary. I was enthralled by decay and eager for more: ailanthus trees growing through cracks in the asphalt; ponds and streams forming in leveled blocks and slowly making their way to the shoreline; wild animals returning from centuries of exile. Such a scenario did not seem so far-fetched then.

Sante's archaeological spirit endures in the photography of Will Ellis, who has explored empty hospitals, barracks, schools, piers, warehouses—a whole geography of urban rot that he documented in the book (and the website) *Abandoned NYC*. These places are the driftwood of real estate, left in place when the waves of life recede and move on. The military no longer actively defends New York against invasion by sea, and so Fort Totten lives on in extravagant obsolescence. Psychiatric hospitals, relics of a different era in the treatment of mental health, when involuntary commitment was the norm, are especially rich incubators of decrepitude. Ellis's photographs lay bare the mechanics of decay with almost medical specificity. They document the way water bloats plaster and crumbles concrete, how pressure bends rebar and wind pulverizes tiles, how sunlight forces its way through diseased roofs.

This kind of imagery has lately been written off as "ruin porn," a voyeuristic fixation on degraded architecture. The eighteenth-century artists who trooped south from Germany to paint the remnants of ancient Rome succumbed to the same prurience. Ruins, whether romantically eroded and overgrown or just stinking and shattered, fascinate because they remind us that even a glittering skyscraper has a life span. There's no more powerful reminder of mortality than architecture that is following its former occupants into oblivion.

Even vibrant, rejuvenated buildings can carry a whiff of death. At dusk, the three-layered sugar cube at the corner of West Twelfth Street and Seventh Avenue turns an almost melancholy blue, as if it were grieving for the multitudes who died there. Until a few years ago, this was the graying, flaking husk of St. Vincent's, a hospital that, because it was situated in a heavily gay neighborhood, became a forward operating base during the war on AIDS. It's worth pausing on the story of this building because, though it, too, was once doomed, somehow it survived as an accidental memorial. St. Vincent's (a.k.a. the O'Toole Building, or the "overbite building") has a lot to tell us about the tricky moral calculus of preservation: how to nurture the old city even as it keeps drawing new people. The AIDS emergency (though not the disease) has passed from New York, and a monument remains in the form of the building that's been restored to pale and blemishless perfection above its glowing base of translucent glass. (A more explicit AIDS memorial occupies the little triangle park across the street.) Each upper floor protrudes over the one below, showing a row of teeth like the tabs left on a sheet torn from a wire-bound notebook.

We almost lost this slightly goofy exemplar of sixties' modernism. Albert Ledner designed it as the headquarters of a now-defunct National Maritime Union. (That's how dated the building became: It evoked a time when Manhattan was still a seaman's base and an organized-labor town.) The *Times*'s architecture critic, Ada Louise Huxtable, didn't love it, but she appreciated its existence. "There is no reason why the [National Maritime Union] could not have . . . added another cheap, dull, routine box with a shiny façade and a big sign to the New York scene," she wrote in 1964. "It decided, instead, to go for architecture. Whatever reservations may be held, New York needs more of those decisions." Then, in the fall of 2008, just as the Great Recession was turning grim and St. Vincent's was suffering its own financial maladies, the hospital hoped to rescue itself by tearing down the awkward building and replacing it with a tower spacious enough to accommodate all the gargantuan new machines that modern medicine requires. And so the Landmarks Preservation Commission (which had jurisdiction because St. Vincent's sits inside a historic district) was faced with a thorny question: whether to allow an ailing hospital to destroy a beloved artifact in order to save itself. The commission decided the overbite building had to go.

As it happened, St. Vincent's went bankrupt before demolition could begin. Later, a different medical institution, Lenox Hill, renovated Ledner's oddity as an urgent-care facility, with more limited resources than a full-scale hospital. The compromise left the neighborhood without a trauma center, but preservationists were pleased. Whether that's a happy trade-off depends in part on whether you're standing on a street corner admiring the building or lying in an ambulance in need of emergency care. There's no easy answer.

The argument over how fast the city should evolve, what deserves to be kept and what can be comfortably swept aside, plays out along a philosophical fault line that runs through New York's history. This city has always been declining and growing at the same time. In 1844 the ever-saturnine Edgar Allan Poe went on an expedition to the still-independent city of Brooklyn and found it bent on forgetfulness and self-destruction. "Brooklyn, you know, is much admired by the Gothamites; and, in fact, much has been done by Nature for the place," he reported. "But this much the New-Yorkers have contrived very thoroughly to spoil." He goes on to describe, disparagingly, a plague of what we would now call McMansions, then continues: "I really can see little difference between the putting up such a house as this, and blowing up a House of Parliament, or cutting the throat of one's grandfather." Poe doesn't just loathe Brooklyn's bad architecture; he considers the growing borough an assault on the senses. "The street-*cries,* and other nuisances to the same effect, are particularly disagreeable here. Immense charcoal-waggons infest the most frequented thorough-fares, and give forth a din which I can like to nothing earthly (unless, perhaps, a gong), from some metallic, triangular contrivance, within the bowels of the 'infernal machine.'"

Six years later, the lawyer, diarist, and member of New York's upper circles George Templeton Strong unsentimentally cheered on the same fevered growth that Poe deplored (in Manhattan, though, not Brooklyn). "How this city marches northward!" he wrote in 1850. "The progress of 1835 and 1836 was nothing to the luxuriant, rank growth of this year. Streets are springing up, whole strata of sandstone have transferred themselves from their ancient resting-places to look down on bustling thoroughfares for long years to come. Wealth is rushing in upon us like a freshet."

Today, the Poes and the Strongs are still battling it out, despairing at all that is being plowed under or celebrating the froth of reinvention. Jeremiah Moss is a Poe-etic pseudonym for an otherwise anonymous man who maintains the engagingly gloomy blog *Jeremiah's Vanishing New York,* which he terms "an ongoing obituary for my dying city." He is the defender of all the undistinguished hunks of masonry that lend the streets their rhythm and give people a place to live and earn a living: bodegas, curio stores, a metalworking shop in SoHo, diners, and dingy bars.

Moss's agenda goes beyond self-indulgent nostalgia; his is a call to arms. "When a store has been there for a hundred years and played a role in the community, we should recognize that the business is important, the interior is important, the family lineage is important," he told me. "Small-business owners watch the street, and they know people. They hold the character of New York; they preserve a visually vibrant streetscape. If you put up walls of glass, you lose all these little stores, and that changes the experience of walking. We also need to protect cultural institutions, places where people can make art and take dance lessons. That's being wiped away. That New York is under attack, and it needs to be protected."

The Strong to Moss's Poe is Nikolai Fedak, master of the blog *New York YIMBY,* who cheers real estate development as the city's life force. I once talked to Moss and Fedak together in a conference call (since Moss wanted to remain anonymous, he refused an in-person interview), and the experience was like playing monkey in the middle with a pessimist on one side and an optimist on the other. Both are smart, observant people who clearly love New York, but the cities they describe are practically irreconcilable. Moss bemoans the disappearance of New York's character. Fedak celebrates its irrepressible force, its growth, its ability to renew itself in each generation, hampered only by outdated regulation. "People from all income levels are valuable, and everyone should be coming to New York if they want to, whether they're poor or rich, and they should have humane housing," Fedak says. "We have to compete globally, and we have a city that was built mostly before World War II, a lot of which is falling apart. If you look at the public housing projects and tenements, at the rats and the gas explosions, at what point do you put the quality of human life above old buildings?"

So where do I fall on the Poe–Strong scale or on the spectrum from Moss to Fedak? Squarely in the middle, though my position fluctuates with my mood. I get enormous pleasure from New York's antiquities, the purely gratuitous terra-cotta carvings that cling to nineteenth-century façades, threatening to rain down debris in a strong gust of wind; the blocks of low-rise townhouses that could be razed for more-efficient living; the Beaux Arts monuments that squeeze the institutions that occupy them into inflexible, insufficient spaces. We have collectively agreed that these works of architecture are worth preserving for their own sake, despite their frustrations.

At the same time, a dynamic city requires an abundance of new architecture, which comes with a concomitant amount of demolition. The most admired, most architecturally resplendent cities are the products of major destruction: Paris, gutted by Baron Haussmann in the mid-nineteenth century; Chicago and London, leveled by fire; Rome, radically reorganized by Pope Sixtus V in the late 1580s; San Francisco, flattened by an earthquake in 1906. I'm not advocating growth through trauma, only pointing out that periods of rapid change can be spectacularly constructive and that the results outlast the pangs. My New York lies somewhere between a museum city and a megalopolis like Tokyo that regularly purges itself of old architecture. That middle ground doesn't come easily. It's an impossible balancing act. Every decision about what to destroy and what to preserve is made in an adversarial situation, juiced by propaganda.

I was born and raised in Rome, where change comes hard and slow. I have spent my adult life in New York, which sometimes feels as though it moves so fast that each sentence I write is out of date by the time I have finished it. From my childhood home I learned the value of old stones. From my adoptive one, I have learned that holding on to them comes at a cost.

Visitors who return to Rome after many years have the reassuring feeling that nothing has changed. The same churches line the same squares; the same kids appear to be hanging out on the same motorbikes in front of the same cafés, although in fact they are, presumably, a new generation of loafers. But that impression of permanence is actually a relatively new phenomenon. Rome was shaped over two thousand years by constant change: It was built, sacked, patched up, allowed to decline, and regularly subjected to large-scale urban planning. Everywhere you go in the old city, you can see each generation's scorn for the one that came before.

New York has that same irreverent energy. But after World War II the cities diverged. While New York went through spasms of urban renewal, slum clearance, and public-housing construction, Rome, traumatized by Mussolini's planning spree during the Fascist era, stopped developing. Building anything in the central city became effectively taboo. The absolutist spirit of preservation, and the ubiquity of buried artifacts, created a culture in which every proposal to widen a sidewalk or build an underground parking garage is mired in controversy and stalled for years. What was once an organic, tumbledown city has hardened into a frozen zone of luxury. One of the pleasures of Rome years ago was its economic diversity. You had outdoor vegetable markets in front of greasy moped-repair shops next to fancy antiques stores. And you had working-class and wealthy people living next door to one another. Today, real estate in the historic center is fantastically expensive. As a result, tourists see a city preserved in amber while the action has moved to the outskirts. That is Rome's beauty, and New York's nightmare.

Similar patterns have emerged here. The Village bears little resemblance to the neighborhood of corner cranks, antiquarian bookstores, jazz clubs, hardware stores, and unhygienic cafés that it was in the fifties. And the parts that have changed the most are those that *look* the same. It has lost its disheveled allure, but aside from suspiciously clean streets, repointed bricks, and leafier trees, many of the Village's vintage blocks remain architecturally untouched. It's the population that has turned over in the last generation, just as it had turned over many times before. It is now a village of the rich, thanks in part to its camera-friendly quaintness. Once, preservationists could plausibly see themselves as defenders of architectural heritage against the amnesiac culture of money. We have learned that preservation, too, can be an instrument of capital and gentrification.

Change does not always tend in one direction. Whether a neighborhood is losing its character or finding it again depends on the reach of one's recollection. Greenwich Village has been scrubbed clean of the scruffy bohemianism of Jackson Pollock's and Jane Jacobs's days, but Henry James might note with pleasure that it also recaptured its original atmosphere of luxe and respectability. "The ideal of quiet and of genteel retirement, in 1835, was found in Washington Square," he writes in the 1901 novel by that name. Its placid comforts were deliberate: Around 1830, the city turned a pauper's cemetery into Washington Parade Ground, setting off a real estate frenzy of the kind that often accompanies a new public park. Developers hired the architect Martin Euclid Thompson to design a row of Greek Revival houses along Washington Square North, which still stands. The square, James continues, "has a riper, richer, more honorable look [than other wealthy neighbor-hoods] . . . the look of having had something of a social history."

It would be nice to think that preservation was a way of stopping time. But you cannot preserve a living thing—you cannot halt its decay or prevent its destruction—without at the same time transforming it completely. We know this intuitively if we're talking about soaking cucumbers in brine, pressing flowers between the pages of a book, or pumping a pretty face full of Botox. Buildings, streets, and cities, too, are animate and complex beings. Whether we like it or not, protecting their physical integrity usually means changing their character, even denaturing their soul. The entrepreneurial owner who fixes up an old warehouse for a small distillery, the nonprofit that recycles an abandoned school into affordable housing, the activist who persuades the authorities to create a historic district—each of these local decisions helps shape a city. Preservation is not just a battle to safeguard expensive antiques but a day-to-day, incremental struggle with a constantly shifting agenda.

The process of triage is often haphazard. Unloved tenement buildings, loathed public-housing projects, prematurely aged mid-century towers, houses too cheap and flimsy to bother with—these things endure, often out of inertia, while churches, treasured views, and historical structures vanish, usually because there's money to be made by destroying them. The preserva-tion movement's creation myth embodies that randomness, beginning as it does with an atrocious loss. In 1964, developers demolished the soaring Penn Station, replacing it with the cramped warren that now lurks below Madison Square Garden. The shock galvanized the city into passing a law that would forbid such outrages. One of the newly constituted Landmarks Preservation Commission's first acts was to designate Brooklyn Heights as a historic dis-trict. In the half century since, the commission has designated 1,400 indi-vidual landmarks and 130 historic districts, where changing a window or restoring a stoop requires a panel of bureaucrats to sign off.

Predictably, that record has produced diametrically opposite reactions. The author Tom Wolfe, who snarls wittily at anyone who would tear down anything, complained in a lengthy 2006 *Times* op-ed that the Landmarks Preservation Commission had stopped protecting history. The agency "has been de facto defunct for going on 20 years," he fulminated. "Today it is a bureau of the walking dead." It was the mayor's creature, and when it suited the mayor to line up alongside developers, he expected preservationists to waggle along. Those same developers that the commission was supposedly sucking up to have had their own harsh words. Steven Spinola, president of the Real Estate Board of New York, has accused the agency of going berserk, of dunking Manhattan in the embalming fluid of historicism for the benefit of affluent nostalgists like Wolfe who want their city to look just as it did in their youth. "Using landmark designation to protect views from penthouse apartments, to freeze architectural style preferences of a few current residents and to promote the self-interests of private parties is a misuse of the landmarks law," Spinola said. "Landmarking the entire city does not leave opportunity to grow."

If we've learned anything in the half century since New York enacted its landmarks law, it's that preservation is a volatile force. To restore a building or a city street, or to keep it from being demolished, is not just an exercise in nostalgia. It's a form of active engagement with the present, and it shapes the future just as profoundly as new architecture and construction does. This is a hard lesson to assimilate. Consider the rationale for designating a historic district: that doing so will preserve the *character* of the neighborhood. So often, though, a preservation triumph goes hand in hand with the area's complete transformation. SoHo was designated in 1973 and then proceeded to morph from an industrial zone to an artists' enclave and eventually into a high-end shopping district. Madison Square North was designated in 2001, spurred in part by the efforts of local residents and business owners to rescue Madison Park from neglect. The restaurateur Danny Meyer did his bit by contributing an unassuming food cart he called Shake Shack. Today the neighborhood's been upgraded to NoMad, and Shake Shack is a billion-dollar public company. I'm not arguing that preservation alone triggered these changes—that would be simplistic—but it certainly helped. Developers and preservationists regard each other with suspicion, and each camp is sure that the other is bent on ruining New York. Builders benefit from a city that has a long and visible history and a rich architectural texture. That's why people want to visit and live here. On the other hand, preservation is an empty pursuit if it doesn't contribute to a vibrant, dynamic city. Preservationists cannot afford to be anti-development, because preservation *is* development.

These debates can get arcane and picayune, but in the furious squabbles over detail you can feel the deep and ancient currents that run through the city's history and our own. The struggle between memory and amnesia is an urban-scale version of the ambivalence that so many of us feel about the passage of our lives. When we move, change jobs, toss a worn old shirt, or sell the trumpet that's been sitting un-played in a closet for years, each of these decisions can feel like a loss one minute and a liberation the next. New York faces a thousand such choices every day, many of them visible to the observant ambler. That's why wandering around a metropolis that rearranges itself at every pass feels like a form of hopeful introspection. If the city can change yet stay true to itself—if it can remember faithfully without getting ensnared in its past, find value in relics that might seem like burdens, accommodate contradictory desires without breaking apart, and keep humming along on the preposterous but indispensable assumption that everything is going to be okay—then maybe we can, too.

ACKNOWLEDGMENTS

When you sit down to write a book it feels like you are alone against the blank page. It's only much later that you stop to appreciate how many others have been sitting quietly in your corner all along. This book is the product of a thousand and one conversations with architects, planners, writers, politicians, developers, preservationists, urban devotees, and New Yorkers who share a fathomless affection for (and often an equally profound ambivalence toward) their city. Some have been particularly generous with their time and insight, even when they had no idea they were contributing to this project: Eric Latzky, Amanda Burden, Janette Sadik-Khan, Carl Weisbrod, Alicia Glen, David Burney, Joseph Salvo, Rachaele Raynoff, Ken Lewis, Jamie Van Klemperer, Roger Duffy, T. J. Gottesdiener, Kenneth Lewis, Elizabeth Kubany, Philippa Polskin, Ken Weine, Jeremy Soffin, Vin Cipolla, Vishaan Chakrabarti, Gregg Pasquarelli, Robert A. M. Stern, Daniel and Nina Libeskind, Michael Manfredi, Marion Weiss, David Childs, Michael Adlerstein, David Fixler, Elizabeth Diller, Jean Nouvel, Claire Weisz, Bjarke Ingels, Raj Patel, Leslie Koch, David Ehrenberg, Andrew Kimball, Regina Myer, Andrew Manshel, Vivian Trakinski, Joanna Lee, Andrew Solomon, Jerry Saltz, Mitchell Moss, Thomas Mellins, Daniel Wakin, and Michael Kimmelman.

Thank you to:

Cindy Spiegel for believing in this book before I did; her wildly efficient assistant and photo wrangler Annie Chagnot; and copy editor extraordinaire Kathy Lord;

My friend first and agent second, Simon Lipskar;

Judy Weinstein for persuading me to donate walking tours at a school auction, setting the whole project in motion;

Ted Moncreiff for his enthusiasm, wisdom, and close reading;

Newsday editors Anthony Marro, Howard Schneider, Phyllis Singer, and John Habich, who gave me the leeway to learn the architecture critic's trade on the job;

Adam Moss, who has made *New York* magazine the finest of perches from which to write about New York City; Chris Bonanos, a true writer's editor, word shepherd, and fellow city geek whom I am implausibly fortunate to have watching over my prose; Jared Hohlt and David Haskell, who suggested ways of looking at the city that would never have occurred to me; former fact-checking queen Rebecca Milzoff and her entire embarrassment-prevention team;

Carol Willis, Eric Gewirtz, James Yolles, Allison Dolegowski, Sylvia Plachy, and Nord Wennerstrom, who helped track down photos and illustrations; Jacob Tugendrajch, Lindsay Turley, Lauren Robinson, and Whitney Donhauser, who put the Museum of the City of New York's sumptuous photo collection at my disposal;

Allan Ceen, who first showed me how to observe and analyze a city street;

My parents, for leaving their native New York that I might rediscover it on my own; and my in-laws, Burton and Cynthia Budick, who welcomed me when I did. Their Berkshires patio became my writer's retreat. As a small child, my son, Milo, asked impatiently when "the station with wings" would be finished. He was in college by the time Calatrava's Oculus opened, and along the way kept me focused on the future while I was meandering into the past.

I can't even plumb the gratitude I feel to my wife, Ariella Budick. The dorm room conversation we began more than thirty years ago has continued unabated, and her thoughts, words, and ferocious love of New York are tightly woven through these pages.

ILLUSTRATION CREDITS

Title page and chapter opener art: Jacques Cortelyou, city map, 1660. Courtesy of New York Public Library.

INDEX

ABOUT THE AUTHOR

JUSTIN DAVIDSON is the architecture and classical music critic at *New York* magazine, where he writes about a broad range of urban, civic, and design issues. He grew up in Rome, graduated from Harvard, and later earned a doctoral degree in music composition at Columbia University. As a classical music and cultural critic at *Newsday*, he won a Pulitzer Prize for criticism in 2002. He lives on the Upper West Side with his wife, Ariella Budick, art critic for the *Financial Times*, and his son, Milo.

Twitter: @JDavidsonNYC